D1806086

Acclaim for Sexual Chemistry

'Science fiction in its purest form.'
– Venue Magazine

'The tales [in SEXUAL CHEMISTRY] are lucid,
darkly humorous and wonderfully inventive; and,
unlike a good deal of SF, the standard of writing is
as high as the imaginative ability . . . Allow yourself
to be seduced and fascinated by the age of Neo-Post-
Ultramodernism, and prepare to be humoured and
stimulated en route.'
–The List

Brian Stableford is one of Britain's most respected writers and critics of imaginative literature. His many novels include *The Empire of Fear*, *Young Blood* and a trilogy consisting of *The Werewolves of London*, *The Angel of Pain* and the forthcoming *Carnival of Destruction*. His non-fiction books include a definitive study of *Scientific Romance in Britain 1890–1950*, and he has edited several anthologies of prose and poetry associated with the Decadent and Symbolist movements of the nineteenth century. He has degrees in Biology and Sociology and lectured at the University of Reading before becoming a full-time writer. He lives in Reading.

SEXUAL CHEMISTRY

Sardonic Tales of the Genetic Revolution

BRIAN STABLEFORD

POCKET
BOOKS

New York   London   Toronto   Sydney   Tokyo   Singapore

First published in Great Britain by
Simon & Schuster Ltd in 1991
A Paramount Communications Company

This edition published in Great Britain by
Pocket Books in 1993
An imprint of Simon & Schuster Ltd
A Paramount Communications Company

Copyright © Brian Stableford, 1991

This book is copyright under the Berne Convention.
No reproduction without permission.
All rights reserved.

Simon & Schuster Ltd
West Garden Place
Kendal Street
London W2 2AQ

Simon & Schuster of Australia Pty Ltd
Sydney

A CIP catalogue record for this book is
available from the British Library
ISBN 0-671-71559-3

Typeset in Galliard 11/13.5 by
Hewer Text Composition Services, Edinburgh
Printed and bound in Great Britain by
HarperCollinsManufacturing

For Bill Russell,
who combines awesome breadth of knowledge
with great depth of imagination, and still
dares to be cheerful.

Contents

Introduction

Mankind now stands at the threshold of a new evolutionary phase.

For 800,000 years, our ancestors were hunter-gatherers, reliant upon the bounty of nature for their sustenance. In the last 10,000 years, our more immediate forefathers have taken control of that bounty by means of agriculture and animal husbandry. We have become the controllers of those species on which we depend for food and other goods, shaping them by selective breeding to suit our purposes. Thus we have sheltered ourselves from the pressures of natural selection.

On these technologies of agriculture and animal husbandry all our accomplishments as a species have been based; they are the foundation-stones of civilisation. Our hunter-gatherer ancestors had other technologies too, but it was not until they settled down to build cities that they really had the opportunity to create and accumulate the two kinds of wealth which gave future generations the opportunity to make progress: the wealth of property, and the wealth of knowledge.

This phase of our evolution has lasted until the present day. The inorganic technology of machinery, which has in recent centuries advanced so spectacularly, has remained parasitic upon the 'organic technologies' of nature which laid down deposits of fossil fuels. We ourselves, insofar as we may be seen as biological 'machines', still rely on plants, animals and micro-organisms as middlemen not only to produce our food, but to maintain the very air that we breathe.

In the future – in the relatively near future – this phase will end. The most fundamental aspects of our relationship with the biosphere are already being altered.

We are now beginning to produce an organic technology of our own, which supplements – and will, in the fullness of time, supersede – nature's technology. Our adventures of this kind began when we made the first stumbling steps in elementary organic chemistry in the last century, but they took a mighty leap forward when we discovered the biochemical basis of nature's technology: the DNA double helix which is responsible for the processes of production and reproduction that constitute life.

We now understand how organisms produce the proteins which are the fundamental materials of life. We are gradually completing our understanding of the nature and operation of genes. On the heels of this burgeoning understanding an ability has already been developed which interferes with the functioning of genes: the beginning of a technology of 'genetic engineering'.

The possibilities of this new technology are tremendous. Genetic engineers will eventually be able to shape the living organisms on which we depend far more cleverly and far more quickly than was ever allowed by the selective breeding on which our ancestors depended. In time, they may produce technologies of artificial photosynthesis which will free us entirely from that kind of dependency, so that we will no longer need plants and animals as middlemen. In due course, the genetic engineers of the future will take direct control of human nature – insofar as that nature is biologically rather than culturally determined – and take their place among the chief architects of future human evolution.

Our descendants will be able to change the world that they live in far more radically than our ancestors did, and will in time be able to free themselves entirely from the tyrannies of nature. We may hope that in such an era, all the problems which currently stem from the impact of our inorganic technologies upon the natural world will be overcome. We may hope to see an end to disease, and an extension of the human lifespan. We may hope to see the emergence of a new Golden Age of achievement.

Where there is hope, though, there is also anxiety. They are two faces of the same coin; the emotional brackets of the power of human foresight and rationality. The technologies of genetic engineering, as they develop by degrees, will permit many projects and possibilities that must seem both hazardous and disquieting. Used well, these technologies might pave the way to paradise on earth; used carelessly or malevolently, they could certainly bring about tragedy of apocalyptic proportions.

This book is an attempt to display some of the possibilities of genetic engineering — to study in advance a few aspects of this new adventure in human evolution upon which we have recently set forth. I have previously done other work with similar intentions, in works of 'futurology' which retain some claim to non-fictional status despite their speculative content. The most important of my enterprises in that vein is a speculative history of the next thousand years, *The Third Millennium*, which I wrote in collaboration with David

Langford; it was published in 1985 but some of its anticipations have already been outstripped by actual achievements (and one sad instance of actual disaster). Although David and I tried hard, while inventing that hypothetical future, to be conscientious in dealing with real possibilities, we were inevitably compelled to deal with many matters bizarre and fanciful. Many of the possibilities inherent in genetic engineering are so peculiar and far-reaching that it is impossible to get imaginatively to grips with them unless one is prepared to deal with the extraordinary and the bizarre.

The stories in this book – all, save for one, written in the wake of *The Third Millennium*, and a few of them set against the same future-historical background – are attempts to dramatise the possibilities inherent in the new biotechnology and the new phase in human evolution which we are now entering. I use the word 'dramatise' without apology, because there are inherent limitations in the capacity which futurological speculations, however eccentric, have to help us to understand the spectrum of hope and anxiety which now extends before us. As an aid to the imagination, stories can be more powerful and more subtle; dramatisation has a vital role to play in helping us confront and come to terms with the future into which we are being rushed by ever-accelerating technological change.

Science fiction stories are not predictions of things to come whose merits and usefulness depend upon their future-historical accuracy; they are explorations of possibility which, while they map out new imaginative territories, attempt to place signposts indicating valuable resources and giving warning of hazards. More importantly, they ask us, in a particularly cunning and pointed fashion, crucial questions about where we might actually want to go – about what futures we do and ought to desire. Stories cannot show us the future in which we will one day find ourselves, and to which we will consign our children, but they can and do interrogate us as to what our hopes and expectations of that future are, and in so doing they can challenge the logic of our answers.

There is an extra function which can be served by a collection of stories of this type, which is to remind us that the future is, after all, replete with alternatives. The actual future will emerge from a vast spectrum of possible futures, steering its course through an infinite wilderness of ifs. The future of mankind will depend on the individual and collective decisions which men make, and if we are to make such decisions wisely we need a keen appreciation of the vast and multifarious range of the windows of opportunity which are open to us.

We all tell ourselves futuristic stories all the time; they are inherent in our daydreams and our career plans, and in our anxious fears for our own old age and adulthood of our children. When the pace of social and technological change accelerates, we all need more help and more practice in writing the scripts for these stories, which are part and parcel of the narratives of our real lives. That is why science fiction and futurology exist, and why they are becoming more significant with every year that passes.

The stories in this book all deal with projects which the advancement of genetic engineering may one day make possible. Their strategy, however, is not to focus on the most probable applications of such technology; that is what futurology attempts to do. The strategy of fiction is to attempt to discover those possible adventures in technology which have the sharpest relevance to the most intimate and most powerful human desires and human anxieties. Sex and death play a very prominent role in the stories in this book, because those are the topics with which our most intimate desires and anxieties are by necessity concerned.

In consequence of this, the collection should not be seen as a series of literary 'portraits' of the future, but rather as a series of caricatures; caricatures carry meaning and implication so much more readily than portraits. The tales are mostly sarcastic in tone, but their dark humour is an aspect of the essential seriousness of the underlying purpose. Human experience is fundamentally ironic. Only by reaching into the realms of absurdity can we measure the true scope of potentiality; only by entertaining nonsense can we cultivate the perspective which lets us see the true limits of sense.

Some of the tales herein are authentically apocalyptic, and the grandiose metamorphoses of future society which are envisaged are usually represented ambivalently rather than with unqualified enthusiasm. I must insist, however, that this should not be taken as evidence of pessimism on my part. Futuristic fiction is, in the main, much more anxious and alarmist than futurology; this has far more to do with the nature of drama and suspense than with the ideals of authors.

Propagandistic visions of pleasant Utopian futures, whatever their merits as political philosophy may be, are always weak and anaemic as fiction; they inevitably lack dramatic tension.

Visions of dystopian Brave New Worlds, by contrast, have dramatic tension in abundance. It is wrong to construe the ending of a dystopian fantasy like George Orwell's *Nineteen Eighty-Four* simply as an expression of despair; it should instead be seen as an argumentative *reductio ad absurdum* which demonstrates the urgency of our need to prevent the triumph of the political ideals and methods employed by its world-rulers. The more downbeat stories in this book should be seen in the same light; if some of their endings seem bleak, it is a result of rhetorical method rather than naked terror.

For myself, I am an optimist: I believe, sincerely and passionately, that the rewards which can come from the wise and constructive uses of biotechnology will more than compensate for the undoubted hazards of careless or malevolent use. That has been true of all past technologies; it will hopefully be true of all future ones. In order to counterbalance the calculatedly ambivalent stance which the stories take, I have appended to the collection the text of one of my more analytically-inclined exercises in futurology, which should suffice to set the argument of the tales in its proper context.

Bedside conversations

'It's not entirely unprecedented,' said the doctor, 'but so far as I know, this is the first time it's happened in the present medical context – which means, of course, that it poses a novel moral problem. I'll have to refer it to the hospital's Ethics Committee, of course, and they'll want to interview you, but I'm certain that the essential decision will be left in your hands.'

Gerald heard what was being said to him, but couldn't find a sensible way to react to it. It was as though his thought-processes had seized up, leaving all the ideas in his head stuck fast, grinding against one another painfully as he tried to force them into motion again.

Dr McClelland waited politely for an answer, but when none came he repeated the last phrase, for the sake of emphasis. 'In your hands,' he said, as though he were bestowing a favour.

Gerald found his voice again. 'What did you say it was called?' he asked.

'*Fetus in fetu*. What happens, you see, is that the fertilised ovum divides, as it does when producing identical twins, but then one embryo develops faster than the other, growing around it. Usually, development of the engulfed embryo is simply suspended and never restarts; even in those cases where it does restart it rarely produces a perfect fetus.'

'This has happened before, then?'

'Oh yes. The first reported case was in the late 19th century, when the French surgeon Dupuytren found an apparently entire fetus in the body of a 13-year-old boy. In England at a slightly later date Blundell tracked the development of a similar fetus in a nine-year-old, which was contained in a sac and connected to the abdominal wall by an umbilical cord. At 31 you may be the oldest person on record to have the problem, but you're certainly not the first.'

'What happened to the two boys?'

'Those particular ones both died. But you needn't worry about that, Mr Duncan; this is the 21st century, not the 19th. You're in no danger at all. The 20th century cases fared better. A surgeon named McIntyre operated to remove a similar fetus from an eleven-year-old boy in the 1920s;

the boy made a full recovery. I found records in three later operations, all successful – but the last one was in 1992, before the first successful experiments in tissue-reconstruction.'

Gerald found a lump in his throat which he couldn't quite contrive to swallow. He was possessed by a perverse mix of emotions. On the one hand, he was deeply relieved that the tumour had turned out not to be malign; on the other hand, he was horrified by the revelation that it wasn't really a cancer tumour at all, but the phantom embryo of a twin brother he'd never had. He pressed his right hand to the bulge which was distending his abdomen to the side of his navel. Four months had passed since he first noticed the swelling, two since he had belatedly become anxious enough to seek medical advice.

'How soon will you need to operate?' he asked, numbly.

'It's not as simple as that,' replied McClelland, patiently. 'That's what I've been trying to explain. It has to go to the Ethics Committee – but I really am certain that the final decision will be left to you.'

'What decision?'

'What will happen to the embryo, of course. That's why there's a new precedent to be established, you see. In none of the cases I've cited could there be any question of the embryo's surviving and coming to term, so the only possible course of action in each case was to remove it. Nowadays, though, we have other options. If we act promptly, it's possible that we could transplant the embryo into a host mother. On the other hand, we could use tissue-reconstruction to stimulate your own cells so that they'd develop a viable placenta. In fact, the Ethics Committee might take the view that the one thing we *can't* do is to treat the fetus as if it were a tumour – they could well conclude that an operation to remove it would count as an abortion, in which case it would be illegal by reason of the 20-week time-limit.

'As far as I can tell, the fetus is at the same developmental stage one would expect of a 24 or 25-week embryo. It's smaller, of course, but I have no evidence to suggest that it's damaged. In my experience, Ethics Committees always look for the closest thing to a precedent they can find – and they're likely to take the view that you should be viewed as if you were a pregnant mother who, for some reason, can't actually give birth.'

'I'm pregnant,' said Gerald, feeling that the notion was more than slightly surreal, 'and I can't get an abortion.'

'That's not unprecedented either,' said the doctor. 'In fact . . .'

'Never mind the precedents,' Gerald interrupted him. 'Let's stick to me. Are you telling me that I might be *forced* to carry this fetus until it's capable of independent life, that you won't cut it out until you're sure that it can survive in an incubator?'

'No, I'm *not* saying that,' replied McClelland, testily. 'The fetus is still viable now, but that doesn't guarantee that you can carry it to term – not, at any rate, without considerable tissue-restructuring to make sure that you can sustain it while it grows. It might be better – indeed, it might be a matter of some urgency – to transplant it into a woman's womb, or into one of the new artificial wombs under test at St Mary's. That's a decision which you'll have to make, but it must be an *informed* decision, morally as well as medically – which is where the Ethics Committee comes in.

'I've already sent in my preliminary report, but the committee will want a more detailed one as soon as I've collated all the data. We can't discharge you – and we must respectfully demand that you don't discharge yourself – until the committee has met and made its views known to you. But you really mustn't worry; what we *all* want is to figure out where your best interests lie, and where the best interests of your brother lie.'

The vital phrase – 'the best interests of your brother' – lingered in Gerald's mind long after the doctor had gone.

'I'm pregnant,' said Gerald, flatly.

'If that's a joke, dear heart,' said Mark Cleminson, 'it's in very bad taste, and it isn't even funny.'

'It's not a joke,' Gerald assured him. 'It's a *fetus in fetu.*'

While he explained, with painstaking patience, he studied Mark's face very carefully.

Mark and Gerald had been together for five years, and married for two. They had married, in fact, a mere three days after the law had at last been amended to permit same-sex marriages. They had, not unnaturally, been carried away by the triumphant feeling that a great victory had been won for justice and equality, and that its potential must be exploited to the full. Alas, Gerald sometimes felt that their relationship had failed to live up to the expectations into which that mortal and political victory had seduced them. Like most marriages made on earth, theirs had fared no better than those supposedly made in Heaven, and he was no longer sure whether or not Mark still loved him – or, for that matter, whether Mark had ever *really* loved him. He couldn't help wondering whether this might be the acid test which would reveal the truth of the matter.

'It's a trifle macabre,' said Mark, when the explanation was complete, 'to think of you swallowing up your little brother-to-be like that. One expects a certain amount of sibling rivalry, of course, but prenatal cannibalism is taking things a *little* too far, don't you think?'

Gerald pursed his lips, but dutifully suppressed his impatient ire. 'It's not a joke, Mark,' he repeated, patiently.

'Oh, cheer up,' Mark retorted. 'Yesterday we thought you might have some dreadful cancer devouring you from the bowel outwards. I'm sorry if I sound flippant, but it's mostly relief, I assure you. You did say that it isn't dangerous, didn't you?'

'It isn't dangerous,' admitted Gerald, 'but it isn't straightforward either.' He explained about the Ethics Committee, carefully gauging Mark's reaction to every point in the chain of argument. He knew that he was going to have to go through the whole thing again, at least twice more. His parents would have to know, and so would his employers. He hoped that it might not be necessary to tell anyone else, but he could hardly avoid the dreadful fear that the media might get hold of the story. It would be news anyhow, but the fact that he was married to another man would give the headline-writers a field day.

He already knew how his parents would react to the story, because they always reacted the same way to everything he did – with pain, shock and horror. They subscribed very heavily to the where-did-we-go-wrong school of rhetoric, and they would try to make him feel as guilty about this as every other respect in which he offended them. In fact, he had a nasty suspicion that his mother, at least, would instantly begin to believe that her life would have been much less trouble if only Gerald had been the embryo which was engulfed.

It was harder to guess how they would react at the office; everyone there had been supremely sympathetic and supportive while it seemed that he might have cancer, but this was something else.

All in all, Gerald felt that he had just undergone an instantaneous role-switch from brave invalid to freak, and he badly needed some reassurance from his first and closest confidant to the effect that other people could ride with the punch.

'That's *repulsive*,' said Mark, when he'd finished. 'Do they seriously imagine that you'd consent to tissue-reconstruction just so that you can carry the fetus until they'll condescend to whip it out? Hell, it's like one of those old 20th century jokes about homosexual couples, which should have been laid to rest with the Dark Ages. Holy shit, they *will* keep it quiet, won't they?'

'I suppose they'll try,' Gerald replied unhappily. 'At least, they will if they remove the fetus. If they don't . . . well, news is bound to get around if I have to put in an application for maternity leave.'

'*Now* who needs reminding that it's not a joke? Thank God it's your decision — it *will* be your decision, won't it?'

'So the doctor says, but it has to be an informed decision, medically and normally. He was very clear about that. Whatever's best for baby . . .'

'Whatever's best for *both* of you. The greatest good of the greatest number, remember. Don't let the bastards talk you into anything. I wouldn't trust a doctor as far as I could throw a feather into a headwind.'

Neither would I, thought Gerald. *That's why I delayed going to see one, and thus made certain that this would become a matter of some urgency.* Aloud, he said: 'I won't. But

Dr McClelland's right – it does have to be an informed decision, and it has to be taken very carefully.'

Mark stared at him, his grey eyes as hard as flints. Gerald couldn't figure it out, now, just why he'd once thought that those were extraordinarily sexy and sensitive.

'Gerry,' said Mark, in a voice which was suddenly rather cold, 'you couldn't possibly think that you might carry this kid around for the next God-knows-how-long. You couldn't possibly.'

'It would only be for three months at the most, Mark,' Gerald pointed out. 'And when all's said and done, he ain't heavy, he's my brother.' He couldn't suppress a giggle, despite the fact that he was trying to be serious. The flippancy, in fact, was only a way of concealing just how serious he was.

An informed decision, medically and morally – that was what it was all about. The doctor was right.

'That's not funny, Gerry,' said Mark, who was, of course, correct for all the wrong reasons. 'That's not funny at all.'

'Your father and I talked about it all night, said Leonie Duncan positively, 'and we're agreed that there's only one thing to be done.'

'Oh yes,' said Gerald, hollowly. 'And what's that, Mother?'

'The baby has to be transplanted, as soon as possible.'

'Well,' said Gerald, dubiously, 'that may turn out to be the best decision, but I'm not sure as yet. Dr McClelland's given me the results of the latest tests, and I had a long conversation with the secretary of the Ethics Committee this morning. He's convening a meeting this evening, so that we can go over the alternatives very carefully. Until then, it just won't be possible to make a final decision, no matter what you and Dad may think.'

'Committees can't make decisions, Gerry,' said Leonie, with the casual air of one stating the obvious. 'The committee that set out to design the horse came up with the camel. It's as plain as day what should be done, and we don't need any committee confusing the issue.'

'But it's *not* as plain as day, Mother,' said Gerald, wearily. 'It's really rather complicated, medically speaking.'

'Well I'm not speaking *medically*,' she said. 'I'm speaking about right and wrong, and there's only one rightful place for that baby.'

She was looking at him so assertively, and yet with such awkward embarrassment, that he was quite confused. Several seconds passed before he suddenly realised what she meant.

'Oh my God!' he said. 'You can't be serious!'

'He's my child,' she said, assertiveness tipping over into naked aggression. 'He's not your child, he's mine. He doesn't belong in an artificial womb, and he certainly doesn't belong inside you. He's my son, and nobody has any right to put him anywhere else but in my womb. I'm willing to do it, Gerry, and I'm willing to go to court to establish my rights.'

'Mother,' said Gerald, feeling once again that strange sense of the surreality of his condition, 'you're 57 years old. What makes you think your womb's in any fit condition to carry a fetus?'

'Don't be ridiculous, darling,' Leonie replied. 'I may be menopausal, but I'm in perfect working order, and if I'm not, I'm certain that it would be far easier to reconstruct my tissues than it would be to reconstruct yours. After all, I *do* have the right equipment, even if it hasn't been used for a while. And afterwards, the child would be with its natural parents.'

'Dad's 63. Are you telling me he *wants* to be a parent again?'

'He already is a parent,' said Leonie decisively. 'It's not a matter of want, it's a matter of fact.'

'If the fetus *is* to be transplanted,' Gerald said,

trying to sound gentle, 'and *if* we decide against an artificial womb, I think it would be best to look for a younger and healthier surrogate mother.'

'Well I don't,' she retorted. 'And if that's what your Ethics Committee decides, or if that's what *you* decide, I'll fight it. This is my baby, and no one else has a better right to carry him and give birth to him, and there isn't a court in the land which would award custody of him to anyone else.'

'Mother,' said Gerald, patiently and soothingly, 'I don't think you ought to be thinking like this. Mark and I would far rather keep the whole thing quiet – we certainly don't want any tabloid publicity. If you go near a court, you'll have every newsvid team in the country baying at our heels. Whatever I decide to do will be in the best interests of everyone, I promise you, but you must see how difficult it is. Imagine it was one of your friends – what would you say if you found out that Margaret Lingard was proposing to have a fetus transplanted into her womb? You'd be horrified, wouldn't you?'

'He's my baby,' said Leonie Duncan, doggedly. 'He's not yours, he's *mine*. My son. My *natural* son.'

Gerald winced at the double meaning, and saw his mother smile thinly. She knew perfectly well what she'd said; he knew perfectly well what she meant.

He knew, also, what Mark would have said had he been there. 'Let the bitch have it, and welcome' he'd have said. Mark didn't usually want Leonie Duncan to have her own way about anything, but this would be too good to miss: in Mark's view, it would be killing two birds with one stone. And he'd be right: one stone, two dead birds. Maybe *really* dead.

'I'm going to see your blessed Ethics Committee,' said Leonie, defiantly. 'I'm going to see them right now, and I'm going to make sure they know what *I* think. An informed decision is what you want, and an informed decision is what you're going to get. They'll give me this baby, *or else.*'

Gerald watched her go, feeling infinitely wearier than he had when she first came in. She always had that effect on him, and he guessed that she always would. Nothing could change that; nothing at all.

'How did the meeting go?' asked Mary Blake, anxious curiosity very evident within her gentle politeness. Mary was Gerald's Head of Department, and his only friend of the opposite sex. Gerald was hoping fervently that she'd be just disinterested enough to provide him with a little honest sympathy.

'Efficiency ponderous would be the best description, I think,' he said. Then, as if quoting from a book of regulations, he intoned: 'The Ethics Committee of this hospital consists of five people: a senior consultant, a hospital administrator, a social worker, a lawyer and a lay adviser. The administrator acts as secretary, the lawyer as chairman.

'Also present at the meeting to decide the fate of Fetus Duncan were Drs McClelland and Digby, expert witnesses. Mr Duncan was duly informed that he had the right to be represented by an advocate, which opportunity he duly refused, it having been made clear to him that the meeting was not supposed to be an adversarial situation, and that everyone's hope was to reach a unanimous decision as to what could and ought to be done.'

'Sounds dire,' said Mary.

'Not really,' said Gerald. 'They had to take pains, you see, to make sure that everything was understood, and everything was taken into account. They weren't just being pompous.'

'And what did they decide, in the end?'

'An Ethics Committee,' he intoned again, 'is not a decision-making body. It acts in an advisory capacity only, but its duty is to advise the hospital as well as the patient, and if it considers the patient's decision to be ill-founded, has a duty to advise the hospital of any such judgement.'

'I mean,' she amended, 'what did you decide?'

'I haven't, yet,' he admitted. 'I have to make up my mind by six o'clock, so that the Committee can meet again and decide whether to endorse my decision or do the other thing. Time is standing still while I ponder the issues involved, weighing the pros and cons as carefully as I can.'

'Of course,' said Mary, 'it's none of my business really.'

'Yes it is,' he told her, dolorously. 'It's your business, and Mark's, and my mother's and father's, and McClelland's. Whatever I decide to do, it will affect other people – that's one of the things I have to bear in mind. There's the surgeon who might have to transplant the fetus, the surrogate mother who might have to carry it, the doctor in charge of the artificial womb which might otherwise have to carry it, et cetera, et cetera. God, wasn't life simple when it was only a tumour which might have metastasised, leaving me with six months to live?'

'Nobody gets six months to live any more,' she said. 'This is 2003. Everything's curable these days.'

'Even a *fetus in fetu*,' he agreed. 'The wonders of tissue-reconstruction. Did you know that more than a hundred men have carried fetuses to term, worldwide? That's in spite of the bans in the EC and America. One hundred and seven successful Caesarian births – mind you, there have been some messy miscarriages too.'

'Wouldn't the transplant option be easier?' she asked. 'Safer for everyone.'

'Safer for the corporation's image,' he agreed. 'Unobtrusiveness is the life-blood of our promotion prospects, isn't it?'

'That's not what I meant,' she said, in an aggrieved tone.

'No,' he admitted. 'I know it's not. And maybe it would be easier in strictly medical terms. Except that I can't help feeling that I might be pitching the poor little proto-person into a bear pit, where various contending parties might contrive to rip it apart while trying to save it.'

'You mean that the artificial womb people may start fighting with the supporters of surrogate mothers? I suppose we're overdue for some kind of test case in that particular debate.'

'Actually,' he said, mournfully, 'I was thinking about my mother. But you're right, of course. The artificial womb people might well be looking for a soft target, and a *fetus in fetu* is certainly softer than a little bundle of cells in its own mummy's tummy.'

'Is Leonie likely to make trouble?'

'Trouble,' he said, 'is far too mild a word for it. Hell hath no fury like a woman's who has finally discovered the perfect way to pay back her only begotten son for being gay.'

'Shit,' said Mary, sympathetically.

'Couldn't have put it better myself,' he said.

'So what *are* you going to do?'

Gerald looked at his wristwatch. Normally he found the old-fashioned display reassuring, but today the second-hand seemed to be going round in an unnaturally hasty manner. He couldn't help feeling that a digital might have had a little more decorum.

'I'll know,' he said, 'in just over two hours' time. Anything sooner would be bound to seem hasty, wouldn't it?'

'I wish you the best of luck,' she said.

'Luck,' he assured her, with a sigh, 'has absolutely nothing to do with it. It's purely a matter of moral and medical reasoning. I have all the necessary information – all that remains is to convert it by the power of pure reasoning into the right decision.'

'I *still* wish you the best of luck,' she said.

'And however the dice come down, I'll do whatever I can.'

'Thanks,' he said, and meant it.

Inevitably, it transpired that when six o'clock came, Mary Blake was the only one who had the decency not to be there and waiting. Leonie Duncan and Mark Cleminson turned up on the dot, and so did Dr McClelland, but Gerald had no intention of making a speech.

'I'll see you one at a time,' he insisted. 'First the doctor, then you, Mother, and Mark last. Please don't argue about the order of precedence – there isn't time for that sort of nonsense.'

He watched Mark and his mother exchanging resentful glances, neither of them quite sure whether or not they had been awarded the most favoured position in the queue. In the end, though, they had to accept it. It was his decision, after all.

When they had both gone, and the door was closed, Gerald told Dr McClelland what he had decided.

'You don't think,' said McClelland, dubiously, 'that it's going a bit *far*? It's at least one step beyond what's strictly necessary.'

'You *can* do it,' said Gerald, 'can't you? It's by no means unprecedented.'

'In itself, no,' admitted the doctor. 'But for this reason . . . you haven't, I suppose, had any leanings in this direction before?'

'None at all,' Gerald confessed, feeling that the seriousness of the occasion precluded a diplomatic lie. 'But circumstances alter cases, don't they?'

The doctor nodded. 'I'll have to refer it to the Committee,' he said, 'but I think they'll go along with it. As I've always said, I think they'd go along with anything you decided to do, except perhaps . . .' He nodded in the direction of the closed door.

'There was never a chance of *that*,' said Gerald.

'Do you think she will go to court, now that you've decided?'

'I hope not. I hope Dad will talk her out of it. But if she does, so be it. After all, I can hardly hope to avoid publicity now that I've made my decision, can I?'

'No,' said the doctor, pensively. 'I dare say you can't.'

'You *can't*,' said Leonie Duncan, angrily. 'It's preposterous. You can't do it.'

'Yes I can,' said Gerald, patiently. 'It's pefectly feasible, and it avoids the worst aspects of both the other solutions. Tissue reconstruction is done all the time – it's just a matter of switching the right genes on and off.'

'It's obscene,' she said. 'It's unnatural.'

'Mother,' he said, quietly, 'everthing that enables us to be human and civilised is unnatural. Wearing clothes is unnatural; speaking languages is unnatural; building houses and roads is unnatural; medicine is unnatural; in fact, every goddam thing which makes life worth living is unnatural. The only *natural* thing in this whole affair is that ridiculous freak of a baby brother which is slowly turning into a king-sized pain in my gut. Nature is all stupid accidents, Mother; human life is about taking reasoned decisions to oppose and overcome the waywardness of nature. That's what I've done. I won't say that it will be easy, but I will defend the reasonableness of my decision in any and every court in the land, if I have to. So you'll just have to go away, and decide what you're going to do, and then do it, won't you?'

Leonie Duncan burst into tears. 'Whatever did we do wrong?' she wailed.

'You *can't*,' said Mark Cleminson, in utter disbelief. 'It's preposterous. You can't do it.'

'Yes I can,' said Gerald, patiently, conscientiously repeating himself. 'It's perfectly feasible, and it avoids the worst aspects of both the other solutions. Tissue reconstruction is . . .'

Mark didn't wait to heaar the rest of it. 'But what about *us!* he complained. 'Don't I figure in this at all?'

'Of course you do,' said Gerald. 'We're married, aren't we? That doesn't have to change, unless you want it to.'

'*Doesn't have to change!* You're mad, do you know that? Mad!'

Gerald studied those hard grey eyes. They looked like the eyes of a blind man, staring but not seeing.

'I suppose you'll tell me now that this is what you've always wanted,' said Mark, converting his sense of injury into a sneer. 'I suppose you've decided that you were never genuinely gay, that you were really a heterosexual woman in the wrong body. Well *I'm* gay, and there is no way I'm going to put up with this nonsense. I'm telling you straight: get this *thing* transplanted — I don't give a damn whether it ends up in your mother, or a machine, or any place else — or we're through. Finished. *Kaput.*'

'Suit yourself,' said Gerald, with a lack of remorse which surprised him more than a little. 'It's only tissue-replacement, you know, not an identity transplant. It needn't even be permanent

— I could change back after I stop breast-feeding. I'd still be *me*.'

'Like hell you would,' said Mark, as though he were spitting out powdered glass. 'Like hell.'

Afterwards, when Gerald was alone (at last!) the doubts began to creep in. He laid his hand yet again on the *fetus in fetu*, wondering anxiously what the pangs of birth would actually be like. Like the torments of hell, perhaps . . . very possibly, in fact. It wasn't something he was looking forward to. It wasn't something he *could* look forward to, but women did it all the time, and by the time he had to do it, he'd be a woman too, at least for a while.

It wasn't simply that he had to become a mother in order to compete with his own mother. It wasn't that at all. It was the *fetus in fetu* whose needs had to be given top priority. Viable it might be, but it was facing a prospect that no proto-human individual had ever faced before in the history of the world. It had to be given every chance; he thought that he owed it everything he could give.

So he'd made his decision.

The trouble with informed decisions, he thought, *is that there's too much bloody information by half.*

But it *wasn't* heavy, and it *was* his brother . . .
and sometimes, he figured, a man just had to do
what a man had to do . . .
That was all there was to it, really.

A Career in Sexual Chemistry

There are some names which are more difficult to wear than others. Shufflebottoms, Bastards and Pricks start life with a handicap from which they may never recover, and one can easily understand why those born into families which have innocently borne since time immemorial such surnames as Hitler and Quisling often surrender such birthrights in favour of Smith or Villanova. People who refuse to change embarrassing names are frequently forced into an attitude of defensive stubbornness, brazenly and pridefully staring out the mockery of the world. For some people, an unfortunate surname can be a challenge as well as a curse, and life for them becomes a field of conflict in which heroism requires them to acquit themselves well.

One might be forgiven for thinking that Casanova is a less problematic name than many. It is by no means vulgar and has not the slightest genocidal connotation. It is a name that some men would be glad to have, conferring upon them as it would a mystique which they might wittily exploit. It is nevertheless a label which might be parent to a host of embarrassments and miseries, especially if worn by a gawky schoolboy in an English inner city comprehensive school, which was where the Giovanni Casanova who had been born on 14 February 1982 first became fully aware of its burdensome nature.

Giovanni's father, Marcantonio Casanova, had always been fond of the name, and seemed well enough equipped by fate to wear it well. He was not a tall man, but he had a handsome face and dark, flashing eyes which were definitely no handicap in the heart-melting stakes. He had made no serious attempt to live up to the name, though, accepting it as a nice joke that he found contentment in placid monogamy. His grandparents had come to Britain in the 1930s, refugees from Mussolini's Italy, and had settled in Manchester at the height of the Depression. Marcantonio therefore came from a line of impoverished intellectuals who had been prevented by social circumstances from achieving their real potential.

Giovanni's mother had also had no opportunity to fulfil her intellectual potential. Her maiden name was Jenny Spencer, and she had been born into that kind of respectable working-class family which would make every effort to set its sons on the road of upward social mobility, but thought that the acme of achievement for a daughter was to be an apprentice hairdresser at 16, a wife at 17 and a mother at 18. All of these expectations Jenny had fulfilled with casual ease.

The whims of genetic and environmental fortune combined to give these humble parents a uniquely gifted son, for Giovanni soon showed evidence of a marvellous intelligence beyond even the latent potentialities of his parents. Nature's generosity was, however, restricted entirely to qualities of mind; in terms of looks and physique Giovanni was a non-starter. He was undersized, out of proportion, and had an awful complexion. A bout of measles in infancy added insult to injury by leaving his eyesight terribly impaired; astigmatism and chronic myopia combined to force him to wear spectacles which robbed his dark eyes of any opportunity they ever had to flash heart-meltingly, and made him look rather cross-eyed. His voice was high-pitched, and never broke properly when he belatedly reached puberty. His hair insisted on growing into an appalling black tangle, and he began to go thin on top when he was barely seventeen. As dozens of thoughtless people were to remark to his face, and thousands more were to think silently to themselves, he certainly didn't *look* like a Casanova.

The class culture of England had proved remarkably resilient in the face of the erodent egalitarianism of the 20th century, and bourgeois morality never did filter down to the poorer streets of Northern England, even when the old slums were demolished and new ones erected with indoor toilets and inbuilt social alienation. Where Giovanni spent his formative years very few girls preserved their virginity past the age of fourteen, and many a boy without a CSE to his name had done sufficient research to write a PhD thesis on sexual technique by the time he was old enough to vote. This tide of covert sexual activity, however, passed Giovanni Casanova by. He was acutely conscious of the flood of eroticism which seethed all around him, and wished devoutly to be carried away by it, but to no avail.

Other ugly boys, who seemed to him as un-prepossessing as himself, managed one by one to leap the first and most difficult hurdle, and subsequently gained marvellously in confidence and expertise, but Giovanni could not emulate them. His unattractiveness made things difficult, and his name added just sufficiently to his difficulties to make his task impossible, because it made even the girls who might have felt sorry for him laugh at him instead. Even the most feeble-minded of teenage girls could appreciate that there was something essentially rib-tickling about saying 'no' to a Casanova.

Giovanni had started out his journey through adolescence bogged down by self-consciousness, and by the time he was seventeen he was filled with self-loathing and incipient paranoia. By then he was already doomed to a long career as a social misfit. He was so withdrawn, having suffered such agonies from his failures, that he had completely given up talking to members of the female sex, except when forced by absolute necessity.

His sanity was saved, though, because he found a haven of retreat: the world of scientific knowledge, whose certainties contrasted so sharply with the treacherous vicissitudes of the social world. Even his teachers thought of him as a slightly unsavoury freak, but they recognised that in intellectual terms he was a potential superstar. He compiled the most impressive scholarly record that his very moderate school had ever produced, and in October 2000 he went triumphantly to university to study biochemistry.

Biochemistry was the glamour science in those days, when every year that passed produced new biotechnological miracles from the laboratories of the genetic engineers. Giovanni was entranced by the infinite possibilities of the applied science, and set out to master the crafts of gene-mapping, protein design and plasmid construction. In everyday life he seemed extremely clumsy and slow of wit, but he was a very different character in the privacy of a laboratory, when he could manage the most delicate operation with absolute control, and where he had such a perfect intuition and understanding of what he was doing that he soon left his educators far behind.

In the new environment of the university, where intelligence was held in reasonably high esteem by female students, Giovanni tried tentatively to come out of his shell. He began talking to girls again, albeit with ponderous caution and unease. He helped other students with their work, and tried once or twice to move on from assistance to seduction. There was a black-haired Isabel who seemed to think him an interesting conversationalist, and a freckled Mary who even cooked a couple of meals for him because she thought he was neglecting himself, but they politely declined to enter into more intimate relationships with him. They could not think of him in such a light, and though they were prepared to consider Giovanni a friend of sorts, the boys they welcomed into their beds were of a very different type. Giovanni tried hard not to resent this, and to see their point of view. He certainly did not *blame* them, but his sympathy with their attitude only made him more disappointed with himself, and even more sharply aware of the mockery in his name.

Transforming bacteria by plasmid engineering was *passé* long before Giovanni's graduation, and he felt that the engineering of plants, though it certainly offered great opportunities for ingenuity and creativity, was not quite adventurous enough for him. He knew that his talents were sufficiently extraordinary to require something a little more daring, and so he channelled his efforts in the direction of animal engineering. His doctoral research was devoted to the development of artificial cytogene systems which could be transplanted into animal cells without requiring disruption of the nucleus or incorporation into the chromosomal system; these made it practicable to transform specific cells in the tissues of mature metazoans, avoiding all the practical and ethical problems which still surrounded work on zygotes and embryos.

Giovanni's early ambition was to apply this research to various projects in medical science. He produced in his imagination half a dozen

strategies for conquering cancer, and a few exotic
methods of combating the effects of aging. Had
he stayed in pure research, based in a university,
this was undoubtedly what he would have done,
but the early years of the new millennium were a
period of economic boom, when big biotechnology companies were headhunting talent with a
rare ruthlessness. Giovanni never applied for a
job or made any inquiry about industrial opportunities, but found potential employers begging
to interview him in the comfort of his own home
or any other place he cared to name. They sent
beautiful and impeccably-manicured personnel
officers to woo him with their tutored smiles and
their talk of six-figure salaries. One or two were
so desperate to net him that they seemed almost
willing to bribe him with sexual favours, but they
always stopped short of this ultimate tactic, much
to his chagrin.

He was so fiercely dedicated to his work, and
had such noble ideals, that he hesitated for a long
time before selling out, but the temptations were
too much for him in the end. He sold himself to
the highest bidder – Cytotech, Inc. – and joined
the brain drain to sunny California, being careful
to leave most of his bank accounts in convenient
European tax shelters so that he could be a
millionaire before he was thirty. He had the

impression that even the most ill-favoured of millionaires could easily play the part of a Casanova, and he could hardly wait to set himself up as a big spender.

Cytotech was heavily involved in medical research, but its dynamic company president, Marmaduke Melmoth, had different plans for this most extraordinary of hirelings. He invited Giovanni to his mansion in Beverley Hills, and gave him the most fabulous meal that the young man had ever seen. Then he told Giovanni where, in his terminology, 'the game was to be played'.

'The future,' said Melmoth, sipping his pink champagne, 'is in aphrodisiacs. Cancer cures we can only sell to people with cancer. Life-expectation is great, but it isn't worth a damn unless people can *enjoy* extended life. To hell with better mousetraps – what *this* world wants is better beaver-traps. You make me a red-hot pheromone, and I'll make you a billionaire.'

Giovanni explained to Melmoth that there could be no such thing as a powerful human pheromone. Many insects, he pointed out, perceive their environment almost entirely in olfactory terms, so that it makes sense for female insects with limited periods of fertility to signal their readiness with a smelly secretion which, if produced in sufficient quantities, could draw every male insect from miles around. Humans, by contrast, make very little use of their sense of smell, and their females are unafflicted by short and vital phases of fertility which must at all costs be exploited for the continued survival of the species.

'All this I know,' Melmoth assured him. 'And the fact that you thought to tell me about it reveals to me that you have an attitude problem. Let me give you some advice, son. It's easy to find people who'll tell me what isn't possible and can't be done. For that I can hire morons. I hire geniuses to say "If *that* won't work, what will?" Do you get my drift?'

Giovanni was genuinely impressed by this observation, though it could hardly be reckoned original. He realised that his remarks really had been symptomatic of an attitude problem, which had manifested itself all-too-powerfully in his personal life. He went to his laboratory determined to produce for Mr Melmoth something that would stand in for the impossible pheromone, and determined to produce for himself some sexual encounters that would put him on course for a career as an authentic Casanova. It was simply, he decided, a matter of strategy and determination.

In fact, Giovanni was now in a position where

he had more than a little prestige and influence. Although he was notionally starting at the bottom at Cytotech, there was no doubting that he would go far – that he was a man to be respected no matter how unlovely his appearance might be.

Thus advantaged, he had little difficulty in losing his virginity at last, with a 17-year-old blonde lab assistant called Helen. This was a great relief, but he was all too well aware of the fact that it represented no considerable triumph. It was a fumbling affair, throughout which he was trembling with anxiety and embarrassment; he felt that his everyday clumsiness and awkwardness, though he could leave them behind in his laboratory work, he concentrated to grotesque extremes in his sexual technique. Pretty Helen, who was not herself overburdened with experience or sophistication, uttered not a word of complaint and made no reference to his surname, but Giovanni found himself quite convinced that in the privacy of her thoughts she was crying out 'Casanova! Casanova!' and laughing hysterically at the irony of it. He dared not ask her to his bed again, and tended to shun her in the workplace.

Deciding that he needed more practice, Giovanni arranged visits to whores whose telephone numbers he found scrawled on the walls of the payphones in the main lobby, and though he avoided by this means the embarrassment of knowing that his partners were aware of his name, he still found it appallingly difficult to improve his performance. If anything, he thought, he was getting worse instead of better, becoming steadily more ludicrous in his own eyes.

Clearly this was what Melmoth would have called an attitude problem, but Giovanni now knew that simply calling it by that name would no more solve it than calling him Casanova had made him into an avatar of his famous namesake. Self-disgust made him give up visiting prostitutes after his third such experience, and he could not bring himself to try to resuscitate his relationship with Helen. He had little difficulty convincing himself that celibacy was to be preferred to continual humiliation.

In his work, however, he was making great strides. Taking Melmoth's advice to heart, he asked himself what would constitute, in human terms, an alternative to pheromones. The dominant human sense is sight, so the nearest human analogue of an insect pheromone is an attractive appearance, but this has so long been taken for granted that it sustains a vast cosmetics industry dedicated to helping members of the desired sex to enhance their charms. Giovanni felt that there was relatively little scope in this area for his expertise, so he turned his attention to the sense of touch.

He eventually decided that what was needed was something that would make the touch of the would-be seducer irresistible to the target of his (or her) affections: a love-potion of the fingertips. If he could find a psychotropic protein which could be absorbed quickly through the skin, so that the touch of the donor could become associated with subsequent waves of pleasurable sensation, then it should be fairly easy to achieve an operant conditioning of the desired one.

Giovanni brought all his artistry in protein-design to bear on the production of a psychotropic which would call forth strong feelings of euphoria, tenderness, affection and lust. This was not easy – understanding of this kind of psychochemistry was then at a very primitive level – but he was the man for the job. Having found the ideal protein, he then encoded it in the DNA of an artificial cytogene which was tailored for incorporation in subepidermal cells, whose activation would be triggered by sexual arousal. The protein itself could then be delivered to the surface of the skin by the sweat-glands.

When the time came to explain this ingenious mechanism to Marmaduke Melmoth, the company president was not immediately enthused.

'Hell's bells, boy,' he said. 'Why not just put the stuff in bottles and let people smear it on their fingers?'

Giovanni explained that his new psychotropic protein, like the vast majority of such entities, was so awesomely delicate that it could not be kept in solution, and would rapidly denature outside the protective environment of a living cell. In any case, the whole point was that the object of desire could only obtain this particular fix from the touch of the would-be seducer. If it was to be used for conditioning, then its sources must be very carefully limited. This was not a technology for mass distribution, but something for the favoured few, who must use it with the utmost discretion.

'Oh shit,' said Melmoth, in disgust. 'How are we going to make billions out of a product like that?'

Giovanni suggested that he sell it only to the very rich at an exorbitant price.

'If we're going to do it that way,' Melmoth told him, 'we're going to have to be absolutely sure that it works, and that there's not the ghost of an unfortunate side-effect. You work for customers like that, they have to get satisfaction.'

Giovanni agreed that this was a vital necessity. He set up a series of exhaustive and highly secret clinical trials, and did not tell Melmoth that he had already started exploring the effects and potentials of the tissue-transformation. In the great tradition of scientific self-sacrifice, he had volunteered to be his own guinea-pig.

To say that the method worked would be a feeble understatement. Giovanni found that he only had to look at an attractive girl, and conjure up in his imagination fantasies of sexual communion, to produce the special sweat that put magic at his fingertips. Once he was sufficiently worked up, the merest touch sufficed to set the psychochemical seduction in train, and it required only the simplest strategy to achieve the required conditioning. Girls learned very quickly, albeit subconsciously, to associate his touch with the most tender and exciting emotions. They quickly overcame their natural revulsion and began to think that although not *conventionally* attractive he was really rather fascinating.

Within three weeks of the experiment's launch four female lab assistants, two word-processing operatives, three receptionists, one industrial relations consultant and a traffic warden were deep in the throes of infatuation. Giovanni was on top of the world, and gloried in the victory of becoming a self-made Casanova. The dignity of celibacy was cast casually aside. Women were

desperate now to get him into bed, and he obliged
them with pleasure. He even managed to overcome some of the limitations of his awkwardness,
and was soon troubled no more by premature
ejaculation.

But the sense of satisfaction did not last. It took
only three months more for him to become thoroughly disgusted with himself all over again. It
was not so much guilt generated by the knowledge
that he had cheated his partners into their passionate desire (though that did weigh somewhat
upon his conscience); the real problem was that
he became convinced that he was not giving them
full value in return. He knew that however dis-
appointing any particular session of love-making
might be, each and every victim would continue
to love him vehemently, but he thought that he
could see how disappointed his paramours were,
in him and in themselves. They loved him, but
their love only made them unhappy. This was
partly because they realised that they were all
competing with one another for his attentions,
but he was convinced that it was mainly because
those attentions were so inherently unsatisfying.

Giovanni could now present to the world the
image of a genuine Casanova. He was talked
about, in wondering tones. He was envied. But
in his own eyes, he remained in every sense a

despicable fraud. It was not *he* that was beloved, but some organic goo that he had concocted in a test-tube; and the women who were its victims were condemned to the desperations of jealousy, the disappointments of third-rate sex, and the miseries of helplessness. Giovanni had not the stomach to be a wholesale heartbreaker; he was too familiar with misery and desperation to take pleasure from inflicting it on others – not, at any rate, on women that he liked and admired.

By the time the royalties began to roll in, when Melmoth's discreet marketing of the discovery to the world's richest men began to pay dividends, Giovanni was again deep in depression and cynicism. Others, he felt sure, would be able to exploit his invention to the full, as the means to illimitable pleasure, but not he. Casanova, the fool, had simply confirmed his own wretchedness. His cup of bitterness overflowed.

It was, as ever, Marmaduke Melmoth who brought it home to him that he was still suffering from an attitude problem.

'Look, Joe,' said Melmoth. 'We got a few little problems. Nothing you can't sort out, I'm sure, but it's kinda necessary to keep the customers happy and the cash coming in. The way we're playing this we have a restricted market, and a lot of the guys are getting on a bit. It's all very well to offer them a way of getting the slots in the sack, but what they really need is something to get the peg into the slot. You ever hear of this stuff called spanish fly?'

Giovanni explained that *Cantharides* was a beetle rather than a fly; that it was a powerful poison; and that it probably wasn't terribly satisfying to have a painfully rigid and itchy erection for hours on end.

'So make something better,' said Melmoth, with that mastery of the art of delegation which had made him rich.

Giovanni gave the matter some consideration, and decided that it was probably feasible to devise a biochemical mechanism which would make it possible for a man to win conscious control over his erections: to produce them at will, sustain them as long as might be required, and generate orgasms in any desired quantity. This would require a couple of new hormones which Mother Nature had not thought to provide, a secondary system of trigger hormones for feedback control, and a cytogene for transforming the cells of the pituitary gland. Even when the biochemistry was in place, people would have to learn to use the new system, and that would require a training programme, perhaps with computer-assisted biofeedback back-up.

But it could be done; there was no doubt about it.

So Giovanni set to work, patiently bringing his new dreamchild to perfection.

Naturally, he had to test the system to make sure it was worth going ahead with clinical trials. Once the genetic transplants had taken, he spent a couple of hours a night in solitary practice. It took him only a week to gain complete conscious control of his new abilities, but he had started with the advantage of understanding, so he mapped out a training programme for the punters that would take a fortnight.

Once again, he was filled with optimism with respect to his own personal problems. No longer would he have to worry about flaws in his technique; he could now be confident that any girl who was caused to fall in love with him would receive full measure of sexual satisfaction in return. Now, he was in a much better position to emulate his famous namesake.

But Giovanni was no longer a callow youth, and his optimism about the future was not based entirely on his biotechnological augmentation. He had undergone a more dramatic change of attitude, and had decided that the Casanova he needed to copy was not the ancient Giovanni but his father Marcantonio. He had decided that the answer lay in monogamy, and he wanted to get married. He was now in his mid-thirties, and it seemed to him that what he needed was a partner of his own age: a mature and level-headed woman who could bring order and stability into his life.

These arguments led him to fall in love with his accountant, a 33-year-old divorcée named Denise. He had ample opportunity to make the fingertip contacts necessary to make her besotted with him, because his fortune was steadily increasing and there were always new opportunities in tax avoidance for them to discuss over dinner. Giovanni orchestrated the whole affair very carefully and, he thought, smoothly, graciously allowing Denise the pleasure of seducing him on their third *real* date. He still felt clumsy and a little anxious, but she seemed quite delighted with his powers of endurance.

His parents were glad when he told them the news. His father cried with delight at the thought that the name of Casanova would now be transmitted to a further generation, and his mother (who looked upon getting married as the only worthwhile certificate of belonging to the human race) was euphorically sentimental for months.

Denise gave up work when she became pregnant, mere weeks after the honeymoon, abandoning to other financial wizards the job of distributing and protecting the spring tide of cash which began to pour into Giovanni's bank accounts when his new discovery was discreetly marketed by the ingenious Melmoth.

Giovanni loved Denise very much, and became more and more devoted to her as the months of her pregnancy elapsed. When she gave birth to a baby girl, named Jennifer after his mother, he felt that he had discovered heaven on earth.

Unfortunately, this peak in his experience was soon passed. Denise got post-natal depression, and began to find her energetic sex life something of a bore. She was still hooked, unknowingly, on the produce of Giovanni's fingertips, but her emotional responses became perversely confused, and her feelings of love and affection generated floods of miserable tears.

Giovanni was overwrought, and knew not what to do. He was slowly consumed by a new wave of guilt. Whatever was the matter, he was responsible for it. He had made Denise love him, and had avoided feeling like a cheat only because he was convinced that she was reaping all the rewards that she could possibly have attained from a love that grew spontaneously in her heart. Now things were going wrong, he saw himself as her betrayer and her destroyer.

When Giovanni became anguished and miserable, Denise blamed herself. She became even more confused and even more desperate in her confusion. The unhappy couple fed one another's despair, and became wretched together. This intolerable situation led inexorably toward the one awful mistake that Giovanni was bound eventually to make.

He told her everything.

From every possible point of view, this was a disastrous move. When Denise heard how her husband had tied her finest and most intimate feelings to chemical puppet-strings her love for him underwent a purely psychosomatic transformation into bitter and resentful hatred. She left him forthwith, taking the infant Jenny with her, and sued for divorce. She also filed a suit demanding 30 million dollars' compensation for his biochemical interference with her affections. In so doing, of course, she made headline news of the enterprises which Marmaduke Melmoth had kept so carefully secret, and released a tempest of controversy.

The impact of this news can easily be imagined. The world of the 2010s was supposedly one in which the women of the overdeveloped countries had won complete equality with their menfolk. The feminists of the day looked back with satisfaction at centuries of fierce fighting against legal and attitudinal discrimination; their heroines had battled successfully against sexism in the workplace, sexism in education, sexism in the language and sexism in the psyche. Though progress had brought them to the brink of their particular Millennium, they still had a heightened consciousness of the difficulties which had beset their quest, and a hair-trigger paranoia about any threat to their achievements. The discovery that for nearly 20 years the world's richest men had been covertly buying biotechnologies specifically designed for the manipulation and sexual oppression of womankind consituted a scandal such as the world of sexual politics had never known.

Giovanni Casanova, who had so far lived his life in secure obscurity, cosily content with his unsung genius, found himself suddenly notorious. His name — that hideous curse of a name — suddenly became the progenitor of jokes and gibes displayed in screeching headlines, broadcast to every corner of the globe. It was constantly features in news bulletins and tawdry comedy shows alike. Overnight, the new Casanova became a modern folk-devil: the man who had put the cause of sexual emancipation back 300 years.

The divorce broke his mother's heart, and her sufferings were compounded when Marcantonio Casanova died suddenly of heart failure. She hinted to Giovanni in a reckless moment that his father had died of shame, and Giovanni took this so much to heart that he seriously contemplated suicide.

Densie, the victim of Giovanni's obscene machinations, achieved a temporary sainthood in the eyes of the women of the world. Melmoth, who had played Mephistopheles to Giovanni's Faust, was demonised alongside him. Thousands of women filed copycat lawsuits against their rich paramours, against Givovanni, and against Cytotech. Giovanni got sacks of hate-mail from tens of thousands of women who believed (usually without any foundation in fact) that his magic had been used to steal their souls.

As storms usually do, though, this hurricane of abuse soon began to lose its fury. Marmaduke Melmoth began to use his many resources to tell the world that the *real* issue was simply a little attitude problem.

Melmoth was able to point out that there was nothing inherently sexist about Giovanni's first discovery. He was able to prove that Cytotech had several notable female clients, who had been happily using the seductive sweat to attract young men. He argued, with some justice, that the cosmetics industry had for centuries been offering men and women methods of enhancing their sexual attractiveness, and that there had always been a powerful demand for aphrodisiacs.

Giovanni's only 'crime', Melmoth suggested, was to have produced an aphrodisiac which *worked*, and which was absolutely safe, to replace thousands of products of fake witchcraft and medical quackery which were at best useless and at worst harmful. He argued that although Giovanni's second discovery was, indeed, applicable only to male physiology, its utility and its benefits were by no means confined to the male sex.

This rhetoric was backed up by some bold promises, which saved Cytotech's image and turned all the publicity to the company's advantage. Melmoth guaranteed that Giovanni's first discovery would now become much cheaper, so that the tissue-transformation would be available even to those of moderate means, and to men and women equally. He also announced that Giovanni had already begun to work on an entire spectrum of new artificial hormones, which would give to women as well as to men vast new opportunities in the conscious generation and control of bodily pleasure.

These promises quickly displaced the scandal from the headlines. Cytotech's publicity machine did such a comprehensive job of image-building that Giovanni became a hero instead of a folk-devil.

The moral panic died, the lawsuits collapsed, and the hate-mail dried up.

On the downbeat side, however, Denise got her divorce, and custody of little Jenny. She did not get her 30 million dollars' compensation, but she was awarded sufficient alimony to keep her in relative luxury for the rest of her life. Giovanni was awarded the Nobel Prize for Biochemistry, but this did little to soothe his disappointment even though it helped his mother to recover from her broken heart and be proud of him again.

Giovanni launched himself obsessively into the work required to make good on Melmoth's promises. He became a virtual recluse, putting in such long hours at the laboratory that his staff and co-workers began to fear for his health and sanity. As he neared forty his mental faculties were in decline, but the increase in his knowledge and wisdom offset the loss of mental agility, and it is arguable that it was in this phase of his career that his genius was most powerful and most fertile.

He did indeed develop a new spectrum of hormones and enkephalins, which in combination gave people who underwent the relevant tissue-transformations far greater conscious control over the physiology of pleasure. As recipients gradually learned what they could do with their new biochemistry, and mastered its arts and skills, they became able to induce in themselves, without any necessary assistance at all, orgasms and kindred sensations more thrilling, more blissful and more luxurious than those which poor human nature, which had been crudely hewn by the hackwork of natural selection, had ever provided to anyone.

Giovanni created, almost single-handed, a vast new panorama of masturbatory enterprise.

For once, Giovanni's progress was the object of constant attention and constant debate. Cynics claimed that his work was hateful, because it would utterly destroy romance, devalue human feelings, obliterate sincere affection, and mechanise ecstasy. Critics argued that the value and mystique of sexual relationships would be fatally compromised by his transformations. Pessimists prophesied that if his new projects were to be brought to a successful conclusion, sexual intercourse might become a thing of the past, displaced from the arena of human experience by voluptuous self-abuse. Fortunately, these pessimists were unable to argue that this might lead to the end of the human race, because discoveries made by other biotechnologists had permitted the development of artificial wombs more efficient than real ones; sexual intercourse was no longer necessary for reproduction, which could be managed more competently *in vitro*. The cynics and the pessimists were therefore disregarded by the majority, who were hungry for joy, and eager to enter a promised land of illimitable delight.

As always, Giovanni was the first to try out his new discoveries; the pioneer spirit which forced him to seek out new solutions to his personal troubles was as strong as ever, and the prospect of combining celibacy with ecstasy appealed very much to his eremitic frame of mind.

In the early days of his experimentation, while he was still exploring the potential of his new hormonal instruments of self-control, he was rather pleased with the ways in which he could evoke rapture to illuminate his loneliness, but he quickly realised that this was no easy answer to his problems. Eight hundred thousand years of masturbation had not sufficed to blunt the human race's appetite for sexual intercourse, and Giovanni quickly found that the reason for this failure had nothing to do with the quality of the sensations produced. The cynics and pessimists were quite wrong; sexual intercourse could not and never would be made redundant by any mere enhancement of onanistic gratifications. Sex was more than pleasure; it was closeness, intimate involvement with another, empathy, compassion, and an outflowing of good feeling which needed a recipient.

Giovanni had found in the brief happiness of his marriage that sex was, in all the complex literal and metaphorical senses of the phrase, *making love*. However wonderful his new biochemical systems were, they were not doing that, and were no substitute for it.

So Giovanni ceased to live as a recluse. He returned to the social world, with his attitude adjusted yet again, determined to make new relationships. After all, he still had the magic at his fingertips – or so he thought.

He looked around; found a grey-eyed journalist named Greta, a Junoesque plant physiologist named Jacqueline, and a sweetly-smiling insurance salesperson named Morella, and went to work with his seductive touch.

Alas, the world had changed while he had lived apart from it. None of the three women yielded to his advances. It was not that he had lost his magic touch, but that Cytotech's marketing had given it to far too many others. When the relevant tissue-transformations had been the secret advantage of a favoured few, they had used it with care and discretion, but now that aphrodisiac sweat was commonplace, any reasonably attractive woman was likely to encounter it several times a week. Because women were continually sated with the feelings that it evoked they could no longer be conditioned to associate the sensation with the touch of a particular person. Greta, Jacqueline and Morella were quite conscious of what was happening when he touched them, and though they thanked him for the compliment, each one was utterly unimpressed.

Giovanni realised that promiscuity was fast destroying the aphrodisiac value of his first discovery. His quick mind made him sensitive to all kinds of possibilities that might be opened up by the more general release of this particular invention, and he began to look in the news for evidence of social change.

The logic of the situation was quite clear to him. As users found their seductive touch less effective, they would tend to use it more and more frequently, thus spreading satiation even further and destroying all prospect of the desired result. In addition, people would no longer use the device simply for the purpose of sexual conquest. Many men and women would be taken by the ambition to make *everybody* love them, in the hope of securing thereby the social and economic success that the original purchasers of the technology had already had. In consequence, he presumed, the world would suffer from a positive epidemic of good feeling. This plague would not set the entire world to making love, but it might set the entire world to making friends. The most unlikely people might soon be seen to be relaxing into the comfort of infinite benevolence.

Giovanni monitored the news very carefully, and realised long before it became generally kown that he had wrought a more profound change in human affairs than he had intended or supposed.

Wars were gradually petering out.

Terrorism was on the decline.

Violent crime was becoming steadily rarer.

Oddly enough, these trends passed unnoticed for a while by the world at large, because the headlines, dutifully following time-honoured custom, carefully selected out whatever bad news remained to be communicated. The majority of people did not begin to wake up to the significance of it all until a much-advertised contest to settle the heavyweight boxing championship of the world was stopped in the third round when the weeping combatants realised that they could not bear to throw another punch, and left the ring together with their arms around one another's shoulders.

Because of these upheavals in the world's routines, the clinical trials of Giovanni's new hormones and enkephalins attracted a little less attention than they might have, but their outstanding success was still a matter for widespread celebration. In 2036 Giovanni was awarded a Nobel Peace Prize to set beside his earlier award, and there was some discussion about the possibility of making it the last prize of its kind, given that the world no longer seemed to require peacemakers. Giovanni became once again the darling of the world's media. He was billed as a modern Prometheus, sometimes even as a modern Dionysus, who had brought into the world of men a divine fire more precious than any vulgar power-source.

Giovanni was still embarrassed by these periodic waves of media exposure. He still felt very self-conscious about his physical appearance, and every time he saw his own picture on newscreen or in a videomag he blushed with the thought that half a billion viewers were probably saying to themselves: 'He doesn't *look* like a Casanova!' He was probably being oversensitive; nowadays it was his face and his achievements which were called to the mind of the man in the street by the mention of the name Casanova; his ancient namesake had been eclipsed in the public consciousness.

In addition, Giovanni no longer appeared to the unbiased eye to be as unprepossessing as he once had seemed. He was now bald, and his bare pate was by no means as freakish as the tangled black hair that once had sprouted there. He still wore spectacles for his myopia, but corneal surgery had corrected his astigmatism, and his eyes looked kind and soft behind his high-index lenses, not at all distorted. His complexion was still poor, but his skin had been roughened and toughened by age and exposure to the elements, and its appearance was no longer offensive. His paleness and frailness could now be seen as appealing rather than appalling.

He was startled the first time that he realised that a woman was using his own aphrodisiac technology upon him, and quickly jumped to the conclusion that she must be one of those people who used it on everyone, but he gradually became accustomed to the idea that he really was admired and desired.

In time, of course, the secretion of aphrodisiac sweat became subject to a new etiquette, whereby indiscriminate use was held in bad taste, and also to be unnecessary as it could now be taken for granted that everyone could love one another even without its aid. Politeness came to demand that a sophisticated and civilised person would use the Casanova secretion occasionally and discreetly, to signal a delicate expression of erotic interest with no offense to be taken if there was no response.

As this new code of behaviour evolved, Giovanni was surprised to find himself a frequent target for seduction, and for a while he revelled in sexual success. Many of the younger women, of course, were interested primarily in his wealth and status, but he did not mind — he could, after all, claim responsibility for his status and wealth, which he had won by effort.

Anyway, he loved them all. He loved every-body, and everybody loved him.

It was that kind of a world, now.

In this way, Giovanni Casanova succeeded at last in adapting to his name. He lived up to the reputation of his august namesake for a year or two, and then decided that the attractions of the lifestyle were overrated. He gladdened his mother's heart by marrying again, and this time he chose a woman who was very like the earliest memories which he had of his mother.

His new bride was named Janine. She had been born in Manchester, and she was embarked on a career in cosmetic cytogenics (which was the nearest thing to hairdressing that the world of 2036 could offer). She was much younger than Giovanni, but did not mind the age difference in the least.

Giovanni and Janine favoured one another constantly with the most delicate psychochemical strokings, and learned to play the most beautiful duets with all the ingenious hormonal instruments of Giovanni's invention. But they also had a special feeling for one another – and eventually for their children – which went beyond mere chemistry and physiology: an affection which was entirely a triumph of the will. This was a treasure which, they both believed, could never have come out of one of Giovanni's test tubes.

With all these advantages, they were able to live happily ever after.

And so was everybody else.

Cinderella's Sisters

Once upon a time there were two ugly sisters.

They were twins, but they were not identical twins; the elder was brown-eyed and brown-haired, while the younger was blue-eyed and blonde-haired. For this reason their surname, which was Dark, fitted the elder, who was named Aurora, better than the younger, who was named Jeanne.

When they were born, Aurora and Jeanne looked much like any other babies, and no one knew that they would grow up to be ugly sisters. Their parents were tolerably rich because Grandfather Dark had made a fortune in the bioengineering business, and so they had the best of everything. Other children envied them for this, but the envy of the others was nothing compared to the envy which existed between the sisters themselves.

How and why two poeple who always had

the best of everything could contrive to be so bitterly jealous of one another it is difficult to understand, but it was nevertheless the case that from the moment of their birth Aurora and Jeanne were rivals. The most probable explanation is that their competition began even before birth, when they struggled for the lion's share of the limited resources available in their crowded womb. Their mother was fond of saying, with tired irony, that Jeanne had never forgiven Aurora for being born ahead of her, and never would be satisfied even if she beat her into the grave.

By the time they were five years old, it was obvious that each of the girls was, in her own distinctive way, very plain indeed. Depsite their different colouring they were of similar build. They were big for their age, with wide shoulders and fat legs, with broad features and lumpy chins. Jeanne's blue eyes were narrow, though, and gave the impression of sly shiftiness, while Aurora's dark ones were round and slightly protruding, giving the impression of a permanent hostile stare. If you looked at the two standing side by side from a distance, you could only tell which was which by the colour of their hair, but when they looked you in the face at close quarters there was all the difference in the world.

It was, inevitably, the children at school who

dubbed them 'the ugly sisters', forcing them to wear the collective nickname from infancy into adolescence. At first, the label was whispered behind their backs – they never could figure out exactly who had coined it – but it was soon invoked to taunt them openly, though usually from a distance; at five, each of them was bigger and stronger than almost any boy, and together they were a fearsome fighting force.

This taunting might have driven them together; it certainly gave them a common cause which they often had to pursue with concerted violent action. In fact, though, it gave them another reason for mutual jealousy, because each girl became secretly convinced that she was the uglier of the two, and each was determined to shift this burden to the other. Thus, while they combined forces to punish any other child who called them both ugly, they would lose no opportunity in private to express scorn and disgust for one another's appearance, particularly in respect of the eyes which were their main distinguishing feature.

This cattiness did not really come naturally to them, and gave a false impression, because they were really fairly placid and by no means lacking in charity or a sense of humour. Sometimes it was hard work for them to be nasty to one another, and it was certainly a duty rather than a pleasure. The rivalry was so deep-rooted, though, that it could not be set aside by any mere surge of regret or sympathy.

Adolescence intensified their self-consciousness in respect of their attractiveness. Their mother had always told them that their bigness was 'puppy fat' and that they would have elegant figures once they had 'grown into themselves' but this proved to be reckless optimism. They both grew up to be very tall, with massive shoulders, hardly any breasts, and thighs like wrestlers. To add insult to injury, they attained their full height at an unusually early age, so that they towered over their peers, male and female alike, throughout the miserable pubertal years.

They had no beautiful younger sister with whom to compare themselves. Indeed, had they had a real Cinderella to maltreat they might have felt a lot better about things, and their rivalry might have ebbed away. Instead, they were forced constantly to compare themselves to a hypothetical Cinderella who was beyond the reach of their abuse: the image of perfect femininity that was enshrined in the mythology of the day: in the world of TV, advertising and romantic fiction. This phantom Cinderella was the very ideal of feminine perfection, who could not ever be proven deficient or out-competed in any way.

As teenagers, Aurora and Jeanne desperately wanted boyfriends, to show the world that they were normal and desirable. They entered into one of the fiercest phases of their rivalry in the attempt to achieve some measure of romantic success, but their desperation only led them to further humiliation.

In the mere matter of timing, Aurora won again, as she usually did, and though she made as much as she could out of her victory in the race, she felt privately that she had only succeeded in lowering herself more quickly to a despicable level of shame. It was easy enough to find boys willing to accept sexual favours from any girl prepared to grant them, but they treated her with such appalling contempt before, during and after the event that she felt horribly humiliated by the whole business.

Jeanne reacted, cleverly, to the fact of having lost the race to give away her virginity by trying to make a virtue of having retained it. Though she was privately anguished by the thought of the joy which, she imagined, her sister derived from her frequent sexual activity, she put on a convincing show of contempt. Aurora never let her know it, but Jeanne's scornful attitude added greatly to her feelings of disgust and self-hatred.

By the time they were 18 years old Aurora and

Jeanne were as miserable as two people could be. The one thing which had held them back from suicide attempts was the bitter suspicion that if they killed themselves they would somehow be conceding defeat in their private war. On their 18th birthday, though, their whole situation was transformed. Ugly they might be, but in their infancy they had been the apples of their grandfather's eye, and he had established a trust fund for them, into which had been paid the royalties from some of his most successful ventures in genetic technology.

This was the first big boom time in the bioengineering business, when mankind stood on the threshold of a vast wonderland of new opportunity, and those trusts had benefited enormously from the boom. When Aurora and Jeanne were told how much they had each become worth, on attaining their majority, they realised that they were richer by a considerable margin than their parents, whom they had previously thought of as being very rich indeed.

They could now buy anything they wanted, and what they wanted more than anything else in the world, was beauty.

The bioengineering boom which had made their fortunes for them had also transformed the business of cosmetic surgery. Biotechnologists had learned how to take control of the processes by which the body's tissues were built and shaped. Work that was done with the scalpel could now be refined with subtler biochemical tools. The operations were delicate and expensive, but for those who had the money fat could be stripped from the body, and the metabolism retuned so that the fat could never reappear. Big bones could be whittled down, and what remained made perfect so that the tendons and ligaments and muscles knitted around them. Breast tissue could be induced to grow, to create a bosom of any size, shape and firmness that might be required. The texture, colour and sheen of skin could be selected from a chart. Every man who had the money could be remade in the image of Apollo, every woman who had the money could be an avatar of Aphrodite.

Aurora and Jeanne went to rival cosmetic engineers; they gave liberal grants to their clinics, financed the training of their staff, and backed their research. In return they demanded to be recreated as rival Helens of Troy.

Their psychicians did a marvellous job. Though Aurora and Jeanne kept their plans a secret from one another, they found that when the job was finished the situation was much as it had been before. From a distance, you could only tell one from another by the colour of their hair; close up, they were quite different. They had both elected to be five foot six in height, with slender waists, well-contoured hips, slim shoulders and modest, well-rounded breasts; from the neck down, there was simply nothing to choose between them. But their new faces were not at all alike.

Aurora had gone into her operation thinking that Jeanne might have an advantage because of her blonde hair (which Aurora had always considered to be her sister's best feature, though no torture would have forced her to admit it). She had briefly considered making her own hair golden, but this would have been tantamount to an admission of the inferiority of her own darkness, and so she had set any such notion aside. Instead, she had decided to make her own hair and eyes even darker, so that they would be almost, but not quite, jet black. To benefit from contrast, she had her skin tone lightened, so that it became almost but not quite pure white. Her lips, which had always been rather thick, she had redesigned to be slimmer, but very red and with a delicate Cupid's bow effect. She chose a relatively thin, straight nose. She acquired long, soft eyelashes, and allowed her eyes to be set a little too far back (in contrast to their previous protrusion) so that they could be artfully shadowed. She had her carriage altered slightly, so that she could look slightly upwards from beneath her neatly-chiselled eyebrows.

Jeanne, on the other hand, had been determined to make the most of her blue eyes, which she privately considered to have been badly let down by her awful lank hair (though wild horses could not have dragged such an admission out of her). She had the irises slightly enlarged, and the colour made perfectly even. She had her hair lightened and given a silvery metallic sheen. For her skin colour, by way of contrast, she chose a tanned look – a golden brown which was in its fashion equally metallic. She abolished the narrowness of her eyes completely, allowing herself to open them wide in an expression of astonished wonder which, she thought, truly reflected the innocence of her cultivated image. She was content to let her lips be soft and relatively full, hardly reddened at all but very gentle. Her adopted nose was just a little bit upturned at the end.

Each sister, when she saw her twin remade, felt uneasy about the striking contrast. Each had confidence in her own decisions, but each was agonised over the worry that the other might prove herself more attractive to men. They were both well qualified to make conquests now, being very wealthy as well as very beautiful. Their remodelling, though fearfully expensive, had hardly dented their fortunes, which grew seemingly of their own accord thanks to the miracles wrought by their investment managers.

Aurora began instantly to shop around for lovers among the wealthy and the wise, the famous and notorious (but choosing from these categories only the most handsome of candidates). She threw herself into a life of hectic seduction and multiple orgasms, keeping score of the men who visited her bed with obsessive accuracy.

Jeanne adopted a different strategy, feeling that it would be an undesirable concession to begin now what she had disdained before, and that Aurora must never be given the satisfaction of thinking that she might be trying to catch up. Instead, she set out to collect admirers and break hearts. She flirted with everyone and slept with no one, casually accepting the adoration of all but reserving her favours for some indefinitely-deferred perfect relationship which would be the ultimate in true love stories. By this means she cultivated a kind of moral superiority over her rival, who was made to seem vulgarly hedonistic by comparison.

Aurora secretly cursed the fact that her sister's frustrated lovers seemed to adore her more extravagantly than her own sated ones, but in public she simply made the most of her appetite for ecstasy, and accused Jeanne of hypocritical frigidity. Jeanne, though coolly contemptuous as far as appearances were concerned, was secretly terrified that this might be the truth of the matter.

The sisters' investment managers were drawn into the conflict just as their cosmetic engineers had been. They began to compete in business, trying to pull off market coups and commodity corners, taking over companies and putting venture capital on the line. They both found this a thoroughly boring and rather too impersonal mode of competition, though, and began to invest more effort in their activities in the world of the arts. They began their own collections, and frequently tried to outbid one another in the auction rooms, though this occasionally resulted in such wildly expensive purchases that the loser had more reason to be content than the winner.

Buying things was, however, almost meaningless as an exercise of rivalry given their vast financial resources, and it gave the sisters much more satisfaction to be given things by their admirers, particularly non-material things which were all the more valuable for having no price-tag. They both sat for portraits by the leading artists of the day. Anton Szulikowski's oil painting of Aurora was said to be as great a work as anything by Titian, and to have brought a touch of Renaissance Classicism to the 21st century. Ojima Okira's coded image of Jeanne, designed to take advantage of all the marvellous sophistication of the new Masterlaser printer was hailed as the first masterpiece of Neo-Post-Ultramodernism, and sold six million copies on disc.

The sisters partronised and cultivated writers as well as artists, and Richard Shelmerdine's 'Aurora Cycle' was generally held to be the work which allowed him to become the British Poet Laureate, while Charles Toussaint's integrated production of text, music and computergraphics, *The Spanish Armada*, ushered in a new era of video-womb drama.

It was soon insufficient for Aurora and Jeanne to inspire works or to give financial support to artists. They both decided at about the same time to star in films.

Aurora chose to take a leading role in one of the holographic epics which were then playing in stadia to audiences of a hundred thousand, and was Cleopatra in *The Rise of the Roman Empire*, directed by Jan van Walwyk. Jeanne was the only real person on camera in the otherwise computer-generated version of *She*, based on H Rider Haggard's famous novel by the aptly named producer/programmer Elaine Quartermaine.

The strain of these appearances was considerable; each sister worried incessantly about the quality of her performance, and dreaded utterly the prospect of her rival gloating over an unkind review.

This mode of competition was more satisfying than commercial competition because it was so very public. It was competition in celebrity, which was for both of them the real heart of the matter. But it was also a hazardous mode of competition, because the risk of humiliating failure was so much greater.

In the meantime, Aurora and Jeanne contrived to be the world's most dedicated followers of fashion. Aurora dressed for preference in black, and Jeanne in white, but each was prepared to attempt daring experiments in colour for special occasions. They each hired private detectives to spy on one another's collections of gowns, perfumes and jewellery, because neither could stand the thought that they might one day appear together wearing the same item of embellishment, and that it might be thought by some innocent observer to suit the other better.

When the fashion world began to absorb the techniques of the cosmetic engineers, so that its leaders began to change their skins as often as their coats, Aurora and Jeanne were of course in the vanguard. Aurora was the great pioneer of artificial bioluminescence, while Jeanne became the key trend-setter of integral ivory.

In the course of these pursuits their cosmetic engineers had once again to begin pushing back the limits of what could be done in remodelling the human body. Nor were the sisters long content with changes of superficial appearance. They had been made beautiful, and they had been made exotic – now they asked to be made talented. Their engineers were ready and willing to rise to the challenge, being just as determined not to be bested by nature as they were determined not to be bested by one another.

Aurora decided to extend her passion for bio-luminescence into the art of dancing, and had her muscles and limbs carefully sculpted and trained. Her solo balletic performances, enhanced by the effect of light reflected and radiated from the many facets of her artificial skin, were quite breathtaking. Meanwhile, Jeanne had her vocal cords completely reconstructed and augmented in order to give her voice phenomenal range and flexibility, and quickly became known as 'the human nightingale'.

Aurora eventually married, not so much because she wanted a husband as because she wanted a wedding – the most sumptuous ever known, with a guest-list such as had never before been assembled. The preparations lasted for nearly a year, and the worry wore her ragged; she took over an entire Mediterranean island for the ceremony and the reception. Her husband, Matthew Roemer, was a theoretical physicist who was rumoured to have the highest IQ in the world.

Jeanne waited for the fuss to die down completely before playing her own hand in this particular game, but any disadvantage she suffered from taking her turn later was offset by the fact of her carefully-conserved maidenly honour, which could be convincingly inserted into a great romance. Jeanne did not simply get married: she fell in love, and her courtship was lovingly tracked by the world's media for nearly a year. She disdained to take any part in making the arrangements; all that had to be done according to tradition anyhow, because she married the heir to the Spanish throne.

The next phase in the competition should, logically speaking, have involved the conception and rearing of their children, but here, without even formally negotiating a truce, Aurora and Jeanne finally drew the line. To give themselves up utterly to this flamboyant warfare was one thing, and their other pawns (investments managers, worshippers, cosmetic engineers and husband) were all volunteers, but to give birth to new persons simply in order to use them as weapons was something else. They both remembered the agonies of their own shared childhood, and the extent to which it had been spoiled by their bitter jealousies. They did not want to see babies born to such spoliation.

If no other proof were available, this reluctance would have demonstrated that Aurora and Jeanne were, after all, basically kind and and loving people. For all their posturing, they never did hurt anyone – at least, not deliberately. Aurora left her trail of disappointed lovers, and Jeanne her caravan of frustrated ones, but they never lied to any of them, or led them to expect anything more than they got, and both shed more than a few tears, albeit secretly, for the miseries which they caused.

While the twins pursued their spectacular careers, further steady progress was made in techniques of genetic engineering. This helped them grow richer still, but it also wrought changes in the world around them. Disease was slowly banished as medical applications of the new technology became cheaper. The development of artificial photosynthesis, coupled with biological desalination, made an exploitable asset out of the tropical sun and sea, and allowed the Third World to escape from the ecological poverty trap. The first techniques of rejuvenation were pioneered by Toshiko Hiroshita and her co-workers.

It was this last development, of course, which eventually attracted the careful attention of Aurora and Jeanne Dark. Once the techniques of rejuvenation by stimulated tissue replacement had proven their worth, they became a focus of intense interest for everyone over the age of forty.

At this point in time the rejuvenating operations were still very expensive, but those for whom money was no problem had every reason to invest all they could in prolonging the time in which they might enjoy their wealth. The older they were, the more they were convinced that youth was absolutely wasted on the young, and the more they believed they stood to benefit from a renewal of vigour.

When the techniques first became available to the very rich Aurora and Jeanne were only 43 years old, and neither showed any immediate hurry to be involved. For several more years they confined their rivalry to the conventional channels, which were by now well-worn, but each took care to keep a watchful eye open, and a considerable financial stake in the sophistication of the Hiroshita techniques. On her 48th birthday, though, Aurora looked at her face in the mirror, and decided that it was beginning to show distinct signs of having been thoroughly worked over, time and time again, by her favourite cosmetic engineer. It was time to consult him about a return to square one. What he told her, though, was rather depressing.

'I can do it,' he told her. 'But there are some things you must realise. What the rejuvenation technique involves is restoring tissue-cells to the primitive, undifferentiated state of blastular cells, in which state they can divide rapidly. These blastularised cells are then allowed to colonise the working tissues, destroying and replacing older cells. It's basically a kind of carefully controlled cancer. It isn't perfect: it means that the damaged structural proteins in your body can be replaced, and that all kinds of junk in your mature cells can be flushed out. But it doesn't set aside *all* the aspects of aging. There will still be copying errors in the DNA of the rejuvenated cells.

'The upshot of all this is that the techniques can restore a man or woman of 60 to the effective age of about 20, but that renewed youth can't last as long as real youth. After a further 25 years the body will appear to be 60 again. A second rejuvenation might restore the appearance of twenty, but that renewal isn't likely to last more than ten years. A third treatment would be useless, probably fatal.

'Those figures, though, suppose normal wear and tear. You're in a rather different position. Your cells have already been worked over very thoroughly by all the transformation techniques at our disposal. They just don't have the same scope as the cells of people who've aged naturally. I can rejuvenate you once, I think, but only once. I can make you seem 20 again, but I think you'd lose that appearance relatively quickly. Say 15 years instead of 25 to get back to real old age, and then, the end of the road.'

Aurora was not particularly surprised by this; she had been warned often about the fact that she was inflicting unfair wear and tear on her body, and that there might one day be a bill to pay for it all.

'It's all right,' she told the engineer. 'I suppose I'll just have to take what I can get.'

'That's not the whole of it,' he told her. 'You do understand, I suppose, that what your rejuvenated tissues will produce is what's programmed into your genes? After you're rejuvenated you won't look like a 20-year-old version of your present self – you'll look the way you would have looked without all the cosmetic remodelling.'

This was an unwelcome shock, and Aurora's

heart sank as she realised what it meant. To be rejuvenated was one thing; to be rejuvenated six feet tall with thighs like tree-trunks and protruding eyes was another.

'But you could do what you did before, all over again,' she protested.

'I'm afraid not,' he said. 'As I said, the cells wouldn't have been *completely* rejuvenated. In some ways, in terms of their intensively recopied DNA, they'd still be aged cells. I've told you often enough that you couldn't keep transforming them indefinitely. I can give you a second lease of life, Aurora, but I can't give you a second lease of the life you lead now. You'll have to live it on nature's terms.'

This news placed Aurora in something of a dilemma. She had naïvely thought that being the first to be rejuvenated would score a point in her ongoing battle with her sister; now it seemed like a kind of surrender. She decided that for the time being, at least, she would forego the pleasure.

When Jeanne, in her own time, made a similar approach to her own cosmetic engineer, she received the same news and she also put aside the idea indefinitely. But this could only be a postponement of the moment of decision, because from that day on there was an anxiety about the way that the two sisters glanced at mirrors, and as the years went by that anxiety deepened into real fear. They knew that they were not aging as gracefully as they would have wished, and that the extravagant way in which they had used the rewards of biotechnology was now taking its toll. They were beginning to look haggard, though they were only in their early fifties.

It was then, for the first time in their lives, that they took very different paths. Always before they had moved along different but parallel tracks. Now, they veered in opposite directions.

When Aurora was 53, she decided that it could not go on. Her intensively-reconstructed body was aging more rapidly than was natural, and her doctor told her that if she did not take the rejuvenation treatment, she might not have long to live; even her natural span of threescore years and ten would be denied her. She decided that she would take the advice, if only on strictly medical grounds. She dearly wanted another fifteen years of youth, feeling that she might make less wasteful use of it this time. She felt that she could face ugliness bravely, having already reaped all the rewards that beauty could bring.

Jeanne felt differently about it all. Having grown used to beauty, she felt that nothing ought to be allowed to force her back to mediocrity. If premature death was the price of retaining her current appearance, she decided, then she would pay it. She demanded that her cosmetic engineers use the methods they had already used so profusely, no matter what the risk, to keep her body in good repair during such time as was left to her. They pleaded with her not to take that route, stressing its awful dangers, but she was not to be persuaded. While Aurora reverted to plainness, therefore, Jeanne continued steadfastly to live life as she always had.

Within two years, Jeanne was on her death-bed.

Jeanne Dark made of her dying a great tragedy, keeping herself fully in the public eye. She built her final travails into a story to compare with the story of her fabulous love affair. If anything, she was more in the limelight now than at the height of her flamboyance, and her beauticians worked around the clock to keep her lovely face fit for the cameras.

When the end was very near, her ugly sister came to visit her.

There was no rivalry left now. Aurora and Jeanne were no longer competing. For the first time in their lives, they could meet one another honestly, with no need to conceal their true feelings.

When Jeanne, in a voice so weak and whispery

that it was impossible to imagine that she had once made of herself a human nightingale, said to Aurora: 'I won, didn't I?' Aurora replied very simply, 'Yes, you won.'

Jeanne was astonished to find that the admission gave her no pleasure at all, and Aurora was equally amazed to find that making it caused her no pain. They hugged one another then, and wept for all the wasted years.

'Are you well?' asked Jeanne, anxiously. 'You do *look* well.'

Aurora touched her jutting jaw and puffy cheeks. 'Yes,' she said. 'I am well. Better, I suppose, than I expected.'

Jeanne looked hard at her sister, and saw that the eyes did not protrude so much after all, and that the big shoulders really did not look too awkward. She tried to imagine the hair blonde and the eyes narrow and blue, but when she did, the picture that emerged was the image of a stranger.

'Mother said I wouldn't be content even if I beat you into the grave,' said Jeanne. 'But in a way, I am content. I hope you don't mind that . . . it's not because you've done wrong – in fact, I know now that you're the one who's done it right. You've chosen to live, and that's always right. No one should be so utterly stupid as to die for vanity.

91

I'm content, I think, because you *haven't* been so stupid. It would be awful, I think, if we'd both done this. I'm glad you didn't . . . glad for the right reasons, I think.'

'I know,' said Aurora, softly. 'I don't mind your being content, though I'd rather you could be content with life than with death. We both know what we did, and we both know what it's cost us. I think we've both been martyred, in our different ways. Like Cinderella's ugly sisters mutilating their feet to try to fit that stupid glass slipper. How is Prince Charming, by the way?'

Jeanne managed a weak smile. 'A tower of strength,' she said. 'We had a bad patch when the relatives became distressed at the lack of an heir, but that's all past now. Now, they don't really want one. The poor lamb will have to wait for another 50 years or more to be king now his father's been rejuvenated. I think, on the whole, I've done him more good than harm, and he's been very good for me. I was very tired of being unsullied. How's yours?'

'Pretty good,' Aurora confirmed. 'I was terrified he'd leave me, you know, when I reverted. I wouldn't have blamed him, either – it wasn't the *real* me he married, when all's said and done. But it's okay so far, and I'm beginning to hope that it really is me he loves and not just the image. It wasn't in the early days, of course, but we've grown used to one another over the years. Married life was nice to settle into after all those years of making a fetish out of finding a new lover every week. It's not that they were all the same, you understand, just that there wasn't *that much* difference. Anyway, I like Matthew; he gets a bit abstracted when he's working, but he's very kind.'

'I'm glad,' said Jeanne. 'You won't waste it, will you? Your new youth, I mean.'

Aurora shook her head. 'I'll try not to.'

Jeanne lay back on her pillow, exhausted by the conversation. 'I'm sorry,' she said, very faintly. 'I think it's close to midnight, you know.'

'You don't have to worry about midnight,' Aurora assured her, with tears in her eyes. 'I'm the one who had to turn back into a pumpkin. You married the prince, remember?'

Jeanne smiled, and in that smile was crystal-lised all the perfection of her carefully-conserved beauty. It was a tragic smile, packed with the power to induce heartbreak in any observer. The sight of it made Aurora cry.

'But you know,' said Jeanne, in the faintest of whispers, 'that damned glass slipper never did fit. Not *really*.'

'I know,' Aurora assured her, taking her by the

hand for the very last time. 'I know that, now. Cinderella was always going to win, whatever we did. In future, though . . . things will be different. People won't have to go through the kind of things we went through when we were kids.'

'I hope you're right,' whispered the younger twin.

Jeanne died a few weeks later, despite all that medical science could do to preserve her overburdened cells.

Aurora didn't have the option of living happily ever after, but she lived as well and as happily as she could, for as long as she could, and she made a pretty good fist of things.

It wasn't enough to score a point off Jeanne, but it was certainly one in the eye for Cinderella.

The Magic Bullet

Lisa had never before had such a strange feeling when going out on a case. She hadn't expected to be called out on any more cases. She was due for retirement in a matter of weeks, having nearly reached her 60th birthday, and had been desk-anchored for the best part of two years.

This wasn't exactly a case, though. The call she'd received hadn't made her position entirely clear, but it seemed that she was not to be part of the forensic team examining the scene. She would be, in essence, an advisor — perhaps best described as an expert witness. She had special knowledge of both the place and the victim. She had been a student in the Applied Genetics Department herself, nearly forty years before, and she'd visited it many times since for purely social reasons. She knew Morgan Miller as well as anyone did, though that wasn't saying a great deal.

Had it just been a police matter the invitation would have been couched in more respectful terms, but it wasn't. Although Miller hadn't been working directly for the Ministry of Defence, any attempt to sabotage research in genetic engineering was construed as a hazard to National Security. Men from the Ministry would be in control, and they would want to question her.

She wasn't looking forward to discussing her relationship with Morgan Miller; it had been part of her private life for far too long, and had never before touched her work as a police scientist.

They hadn't told her over the phone whether anything had happened to Miller; they'd said that they were still trying to make contact with him. She inferred, though, that something had. Whatever the true extent of this affair turned out to be, it surely wouldn't stop with arsonous assault on Morgan Miller's mice.

When she thought of it like that, it seemed simply absurd; firebombing a thousand mice was one of the most ridiculous crimes imaginable. The apparent stupidity of it, though, was sinister. Miller's mice had been breeding away, generation after generation, for nearly four decades, undisturbed and unconsidered by anyone else except Miller himself. Now, it seemed, they had become important enough to be worth destroying.

Lisa found that thought profoundly disturbing. It suggested that Morgan Miller had been keeping secrets from her.

One secret, anyhow.

She didn't like that idea. It hurt her pride. It might also make her look stupid to the Men from the Ministry, which was bad from a personal point of view, and bad because of her position in the police force. It was little consolation to know that Morgan Miller had always been, by nature, a very secretive man, a man who liked to be a law unto himself.

The scene, when she got there, was chaotic. The fire was out, but the firemen were still wandering around, and the mess they had made was awful. There was wreckage everywhere, and stinking foam soaked the walls and the floor. The forensic team had already moved in, and they acknowledged her arrival with embarrassed nods of recognition. The only other familiar face was the caretaker, Tommy, who had been in the job for twenty years, and knew her as an occasional caller. Now, she obviously seemed to him a sympathetic figure – a possible ally against the uniformed officer and the slings and arrows of outrageous fortune. The mournful look he gave her was a faint but heart-rending echo of her own feelings.

'Hell, Miss Friemann,' he said, desolately. 'That's his whole damn life. What in the world is he going to *do*?'

He always called her 'Miss', never 'Doctor' (let alone 'Superintendent', which was her theoretical rank as a senior police scientist). She didn't mind in the least; she felt that she was a partner in the tragedy, not just a part of the bureaucracy of investigation.

Lisa looked around at the blasted cages: the smashed glass, the twisted wire, the shards of plastic; everything was blackened, the odour of a thousand roasted mice mingling with the last traces of the acrid smoke and the vapour from the slimy foam.

'Did you try to call him?' asked Lisa. It was four in the morning, and Professor Miller ought to be tucked up safely in his lonely bed, though she was rather afraid that he wasn't.

'He doesn't answer his phone,' said Tommy, sadly.

'Is he away?'

'Not that I know of,' the old man replied, still shaking his head in disbelief. 'Why, Miss . . . ?'

'Who else did you try? Did you manage to contact Stella?' Stella Filisetti was Miller's latest research fellow. Lisa presumed that Miller had been conducting a desultory affair with her, in parallel with the desultory affair which he had long been conducting with Lisa. It tended to be his habit. Lisa did not mind, not in a strictly jealous fashion, but she couldn't help wondering whether Stella was in on the secret that had made Morgan Miller a target.

'I phoned her right after I called the fire brigade, but she didn't answer. I'm sorry, Miss, maybe I should've called you, too, but I don't have your number. I didn't know at first it was a police matter. All I saw was the smoke. I phoned the brigade right away, then the Professor and Dr Filisetti. Then I came to see if there was anythin' to be done. Not a damn thing, Miss. Couldn't get past the door. Saw no one. Sorry.'

The fire chief, who recognised Lisa from way back, came over to tell her that it had been a well-made bomb, with a considerable charge of plastic explosive as well as the incendiary material. Someone had certainly intended to make a mess. Lisa let him finish before telling him that she wasn't officially in charge. She would have liked to put some questions to the uniformed men, and to her own team, but had to be careful of protocol, and decided to wait for a more convenient moment.

The heavy mob arrived, in dark raincoats which were meant to be unobtrusive, but seemed as distinctive as any uniform. Lisa had some contact with the Ministry on a regular basis, but she didn't know these men, and didn't even know what cryptic initials would be used to identify their Department.

It was easy enough to work out why they'd involved themselves so quickly. When someone tried to destroy the work of an experimental scientist, the most likely reason was that he'd discovered something which it was to someone's advantage to know. Commercial advantage might be the relevant issue – commercial concerns had motivated many a firebomb in the past – but where genetic engineers were concerned, the Ministry was always anxious, always sensitive.

One man, a tall, dapper individual in his fifties, introduced himself to Lisa as Peter Smith. It had to be true; no one used Smith as a *nom de guerre* any more. It was decidedly *passé*.

'We may have to warn your people off this one, Dr Friedmann,' said Smith. He was trying, but not too hard, to sound apologetic. 'It could be our baby.'

'Have you found Miller?' asked Lisa, not wanting to get involved in a dicussion about jurisdiction.

'Not yet. Your people and mine have already gone to his home. I'm on the way there myself

– I came here to collect you. We understand that you knew Professor Miller well, and could tell us something about his work.'

'Stella Filisetti could tell you more.'

'We haven't been able to locate her yet.'

Lisa took this to imply that Stella Filisetti was suspect number one, but she didn't pursue the point.

Lisa let Smith guide her out of the lab, and back down to the car park, where a black Renault was waiting for them. The Ministry didn't like to use Japanese cars.

It wasn't far to Morgan Miller's house – the Professor liked to be able to walk to work. Lisa had been there many times before; Miller had lived in the same place throughout the years that she'd known him. It was a big house, with a small but lushly overgrown garden, and ivy crawling all over the walls. It looked horribly decrepit in the cold grey light of dawn, but it always had. It had been built at the very end of the 19th century, more than 150 years ago, and no amount of regular patching-up could conceal the fact that it was ancient. Miller must have bought it soon after the turn of the Millennium.

As Lisa got out of the car and walked to the door she tried to remember how old Morgan Miller was. She added it up, and made it 77, give or take a year. It was a wonder he was still working, but the University wouldn't force him to retire. He'd been trained during the golden age of genetic engineering, before the greenhouse crisis and the energy drought and the Great Economic Collapse. His skills were worth retaining, even though he'd never really fulfilled his early potential as a researcher. He'd won no prizes, had made no breakthrough to fame. He was just the eccentric man with the mice: an institution; a legend in his own lifetime.

There was a uniformed inspector standing on the threshold – waiting, obviously, for Peter Smith. Lisa's heart sank as the inspector caught her eye and looked up, indicating that she should follow his gaze. One of the first floor windows was doubly spider-webbed with cracks where two bullets had gone through it. Smith nodded to the waiting policeman, and the door was opened for him. Lisa followed him in, knowing what they were going to find.

It wasn't as bad as she expected. He wasn't dead. Both bullets had hit, but neither wound was fatal. He had bled all over the bed, but he was still breathing. It wasn't difficult to work out where the bullets had come from: a roof over the road. The mobile hospital arrived less than a minute after the Renault, and the duty surgeon moved past them, clearing the room while the support staff erected a sterile tent.

Lisa, with an entire career of examining corpses behind her, was by no means squeamish. To see someone you've known all your life go under the knife is hard for anybody, though. She felt frozen up inside, too stunned to begin thinking seriously about the questions that came into her mind. She knew, though, that Peter Smith would soon be directing those questions at her. The fact that she didn't have the ghost of an answer was unexpectedly distressing. Morgan Miller had been shot, and she, his friend, lover and supposed confidante, couldn't begin to guess why.

She sat down in an armchair that she remembered only too well, in the room he used as a study, and stared at the mute screen of the wordprocessor on the desk. Smith was still talking to the men outside, in the hallway, and she relaxed into a moment's respite, letting her eyes roam over the disc library that filled two walls of the study. Thirty thousand discs, Miller had boasted to her. His own notes and records filled several hundred; the rest was all published stuff – journals, textbooks, reports, theses. There was no fiction, no light relief. For that, he watched broadcast TV or bought video-tapes. He had once told her, unashamedly, that he had never read a novel since leaving school.

It didn't take long for the Men from the Ministry to catch up with the state of play. They had no real witnesses to question, but they had Lisa. From their point of view, she was their only lead, until they could find Stella Filisetti – which might well take some time, if she really was involved. If she was, she was obviously not alone. The firebomb and the shooting presumably had different perpetrators. Lisa knew that one plus one added up to a conspiracy, and that Mr Smith from the Ministry was going to be worried about it.

Amazingly, Smith – who was still being scrupulously polite – made her a cup of tea.

'While we wait,' he said, evenly, 'I'd be obliged if you could tell me all that you can about Professor Miller's work. We have no file, you see, and I understand that you . . . ?' He left the sentence dangling, with polished discretion.

'I knew him socially,' said Lisa. 'We did talk about his work – but all his records are here. They could tell you far more than I.'

Smith let his own gaze travel over the serried ranks of discs. 'In time,' he said, 'we can have a team go through them. But we need to act in the meantime, and we need everything you can give us, as I'm sure you understand. Had he any enemies?'

'He had one,' replied Lisa, levelly. 'But I haven't the slightest idea who or why. I assure you that I'm not being unco-operative. I really don't know.'

Smith smiled, weakly. 'You know more than we do,' he pointed out. 'Suppose you tell me just what kind of man he was?'

Lisa sipped tea, and wondered what the answer to that question really was.

'I'll tell you what I can,' she promised. 'I want to work it out in my own mind, too. He was a friend of mine. A very good friend.'

Smith smiled at her, not knowingly, but smoothly, and she realised that she wasn't just a witness. Until they had checked her file very carefully, she was suspect number two.

Clearly, even the Men from the Ministry always began their investigations with *cherchez la femme*.

'I suppose it was unusual in those days,' said Lisa, 'for a student of biology to get a police scholarship. But police work and forensic science were becoming ever more intricately involved with one another, and identification by gene-typing was on its way to becoming standard. Most of the police scholarships were going to computer scientists, because computer-related crime was seen as the boom area. I suppose I was interested in Applied Genetics first and police work second, and it was really in the interests of financing my studies that I took up the police scholarship.

'Before the Crash there was a flood of research money for all aspects of applied genetics. Genetic engineering of bacteria and plants was already making an economic impact on food production, and there was intense interest in the possibility of engineering animals for meat production. We could see the energy crisis coming, of course, and the rise in sea level due to the greenhouse effect had really begun. Everyone knew that the entire world agricultural system was on the brink, and the developed nations all wanted to make progress in factory farming, to take food production out of the fields. So the Department, in the days when I was a student there, was heavily committed to the development of techniques for animal engineering.

'Morgan Miller, in those days, was in the very forefront of his profession. His mice have become a bit of a joke over the years, but at that time animal engineering was all the rage. What the engineers were learning to do to mice was just the first step toward engineering pigs, cattle — and it was all the more exciting because of the difficulties.'

'Don't get too technical,' Smith warned. 'I'm no expert.'

'Bacteria and plants are easy to engineer,' Lisa explained, 'because they can reproduce asexually. You can only introduce new genes into a very small number of bacterial cells in a culture, but if you introduce a gene conferring immunity to a particular antibiotic you can easily isolate the transformed cells and obtain a pure culture which multiplies very rapidly. Plants produce vast quantities of seed, and it's not difficult to inject new genetic material into the seeds — when they develop you only need one usefully transformed plant, because you can then clone it easily.

'Transforming mammals is a very different matter: mammals produce relatively few egg-cells, which are fairly delicate. If you extract them from an ovary, fertilize them *in vitro*, and then pump new DNA into them you spoil nine hundred and ninety-nine out of a thousand, and even the odd one that begins to develop usually aborts very quickly. Producing a transformed organism is extremely difficult.

'Several people in the Department, including Miller, were trying to solve this problem. They were trying to find a way of getting new DNA into a mammalian egg-cell without having to remove it from its ovary. They were trying to create artificial viruses which would seek out and invade egg-cells, while leaving ordinary cells alone, integrating their DNA with the chromosomes of the eggs. They called these artificial viruses MB viruses. MB stands for *magic bullet*. They hoped that once the basic techniques were proven, they could rapidly move on from experimental animals to real practical applications.

'The MB viruses weren't too difficult to develop, though it wasn't easy equipping them to infect egg-cells alone. But egg-cells are differentiated within the body by biochemical markers, which can be used to trigger the viruses. I don't know the very intimate details, because it wasn't specifically my field. Professor Miller wasn't my own teacher, once I got beyond the elementary stages — he was a friend.

'I know that Morgan's research ran into problems, though, after the development of the MB viruses. It's all very well to transform the egg-cells inside a female mouse; you still have to turn those egg-cells into new mice, and you still have a dreadful wastage rate. The vast majority of the female mice that Morgan shot with his magic bullets simply turned up sterile, because the transformed ova weren't compatible with ordinary sperm. On the very rare occasions when a transformed mouse was born, it was no use – you can't take cutting from a live mouse the way you can from a plant. In order to breed you need two mice of opposite sexes with identical transformations – a real billion to one shot.

'So the research was blocked. Gradually, over the years, a lot of workers abandoned the whole line as a blind alley, but Morgan wouldn't give up. By degrees, he lost his place in the forefront, and I suppose he eventually got left in a backwater. He wasn't bitter about it, though – he really wasn't interested in fame or fortune. His pride wasn't invested in his reputation, it was all tied up in his work. He persisted with his magic bullets: experiment after experiment, generation after generation. Everyone respected him for it, I think, even though they did make sarcastic jokes about it.

'I remember that Miller was always impressed by one strange fact about mammal egg-cells, and that was the way that nature wasted them. Male mammals produce sperm throughout their lives, as long as the testes are capable of it. By the time a female mammal is born, though, she has all the egg-cells she's ever going to have, and she loses most of them long before she reaches puberty and becomes fertile.

'The peak number of egg-cells is actually

reached – oddly enough – in the early embryo, and millions of them die before the female is even born. I can't remember the exact figures for mice, but I do recall that the human female starts off with about seven billion egg-cells, in the fifth month of gestation. By the time she's born, she has only two million, and by the time she reaches puberty, she's lost the vast majority of those. She runs out altogether long before the end of her life-span; that's when she reaches the menopause.

'What kind of evolutionary sense that makes, I don't know, but I do know that it was something that fascinated Morgan Miller. He told me once that if only he could transform those millions of cells in such a way as to protect them from degeneration, then he could take the ovaries from a new-born mouse and have a vast population to aim his magic bullets at – and then, if he only had some way of making those embryos develop outside the body, in artificial wombs, he would have the odds on his side instead of against him. That was the idea which seemed to dominate his research during the last twenty or twenty-five years. That was the key, he believed, to developing efficient techniques for the genetic engineering of mammals.

'I can't tell you how far Miller got with his work,

but I know he didn't reach the end. He never did produce a pair of true-breeding engineered mice. He didn't even manage to develop the artificial wombs necessary to his grand plan. As far as I know, all he ever managed to do was produce generation after generation of sterile mice, shot so effectively by his magic bullets that they might just as well have been dead.

'He managed, I suppose, half a dozen live births of transformed mice every year, but never a pair. He induced giantism, contrived some interesting alterations of fundamental biochemistry – produced, in fact, some fascinating freaks. But without a way of establishing a breeding population, it all came to seem rather futile.'

'But somehow,' said Smith, 'he discovered something that made him worth killing.'

'It looks that way now,' said Lisa, 'but your guess is as good as mine as to what it might have been. The mice are all dead, Miller may not pull through. And his lab assistant . . . ?'

'Think she's the one?'

Lisa shrugged. 'Never really knew her. Didn't look to me like a dab hand with a high-powered rifle. Have your people come up with anything in her background?'

He shook his head. 'Nothing obvious. Thirty-two years old. Unmarried. Good degree in Applied

Genetics, doctorate from Oxford. Came here eight years ago. Politically active, but only with radical feminist groups. Votes Green. No relatives outside the country, in spite of her name. Clean credit record. No significant ties with industry.'

'In that case,' said Lisa, 'it looks as if we'll just have to wait for Miller. If the surgeon can save him, he can give us the whole story. If not . . .'

Smith didn't look particularly optimistic about that. He obviously didn't expect a man in his seventies to survive two bullets in the torso. His thoughts were already dwelling on other lines of inquiry.

'He never married, did he?' asked the tall man, trying to sound as if he were merely making conversation.

'No,' said Lisa. 'He was wedded to his work. An essentially solitary man. He liked his relationships casual and occasional. It suited him.'

'And you never married either?'

'No,' she said, levelly. 'Two of a kind. Three, if you count Stella.'

'You could say that he used you both,' he suggested, calmly.

'Or that we used him. Nobody shot him out of jealousy, Mr Smith. And I doubt if Stella shot him because she was a radfem – even though he was a trifle Victorian in his attitude to women. Did you find the weapon?'

He shook his head.

'If he does die,' said Lisa, grimly, 'I don't think you'll find out why until you've searched those discs with a fine-toothed comb. Time seems to be against you,.'

'Against us, Dr Friemann. This is a police matter too. And for you, a personal matter. We've checked your record too, as you knew we must. I'm satisfied that you're in the clear, and I know that we can rely on your co-operation. I hope you won't take it amiss when I say that I'd rather it *was* a personal matter.'

Lisa stared at him, feeling that she was on the brink of exhaustion. She had become unused to missing her sleep. 'It wasn't personal,' she said, confidently. 'No one had anything personal against the mice.'

For once, Smith couldn't contrive a smile.

Behind him, the door opened and the surgeon came in. Bluntly, he told them both that Morgan Miller would be lucky to last two days, and might only last a matter of hours if he were hyped up with sufficient drugs to make him available for questioning, instead of being allowed to rest.

The Man from the Ministry didn't even glance at Lisa.

'Do what you need to do to wake him up,' he said. 'We have to have the answers, and we can't wait.'

Miller was still inside the sterile tent which the medical team had erected by his bed. A senior paramedic remained when the mobile hospital took off; she was the official death watch. Smith told her to leave the room, and she obeyed without question. He let Lisa stay, though, probably not because he trusted her, but because he thought her presence might help to rally the patient's ailing spirits.

As far as Lisa could judge, the professor's spirits would need all the help they could get. He was very weak. If there'd been any real chance of his making a recovery, the surgeon would never have allowed him to be pumped full of drugs to bring him back to consciousness.

Smith didn't waste any time. 'Professor Miller,' he said, 'we need to know who shot you, and why. They bombed your laboratory too. It's all destroyed.'

Morgan Miller stared at his interlocutor, but didn't seem to understand. Smith frowned, and looked across at Lisa, appealing for help. She took a gentler line.

'Morgan,' she said softly, sitting down on the edge of the bed. 'It's Lisa. Lisa Friemann.'

He shifted his gaze to meet hers, and blinked in recognition. 'Lisa,' he said, faintly. He seemed surprised by the fact that he was able to talk. He paused for a moment, obviously preparing to say something more. Smith tensed, waiting eagerly, but all Miller said was: 'It doesn't hurt.'

'No,' said Lisa, 'it won't hurt.'

'Bad though,' croaked Miller, 'isn't it?'

'Pretty bad,' admitted Lisa. 'I don't suppose you remember being hit – you must have been asleep.'

'Bad dream,' he murmured. 'Very bad dream.'

'You were shot, Morgan. Someone fired from across the street. You were hit twice.'

The man on the bed managed a very weak smile. 'Magic bullets,' he said.

'That's what we want to know,' Smith intervened. 'Tell us why.'

Lisa looked up at the Ministry Man. 'Unfortunately,' she said, drily, 'I think he was only making a joke.'

'Then you'd better tell him,' said the tight-lipped Smith, 'that we don't have time for jokes.'

Lisa returned her attention to Morgan Miller. 'Morgan,' she said, 'who would want to burn the mice? They're all dead, Morgan – all the mice. Who would want to do that?'

A few seconds went by while Miller struggled to digest this information. Then tears came into his eyes, and Lisa knew that she was getting through.

'All dead?' he queried, his voice trembling.

'Burned to death,' she said. 'All burned. Who would do a thing like that?'

Miller opened his mouth to speak, but no words came out. He had been looking at Lisa, but now he looked beyond her, at Peter Smith.

'Who's he?' he asked. There was a slight catch in his voice because of the tears.

'My name is Peter Smith. I'm from the Ministry of Defence. We need to know why someone might want to steal the results of your work – or to put a stop to it. We need to know what you found out.'

'Defence?' repeated Miller, dazedly. At first, Lisa thought that he was simply unable to understand. But then he added: 'There isn't any defence.'

Lisa imagined the effect that words such as those must have on a man like Smith. All kinds of memories must be coming back to him, of the so-called Plague Wars, which might not have been wars at all, but which had wiped out a third of the human race in the early part of the century.

'What . . . ?' Smith began, but Lisa silenced him with an irritated gesture.

'Tell us where to look, Morgan,' she said. 'Give us the reference. It must be in your files somewhere. You needn't try to tell us. Just tell us where to look.'

But Miller turned his head away, and refused to look at either of them. His brow was furrowed, as if he was as deep in thought as the drugs would let him be. Smith opened his mouth again, but caught Lisa's eye and shut it. They waited. Finally, Miller said: 'It's hidden. *Nobody* knows.'

'Somebody burned the mice,' said Lisa, patiently. 'Whatever you had hidden, somebody knows now. You have to tell us what it is.'

Miller moved his head from side to side, still not looking at them. The drugs were inhibiting his motor responses, but they couldn't entirely cut out his agitation.

'Don't try to move,' said Lisa. 'You have to conserve all your strength. The more time it takes, the more strength you waste. For God's sake, Morgan, tell us now, and then you can rest.'

But all Morgan said in reply, his words heavy with drug-sodden anguish was: 'Nobody knows. Nobody knows.'

'Then you must tell us now,' said Lisa, soothingly. 'You *must* tell us. You have to tell someone, Morgan. You can't carry secrets to the grave.'

Smith frowned at her, obviously uncertain how sensible it was to let Miller know that he was dying, but he said nothing. He was apparently content to defer to her judgment.

But Morgan Miller didn't respond to her plea. When Lisa had come into the room she had not been sure that Miller had anything to tell them, but what was happening now was bewildering. She felt herself growing angry – angry because Morgan Miller was nursing some secret which he had never shared with her, and which he still would not share, even though he was on his deathbed. The security angle, if there was one, did not distress her overmuch; what she felt was a sense of personal betrayal.

'Professor Miller,' said Smith, sternly, when he saw that Lisa wasn't going to get any reply. 'You have to tell us everything. It's absolutely necessary.'

Miller looked at him, and curled his wrinkled lips. His eyes seemed very bright. 'What will you do?' he asked, hoarsely. 'Torture me?'

'What the hell is going on here?' demanded Smith of Lisa. 'What is he playing at?'

It was Lisa's turn to frown. 'We don't understand, Morgan. We don't understand why you won't talk to us. We're trying to catch the people who shot you – the people who bombed the mice. Was it Stella Filisetti, Morgan? Has she any reason to do this?'

Miller tried again to shake his head, and managed to move his right hand from beneath the blanket on the bed. He tried to wipe the tears from his eyes, but he had great difficulty controlling his hand.

'Stella?' he said, more as if he were talking to himself than answering the question. '*Must* be Stella. How . . . nobody knows! *Nobody knows*.'

There was a sharp rap on the door, and Smith turned to open it. Lisa couldn't see who it was, nor could she hear what was rapidly whispered. When Smith turned round, though, he was clearly in an agony of indecision. He beckoned her over to the door.

'They've located Filisetti,' he said. 'She's under observation. We've got to pick her up. We need to find out how many others are involved, nip the while thing in the bud even though we don't know what's it's all about.'

'Let me stay here,' she whispered. 'I think I can get him to explain, if there's time. I stand a better chance alone – if there's anyone in the world he trusts . . .'

Smith hesitated, but then nodded. He crossed swiftly to the bed, leaning over the plastic tent to look at Morgan Miller, who had closed his eyes. There was no way to be sure that he would open them again. Smith turned back, nodded curtly at Lisa, and then left.

Lisa went back to the bedside, and pulled up a tattered old armchair, over whose worn back she had deposited her clothing on so many occasions. She sat down, and now that she was unobserved, she began to weep. She had not wept for many years, and hoped that she never would again.

Lisa would not have said, had she been asked – or even if she had posed the question secretly to herself – that she loved Morgan Millar. She *had* loved him, long ago, but had long since outgrown it, as she had outgrown all passion and almost all affection. There remained, however, a sense in which Morgan Miller was closer to her than any other human being, and he was dying on *their* bed, where an assassin had shot him while he slept – as he usually did – alone. If this was not an occasion for tears, there could surely be no other.

For several minutes, she was content to let the silence last, to secrete herself within her grief.

Then she stood up again, went to the bedhead and removed the bug that Smith had planted on its rear side. She wrapped it carefully in a handkerchief, and put it in her pocket.

'You bastard, Morgan,' she said, in a low tone. 'You have to tell me. You hear me? You *have* to tell me. I'm surely entitled.'

Morgan Miller opened his eyes again.

'Jesus, Lisa,' he said, faintly. 'They really did it. They really killed me.'

'Yes they did,' she said, levelly. 'It's a miracle you've got the time you have. Whatever it is, someone knows about it. *I want to know too.* I've never asked you for anything else. Never. But I want to know, Morgan. *I want to know.*'

Morgan Miller smiled a kind smile that she had seen on his faded lips a hundred times before – a smile of confident superiority. She had never liked it. She sat down in the armchair again, and waited.

'Lisa,' he said, quietly, 'you're not going to like it.'

'Tell me anyway,' she said, in a cold, sardonic tone that *he* must have heard a hundred times before, and probably liked no better. 'You wouldn't want to go to your grave keeping secrets from the only woman you ever really loved, now would you?'

'Hell no,' he said. 'Now how could I do a thing like that to you?' His voice, as he said this, was little more than an icy whisper.

He paused for some time, while Lisa waited, calmly.

Theirs had always been a relationship which had made many demands on her patience and insensitivity.

'It was a pure fluke,' said Miller, keeping quite still and relaxed. His voice was faint, but no longer hoarse. He had rallied somewhat, and his state now seemed almost trancelike. 'A real shot in a million. I've tried to work out the biochemistry, but I never could. The key protein is some kind of controller, like the ones which determine the switching on and off of selected genes in different kinds of specialized cell.

'It was a bullet virus – one of those I adapted specifically to infect oöcytes. It was intended to preserve the egg-cells, cut the wastage rate. It preserved them, after a fashion. It stopped them dying off so fast, so that the infected mice were born with something like ninety per cent of the egg-cell store intact. There was no somatic transformation – at first I didn't think I'd achieved anything at all, except that the oöcytes could be preserved in any infected female. I kept a number of the mice alive, to track the oöcytes through the lifespan. When they reached the right age, puberty didn't happen. No ovulation. The mice were sterile. Seemed even more useless, then, but I kept monitoring, just in case.

'I sectioned a lot of tissue, just to track the rate of degeneration, without seeing anything unusual. The rate was still very slow. Then I caught the anomaly – an oöcyte that had started dividing, forming what looked like a tumour. Not a virgin birth, you understand; it wasn't forming an ordinary embryo, and the new cells looked to be dispersing, like a cancer in metastasis. It looked then as if the virus was a killer, and I kept the remaining live mice under observation to see what would happen. I waited for them to show external symptoms, but they didn't.

'I waited, and waited, and the damn things didn't die.

'They didn't die at all. Ever.'

He paused to draw breath. Lisa waited, impatiently, for him to continue.

'Eventually, I figured it out. The oöcytes which were developing were producing new juvenile cells which gradually displaced the maternal cells *in the mother's body*. They were producing new individuals, all right, but not *separate* individuals. As the mother got older she became a mosaic, except that the new cells weren't genetically different: these freak oöcytes were diploid clone-daughters of the original. They were rejuvenating the host body, over and over again. Instead of living the one lifetime programmed into its originating egg-cell, each mouse was living a whole series of lifetimes, cannibalizing her own egg-cells.

'I'd infected the damn things with immortality.

'Remember the old joke about the chicken just being an egg's way of making another egg? DNA has always been immortal; our chromosomes live for ever, they just use organisms as a way of swapping their individual genes around. Bacteria and protozoans generally don't bother – their cells just keep on dividing. It only needed a little genetic nudge to put the mouse chromosomes on a new track, so that they express their immortality through a series of individuals who would just grow up to displace one another inside the same body, shedding the aged cells just as a growing snake periodically sloughs its skin.

'I had a complete gene-map of the bullet virus that had done the trick. Its infective capacity was mouse-specific but the active DNA wasn't. I knew that I could tailor a virus to do the same thing to human egg-cells. Two or three misses, maybe, but the technical part of the problem wasn't difficult at all. Armed with that gene-map, anyone with a decent lab could do it. But without the map, even knowing that it could be done, it would be impossible. You know how many ways there are to perm four bases into a string of DNA a hundred units long. I knew it would be hundreds of years before anyone else turned up another fluke like it.

'So I hid the map.'

Lisa had listened so far in silence, no wanting to break the rhythm of his speech because she feared that if the flow were once switched off it might be very difficult to get it going again. Now, though, Morgan Miller had stopped of his own accord, and he was watching her with his bird-bright eyes, waiting for her reaction. It was as if he were challenging her to work out the pattern of his motives for herself.

'You discovered immortality,' she said, sarcastically, 'and you decided to keep it a secret between you and the mice?'

He nodded slightly, but said nothing.

She realised that she had left something out. 'You discovered a way to make *females* immortal,' she corrected herself. 'Only females.'

He nodded again.

'What have you been doing?' she asked. 'Trying to find a magic bullet that would transform sperm-cells the same way? In the interest of fair play?'

'It wouldn't have worked,' he said, softly. 'A sperm-cell doesn't have the supporting bio-chemical apparatus. It's just a bundle of chromosomes. Its genes can only become active after invading another cell – like a virus, in a way. In biochemical terms, males have always been parasitic on females. When oöcytes can do it on their own, a species doesn't really need males.'

Lisa though about the implications of what Morgan Miller had discovered, and what he had done – or not done – about it.

'How long ago, Morgan?' she asked, eventually.

He tried to shrug his shoulders, but couldn't. 'Forty years,' he said.

Forty years ago, thought Lisa, coldly. *I was in love with Morgan Miller then, and my body contained hundreds of thousands of egg-cells. Hundreds of thousands of potential lifetimes. And he knew; even then, he knew.*

She had known, of course, that Morgan Miller had not loved her, and that he never would. He would never have given her a child. Why should she be shocked because he had known a way by which he might have made her an elixir of life, and had not even tried?

Whatever happens now, she thought, *it's too late. I'm too old, and there are no more egg-cells left.*

Stella Filisetti, she remembered, was young enough still to be carrying viable egg-cells.

'Why did you tell Stella?' she asked.

'I didn't. Must be clever than I gave her credit for. A dozen immortal mice in a population of a thousand, all looking alike. I thought they were well enough hidden even in plain view. She always liked the mice, though; she had a curious silly fondness for them. Sentimentality is *so* out of place in a biologist.'

'You bastard, Morgan,' said Lisa, levelly. 'If she hadn't set you up, I swear I'd shoot you myself.' She was surprised, as she said it, how tempted she was. It was odd, in a way, because she felt no white heat of passionate rage. If, as she felt tempted to, she were to rip aside the sterile tent, pick up the pillow and smother him, she would be doing it quite coolly.

She knew, though, that there was no point.

'Well,' he said, softly, 'it's out now. Once she knew there was something hidden, she must have gone through my files very carefully. I had too many copies of the map, I guess. Maybe I should have destroyed it, if I really wanted to save mankind.' He put a faint stress on the word 'mankind', to emphasise that he meant just that, and no more.

'Did you?' asked Lisa. 'Want to save mankind, that is?'

He grinned, 'I rather liked the world as it was,' he said. 'In spite of the greenhouse crisis, in spite of the plague wars, in spite of the energy shortage, in spite of the economic collapse. Not a bad world, for one such as I. I'm glad I had no sons, though – Stella's people will make sure that the future's very different.'

'Smith's men have found her,' Lisa told him. 'There's every chance that they'll get the map back, if she hasn't already run off and distributed a thousand copies. I don't suppose she has. The fact that they bombed the lab and tried to kill you suggests that they didn't intend making their little discovery public. I think they want to keep it to themselves. Not so sentimental after all, you see.'

He grinned again. 'So much for the spirit of sisterhood,' he said.

Lisa studied his face carefully. 'Why didn't you tell Smith?' she asked.

'Didn't have time.'

'Yes you did. You held back. You waited

for him to go, and then you told it all to
me. Why?'

'Why'd you wrap up the bug?' he count-
ered.

'It was making me self-conscious. I thought I'd
like us to have a little privacy.'

'I don't like the men from the Ministry,' said
Miller. 'My first inclination is always to tell them
nothing.'

'It seems,' observed Lisa, 'that your first inclination is to tell *everyone* nothing.'

'I told you.'

'Forty years too late.'

'Too late for you, perhaps. But I never thought
of you as a selfish person, Lisa. It was something I always admired in you. Authentic altru-
ism. A sense of duty. You've always been my
favourite.'

Lisa watched him, knowing that he was playing
a kind of game. He was teasing her, playing cat and
mouse. There he was, on his deathbed, enjoying
the idea that the future of the world might still
be his to determine, his to play with, and his to
dispose.

She still felt a little like killing him, but she
didn't intend to do anything of the sort.

Instead, she knew, she would wait, and listen,
and see what he decided to do.

If he wanted to, he could tell her where to find another copy of his map. If he wanted to, he could die silent, leaving it for the painstaking Mr Smith to seek out with his fine-toothed comb. She didn't need three guesses to know what Mr Smith would do with it.

There was a long pause while they watched one another, waiting to find out which one of them would break the silence, and what he, or she, would say.

Agents of the Ministry of Defence arrested Stella Filisetti later that day. Within a matter of hours, they had made seven more arrests. Following a trial – which was held in secret because of its implications for national security – eight women were eventually sentenced to indefinite imprisonment in an unspecified location.

When Peter Smith returned to Morgan Miller's house the professor was still alive, and he remained alive long enough to repeat all that he had told Lisa Friemann. Smith's men then began a very carefuul and exhaustively thorough search of Morgan Miller's data-discs, looking for the crucial gene-map.

They also began an intensive search for Lisa Friemann, but by the time they found her, it was too late.

By then, far too many people had seen the map, and the world was already embarked upon its new era.

The Invertebrate Man

When he was five years old Patrick O'Connell knelt on a thumbtack. The point went in just beneath his kneecap, and he had thrown himself down with such abandon that it was driven in all the way. He howled with pain, rolling and writhing on the floor, instantly attracting the anxious attention of his parents. It took them three minutes to figure out that he had a thumbtack stuck in his leg. His father promptly removed it, but Patrick continued to howl and wail.

He wept for something like seventeen hours, and in so doing exhausted the patience of his father, his mother and the doctor they called (who pronounced him okay but gave him a 'painless' tetanus shot just in case). Patrick saw their sympathy turn to annoyance, and would have stopped crying if he could, but to his dismay he found himself unable to stem the flood of tears. It was not the pain, which had faded, and it was not the shock, which wore off along with the pain. It was something else, as if a trigger had been pressed inside him which made it impossible for him to exert his will and obey his father's urgent command to 'pull himself together'.

It was not until he had cried himself to sleep that the incident was finally closed, but by that time he had heard a terrible statement uttered by his irritated father. 'I don't care what you say,' said Steve O'Connell to his wife, *'that kid has no backbone.'*

This judgment was unfair, and what was said then in the heat of the moment was never repeated with malice or said directly to Patrick, but for some reason it stuck in the memories of both father and son.

Patrick was no more prone to get hurt than any other boy, and was probably no more scared of the pain. Nevertheless, if he *was* hurt he tended to over-react. He would cry and cry, unable to stop himself though he thought he might die of shame, and he always interpreted this reaction – as did his father – as physical cowardice. More than once, while lying in bed straining his ears to eavesdrop on his parents' discussion of his 'problem', he heard his father say: 'There ain't nothin' wrong – he just ain't got the backbone.'

At school he was bullied, partly because he

was fairly small for his age, but mostly because he reacted so *well* (in the eyes of the bullies) to ill-treatment. The sympathy of those in authority, like the sympathy of his parents, was at first given in abundance, but ultimately withdrawn. People pitied him for being hit, but they could not pity him for his pathetic failure to 'pull himself together'.

Mercifully, childhood passed, and if Patrick's 'problem' did not altogether disappear, at least its manifestations became less frequent. He gradually perfected the art of avoidance, steering clear of hazardous situations. He isolated himself from his dangerous peers and courted the good opinion of his teachers by becoming a model pupil. Reading became his main pastime and pleasure, valued more because it was an escape into safe abstraction than because of the information about the world which it gave him. When he was not reading, he still preferred to be on his own, and he liked to wander off into the woods surrounding his small-town Californian home, where he would watch the everyday routines of nature – especially the behaviour of small things, like spiders and insects, with which he came to feel a certain identification. They too were commonly disliked and despised, and they too had no backbones.

In his teens, he had regular sessions with the school therapist, who happened to be going through an Adlerian phase at the time and was finding inferiority complexes everywhere. She told him that he was only afraid of fear, and that his academic success was due to a desperate fear of being inferior to others, which drove him to over-achieve and yet remain unsatisfied with his achievement. She told him that his uncontrollable crying when injured was a manifestation of a deep-seated anxiety about failure, which was in typically paradoxical fashion *causing* a kind of failure. If only he could face up to all this and understand it, she opined, he would be able to overcome the difficulty.

Patrick was grateful for this advice, though he did not take it in quite the way it was intended. He came to the conclusion that what he needed was a more fully worked out inferiority complex, and he set out to intensify that pattern in his behaviour which the therapist had identified as a chief symptom of his neurosis.

He decided that he must assert in every possible way his superiority over others, to prove beyond a shadow of a doubt that however much they despised him they had no right so to do. He intensified his studies, and his determination to be a man of learning, but that was not enough.

What he really needed, he eventually concluded, was to put himself constantly in situations where most people would be afraid, but where he felt quite secure.

He had noted that a great many people harboured some degree of phobia about such spineless creatures as spiders, centipedes and scorpions, while he had none at all. Most people were afraid of things without backbones – and was he not a boy without a backbone himself? He resolved to get his own back on the world, by trading on the fears which others had and he had not, just as the bullies at school had traded on the fears he had, but they had not.

He resolved, in fact, to make a career out of an ironic play on words. To demonstrate to the world that he was not spineless, he set himself on the road to becoming an Invertebrate Man.

Patrick began to keep insects at home, starting with stick insects and moving on to preying mantisses. He relished the alarmed reaction of his parents, and the refusal of his mother to clean his room. The new dimension of privacy was an unexpected bonus.

He was soon specifically forbidden to add more fearsome creatures to his collection, but now that no one checked on the population of his vivaria he soon began to diversify into arachnids; two so-called 'wind scorpions' (actually solifugid spiders) became his most prized possessions. By the time he was a year or so into his new hobby he had a dozen glass tanks and was beginning to venture into breeding his specimens so that he could become a supplier as well as a customer of the shops which had initially set him up.

He often carried his more alarming pets around in his pockets, sometimes producing them in public places and stroking them lovingly. He kept scorpions in jars, tempting them to release the poison from their sacs by stinging bits of apple which he lowered into their reach on bits of string, for the benefit of fascinated audiences. They rarely stung him, and even when they did it was never like that awful thumbtack. The first few times it did hurt him, though he did not keep the more dangerous species, but he soon built up a tolerance which allowed him to improve his public performances by permitting himself to be stung. He delighted in the horror-stricken reactions of those he entertained, and the way they took it as a testament to his courage.

His tolerance to arachnid toxins allowed him to become confident and comfortable in handling the bigger and more horrid-seeming spiders, but he never took senseless risks, and certainly never tried to get used to the likes of *Lactrodectus mactans*, the black widow. He took great delight in the fact that he handled his pets so well that they treated him almost as one of their own.

He never went in for such practical jokes as leaving his pets in other people's lockers or lunchboxes. This was not because he was worried about people being frightened half to death when they found them, but because he was anxious that no harm should come to his spiders as a result of reckless over-reaction. He was not so much concerned with frightening others as with demonstrating his own immunity to their fears, confirming his carefully-cultivated moral superiority. After a time, though, he ceased to make ostentatious displays of his familiarity with ugly arachnids. Once his reputation was secured, there was no need to show off any longer.

He enjoyed one moment of triumph when, at the age of seventeen, he was approached by three teenage muggers. The biggest and ugliest of the muggers showed Patrick a cut-throat razor. Patrick showed the mugger a Mexican red-legged tarantula. It was the muggers who ran away, empty-handed.

By the time he went to college, Patrick's 'difficulty' seemed to be a thing of the past. He had secured his own release, at the cost of driving himself to unusual academic achievement and estranging himself from his parents, who now regarded him as an alien being with inexplicable drives and desires. At college he studied Zoology, and then did post-graduate research in the application of genetic engineering techniques to the modification of invertebrate species.

The first great success in the industrial application of genetic engineering techniques to invertebrate species had already been scored by John McBride, working with the silkworm *Bombyx mori*. Patrick's work followed on from this, meddling with the genes controlling the production of the spidersilk that various web-spinners produced.

His achievements in altering the properties of these spidersilks gave rise to no immediate commercial applications, but they did demonstrate potential. After receiving his doctorate, therefore, he joined IBEX – the multinational corporation for which McBride worked – and expressed enthusiasm for working in collaboration with the great man.

'You do realise,' said the personnel officer, 'that he's in Baltimore?'

'That doesn't matter,' said Patrick. 'I'm quite prepared to travel.'

'Not Baltimore in Maryland,' she explained. 'Baltimore, County Cork. The West of Ireland.'

Patrick was already committed. He simply shrugged his shoulders.

'Oh well,' she said. 'With a name like yours, you'll probably fit in there just fine.' The way she said it suggested that Baltimore, County Cork, was not her favourite place on earth. Several months later, in fact, Patrick realised that from the point of view of the corporation's personnel department, Baltimore was the armpit of the organisation, to which hardly anyone wanted to go, and from which almost everyone wanted a transfer. Nevertheless, it was there that fate took him, and he set off willingly to meet his destiny.

Patrick began to get some idea of why working in Baltimore would be no picnic when he was in the minicab which took him on the last leg of his long journey, from Cork airport to the shores of Roaringwater.

'Around here,' said the cab driver, 'they call it the Frankenstein Factory. Not me, of course — I know better. I know there's no monsters made there . . . or if there are, they don't hire minicabs.' He laughed at this, and Patrick marvelled at the fact that it was possible to laugh in an Irish accent as well as speak in one.

Patrick did not reply, but simply looked out of the window. There was not much to see; the sky was a solid leaden grey and it was raining. He was to see a great deal of grey sky and rain; by Californian standards the climate in County Cork could only be described as dismal.

He further realised why this was not a popular spot when the Director showed him around the various sites. To describe IBEX's Baltimore establishment as unlovely would have been a colossal understatement.

'As you're an Invertebrate Man,' said the Director, who was named Nijssen, 'you'll be in the warehouses on the south shore. You're not in the Marine Section, of course, but we keep all the inverts together. Most of our work is with prokaryots, and that's scattered between the holding tanks on the north shore, and the cracking plant and distillation towers inland. There's another installation out on Cape Clear, but that's triple-X security and the likes of you and me aren't even allowed on the island.'

Patrick's confusion regarding the references to holding tanks and a cracking plant was short-lived. Although it was now given over completely to biotechnology, the Baltimore station had once been IBEX's toe-hold in the great Celtic Sea oil boom of 1999. Corporations with more considerable oil interests had built their own stations in the east, near Rosslare, or in West Wales on St David's Head, but IBEX had taken advantage of some lavish grant aid offered by the Irish government and the EEC to assist the development of counties Cork and Kerry.

When the oil petered out between 2007 and 2011 IBEX had had the choice of paying back the grant money or converting their now-useless oil terminal to some other use. Then some enterprising executive in New York had one day been struck by the uncanny resemblance between a schematic diagram of a proposed continuous-culture system for breeding engineered bacteria and a map of the tanks and towers of the Baltimore terminal. So the holding tanks and the distillation towers had been adapted into fermenters where transformed micro-organisms could multiply, producing insulin, interferons, enzymes and hormones by means of transplanted genes.

Although the Atlantic waters which washed the shores of Cork were rather cool (despite the beneficial effects of the Gulf stream) for rearing the crabs, lobsters and oysters which were the focal points of IBEX's marine invertebrate research and development, that work too had been transferred here from the balmy Caribbean. With it had come the burgeoning Terrestrial Invertebrate Section, formerly distributed through a variety of university laboratories until the great John McBride had shown up its real potential and had persuaded IBEX's accountants that here was an underfinanced area where some lucky corporation was going to make a killing.

Some members of the local population had not wanted the oil terminal in the first place, had been suitably holier-than-thou about it when the oil gave out, and were even sourer about the adapted facility, which they considered a nonsense. On the other hand, some were all in favour of the so-called Frankenstein Factory, because it was the only possible source of employment for them. This situation was further confused by other attitudes, and on this topic Patrick heard a good deal from the great John McBride, who considered himself a broken wreck of a man, and blamed it all on Baltimore.

'O'Connell?' he said, on being introduced to his new assistant. 'I suppose your grandfather came from these parts and you imagine that you're returning to the native soil where your genetic roots are buried?'

Patrick assured him that this was not so. If some ancestor of his had carried the O'Connell name to America during the Great Famine of the 1840s, the family had long since forgotten him. No anecdotes of banshees and potato blight had been handed down over the generations.

'Ach, it doesn't matter,' said McBride. 'They'll probably take to you anyhow. Are you Catholic?'

'I'm an atheist,' Patrick told him.

'Aye, I've no doubt. But around here there are Catholic atheists and Protesent atheists, and you'd better be the first. Now, I'm the other. My grandfather emigrated to the States in 1927 – and he was a bloody Ulsterman. In the eyes of some of the locals, that makes me kin to the Devil himself. They look at me almost as if I were an Englishman!'

Patrick eventually discovered that this was an exaggeration, and that the inhabitants of Baltimore were no more bigoted than the human average, although the targets of their unreasoning dislikes seemed odd to the foreign eye. The local people reacted with instinctive negative feeling to three breeds of men: they were jokingly contemptuous of the men of neighbouring Kerry; they were not-so-jokingly contemptuous of the English; and they despised the Ulster Scot, for crimes committed over the course of three centuries. It was true that despite McBride's American nationality (aided, perhaps, by the curious shadow of an Irish accent which he somehow retained) they really did consider him an Ulsterman and an invader. By the same token, Patrick (though his accent was pure California) came to be seen as a kind of honorary Irishman.

This difference in Patrick's and McBride's status was nowhere more obvious than in their home. When IBEX had built the Baltimore station they had raised four small apartment blocks and bought up half a dozen of the largest houses in the neighbourhood to house their employees. Because biotechnology proved to be less labour-intensive than the oil business, at least in respect of highly skilled staff who could not be found locally, much of this accommodation was no longer required for imported Americans, and as part of its unceasing effort to maintain good public relations IBEX let the remainder at peppercorn rents to needy families. Patrick and McBride were senior enough to be given large apartments in a pleasant old house, but of the other three apartments two were occupied by the Flynns and the Flanagans, who crammed them to bursting. Patrick was never quite sure how many children there were in the two families, because they were never still enough to be counted, but there were at least a dozen and a half all told, of ages ranging from a few months to the darkest years of awful adolescence.

The father of the Flynns worked in the old cracking plant, while the Flanagans' only claim to corporation support was that the eldest daughter was a word-processor operator in the Marine Section. The Flynns and the Flanagans were not bad neighbours, given that there were so many of them – they could hardly help being more than ordinarily noisy – but Patrick soon found out that McBride was virtually at war with them, and had been for years. The adults treated him with polite scorn, but the children were liable to bait and insult him at almost every opportunity. When Patrick arrived, by contrast, the adults treated him with calculated *bonhomie* and the children with deliberate respect, as if to exaggerate by comparison their distaste for McBride. Sometimes it seemed that McBride could hardly bear to live in his ground-floor rooms when the children were about, and he would often retreat into a secret sanctum which he had established in the cellars, whose door he protected with a padlock and bolts. Patrick soon found out, though, that his own acceptance would not protect him from a stream of jokes about Frankenstein and making monsters; this seemed to be the only vocabulary the Flynns and the Flanagans had for thinking about any aspect of genetic engineering.

Despite these difficulties, Patrick did find some things to like about Baltimore. His other neighbour, who shared the ground floor of the house with McBride and the Flanagans while Patrick shared the first floor with the Flynns, was Dr Annabel Crozier, a small, dark and female Invertebrate Man whose speciality was molluscs. Patrick fell gradually but completely in love with her. The feeling was mutual, and if this were Dr Crozier's story their affection might have played a much greater part in it; in the schema of her life love was something much more significant and satisfying than slugs and snails. But Patrick, for all that his 'problem' was far behind him now, had only a small part of his ambition to spare for emotional entanglements. He was still first and foremost an Invertebrate Man, and his relationship with Annabel, though it brought him much joy, took second place in his mind to his less intimate but more problematic relationship with John McBride.

McBride was not quite what Patrick had expected. Knowing him only through his published papers, Patrick had recognised him as a man without peer in the field of Invertebrate Biology. He had assumed that McBride would be an aloof and distant figure, calm and abstracted, ruthlessly efficient and inhumanly self-controlled.

In fact McBride was none of these things – at least, not consistently. He was a strange patch-work of a character: paranoid, hyperactive and hard-drinking. He could be jovially manic and angrily melancholic. He was nervously verbose in conversation, but capable when working of astonishing concentration and delicacy of touch. If he *was* a genius then he was in the Edisonian rather than the Einsteinian mould; a 99% perspiration man. He worked quickly and prolifically, running dozens of experiments side by side on a frenetic trial and error basis, never losing track of anything.

The lines of research on which McBride was working for IBEX were varied. His principal research was into the applications of biotech-nology to pest control. He *was* transplanting pheromone genes into bacteria so that the phero-mones could be produced in quantity and used to lure mosquitoes, termites and cockroaches into traps. He was also working on specific pesticides which would kill their targets in droves without harming other species.

In addition to these main lines, McBride had been continuing his silk research, which Patrick would be required to take over and broaden.

He had also been working with bees, trying to emulate the animal engineers who had developed meat-yielding tissue-cultures by developing tissue-culture structures to produce honey, beeswax and royal jelly on an industrial scale. This too would become Patrick's province, but McBride intended to keep control of his research into the possible medical uses of arachnid toxins as muscle-relaxants. He candidly explained to Patrick that if there was a Nobel Prize for medicine going, he wanted it for himself.

McBride was also conducting some more peripheral experiments of dubious commercial application. One involved the butterfly *Papilio dardanus*, celebrated for having variants whose brightly-patterned wings mimicked several different model species. Mc Bride was trying to figure out how the colour patterning was genetically controlled, with a view to producing new variants whose patterns could be designed to order.

'If these boys can mimic half a dozen different models,' he told Patrick, 'there's no reason why we can't produce pictures on their wings – any image you care to name.'

McBride's successes in this private quest were already quite startling, though he had yet to persuade Nijssen that there was any market for designer butterflies. IBEX were not heavily involved in the arts, certainly not in speculative *avant garde* developments.

With all these things going on, it was not surprising that McBride's labs were in a mess. He had half a dozen research assistants and thirty lab technicians, but he kept them all so busy in their own areas of responsibility that they simply took up their stations in the sea of chaos and left the captain of the ship to look after the whole enterprise. Equipment was continually being appropriated and moved, and it was necessary to hang DO NOT TOUCH notices everywhere to preserve apparatus from being plundered.

McBride's car was just as cluttered, not simply with paper but with all kinds of glassware and gadgets.

'I try a few things at home,' the great man explained, airily. 'We don't all have rich love-lives to fill up our leisure time.'

Such comments were intended as jokes, but there was an underlying bitterness in them. McBride envied him his happiness with Annabel, though not because he admired her himself. Annabel told Patrick that McBride had been deeply in love with one of her predecessors, but that something had gone wrong and she had transferred back to the States. The failed affair had marked the beginning of McBride's drinking problem.

Patrick was much fonder of order and discipline than his mentor. He tried to set things straight at the lab, but soon had to give up. He settled instead for keeping his own work under strict control, and turning a diplomatically blinkered eye to the rest. He was constantly amazed by the quality and the quantity of the work that McBride got through. Alcoholic McBride may have become, but he was a workaholic first and foremost. He bequeathed his most celebrated research to Patrick lock, stock and barrel, having lost all interest in it.

'What you need to do,' he said, 'is breed bigger worms. Then start buggering about with the silks. That stuff with spidersilk was all good practice, but scale is the problem. Maybe it would be best to work up tissue-culture sub-organisms, but in the meantime go for bigger worms. Great fat things that can produce thick thread by the yard.'

'I don't know,' Patrick told him. 'Giantism in inverts produces so many problems. Oxygen supply to the tissues . . . mechanical support.'

'Ach,' said McBride, 'that's garbage. Too many prissy characters with no imagination tutting at old Hollywood films. Transplant a gene for haemoglobin into the little darlings and turn them into expert oxygen-moppers. Forget the mechanical problems – the worms don't have to fly once they turn into moths. Anyhow, the hydrostatic systems in insect legs are more powerful than they're given credit for. Remember the Golden Age? Those beautiful dragonflies! If inverts have stayed small for the greater part of their evolutionary history, it's because it was economical, not because it was impossible to be big. Don't underestimate your playmates, Patrick. And if in doubt, squirt a bit of helpful DNA into the little sods. Remarkably adaptable, invert eggs. Take care, and you can do anything with the little darlings you want to. Take my word for it.'

Patrick took his word for it, and never found his advice poor. And as his respect for McBride was confirmed, so McBride's respect for him increased. Patrick got the impression that McBride had been a lonely man all his life, and could not help but wonder whether there was some strange and shameful secret in *his* personal history that somehow paralleled his own, though it was not a matter he could ever discuss. McBride made friends with Patrick, taking the younger man completely under his wing as protégé and confidant. Patrick grew to like him very much, and to pity him desperately for the way the Flynns and the Flanagans used the Frankenstein label to taunt him.

The pity disappeared though – never to return – when he found out what McBride was doing in his secret sanctum in the cellars of the old house where they lived.

Patrick had been in Baltimore for nearly a year when McBride decided to let him in on the big secret. Even then, it happened only because the great man was maudlin drunk and Patrick had spent two hours with him in one of Baltimore's several public houses trying to persuade him that it was time to go home.

McBride began by complaining, as he often did, about the supposedly disgusting habits of the Flynns and the Flanagans, diversified into more general calumnies against the Irish, and then progressed to complaints against IBEX, the scientific community and the world as a whole.

'I tell ye, Patrick,' he said, his speech very slurred, 'the world as it is is no place for the likes of us, and the sooner we blow it to hell and are gone the better. Nuclear winter's the thing – crucify the entire bloody ecosphere, and let the inverts have it back. They're the boys that will do it, Patrick – the cockroaches and the spiders, the snails and the worms. It's their world, Patrick, an' always has been. People are just a temporary aberration.'

When they got back to the house Patrick had to carry McBride across the threshold, but the older man soon began to revive. He resisted Patrick's attempts to open the door of his apartment, dragging him instead to the padlocked door that led down to the cellars.

'Ye're a good boy, Patrick,' he said, 'an' I'll show ye somethin' that'll warm y're old heart. 'Cause y're an invert man like meself. An' I know y'll understand.' With Patrick's help, he extricated the key to the padlock, and released it. He ushered the younger man through, and quickly bolted the door behind them, then led the way down the stone steps.

Patrick was surprised to find the cellars very warm. The gas-fired boiler which ran the house's central heating was in a cupboard on the ground floor, but there was obviously another heating system down here. The steps were flanked by whitewashed walls, and it was not until they turned the corner at the bottom that Patrick realised how extensive the cellars were, and how completely McBride had made them his own.

He had expected the mess, of course, but not the sheer profusion of apparatus, which must have been appropriated from the warehouses over a period of ten or twelve years. He was not surprised to find vivaria, with living specimens, but the nature of those specimens came to him as a complete shock.

There was a certain irony in this, because many people would have found in those glass cases the perfect fulfilment of their anxious expectations. John McBride had been making monsters, and had clearly brought to the task at least as much expertise and imagination as he brought to his more orthodox labours.

With an eerie thrill of recognition, Patrick realised that most of the creatures in the vivaria were solifugids – the sun spiders and wind-scorpions which had so impressed him in his youth with their grotesqueness. But he had never seen solifugids like these.

It was not simply that they were huge (McBride had clearly spoken from experience in declaring that common theories regarding the impossibility of giant invertebrates were misguided) but that they were decorated so garishly. Patrick was looking at spiders whose bodies were the size of footballs and whose leg span must be all of four feet, their great bulbous bodies patterned as brightly as the wings of the *Papilio* butterflies in the labs.

These patterns were no mere mosaics – they were crude pictures. Each spider-body was formed as a human head, with the hairy crown toward the rear and an open, screaming mouth on top. At the front of the spider's head the eyes and mouth parts were virtually lost in a riot of scarlet, which simulated the region where the fake human head had been torn from its body.

For more than three minutes, Patrick simply stared about him, looking from one glass case to another. In the end, all he could find to say was: 'Jesus!'

'I wanted to do it at the labs,' said McBride, suddenly sounding more sober. 'The bastards wouldn't let me. So I did it here. Twelve years' work, Patrick – me *magnum opus*.'

Patrick went through an open door into a further room. McBride leaned through the doorway to switch on the light for him. There were more vivaria, more giant spiders. These were black and hairy wolf-spiders – not as large as the solifugids, but the kind of thing that might feature large in anyone's nightmares.

'They said it couldn't be done,' observed McBride, with evident pride. Patrick could hear in his tone the unmistakable symptoms of an inferiority complex of huge dimension, but whether it was as conscious and calculated as his own he could not tell.

'Why, John?' he asked, faintly. 'For Christ's sake, why?'

'All genetic engineers are monster makers,' said

McBride, sounding as if he had sobered up. 'You know that, Patrick. "Dr Frankenstein, I presume . . ." You've heard it all. "Made any good monsters today, Doc?" But you understand, Patrick, what's involved. Works of art, dear boy. Some day, when oil painting is long forgotten, the world's great artists will be working in living clay.'

'Does anyone else know what's down here?' asked Patrick.

McBride shook his head, sorrowfully.

'I showed someone,' he said. 'Once. She didn't understand. But I knew *you*'d understand.'

Patrick realised that this was the lost love that Annabel had told him about, and that it was what the woman had seen in this cellar which had spoiled the relationship. Patrick understood that – but what McBride was asking him to understand was something else again.

'It's brilliant, John,' he said, unable to prevent himself from adopting the kind of humouring tones he might have used to talk to a madman. 'But aren't they dangerous?'

'Of course not,' McBride told him. 'Maybe not so harmless as they are normal size, of course, but not difficult to handle. The tanks are closed, and they breathe a special oxygen-rich mixture. When I handle them I give them a whiff of nitrous oxide. They couldn't live long in ordinary air –

they'd choke to death within a day, in spite of their added haemoglobin.'

As he spoke, McBride waved his arms at the cylinders of oxygen connected by feed-tubes to the vivaria, and at the pressurised plastic beakers of nitrous oxide which littered the space under the benches. 'Of course,' he added, 'they can't scuttle along like the little ones. I wonder whether that makes them a bit less effective. What alarms people is the way they move, not just the way they look.'

McBride went into yet another room, and turned on the light. Patrick followed him, stepping gingerly over the litter of plugboards and electric cables that formed coloured webs over the floor. There were more vivaria here, but most were unoccupied. Two held specimens rather less impressive, at least in terms of sheer size, than the ones in the other rooms – spiders with bodies no bigger than a man's fist, and legs to match. They were black, with red patches. Paradoxically, they gave Patrick the worst thrill of fear he had yet felt. They were females of the species *Latrodectus mactans*: black widows.

'What do you intend to do with them?' he asked.

'I don't intend to *do* anything,' McBride told him. 'It's art for art's sake.'

'What do they eat?'

'They're not particular. Insect grubs, mostly. They're easy to grow in giant sizes. Then again, there's always the failures. Waste not, want not. Spiders aren't squeamish about cannibalism.'

Patrick continued looking about him, searching for some clue that would make sense of it all. There was so much mess, and these nightmare creations living in its midst seemed almost surreal. It was as though the laboratories in the old warehouses were the respresentations of McBride's consciousness, while this secret subterranean realm was the embodiment of his subconscious, populated by the unrepressed forces of creativity which knew no guilt or social responsibility.

'You don't like people very much, do you, John?' said Patrick, quietly. 'What is it that you're afraid of, that makes you so desperate to show that you don't share their fears?'

In saying this, Patrick thought he was demonstrating that McBride's confidence in him was not misplaced, and that he really did understand. But it wasn't the understanding that McBride had been looking for.

'Don't be such a prick, dear boy,' he said. 'It doesn't suit you.'

'No,' said Patrick, 'I don't suppose it does.' He

left the cellars with the defeated air of one who has discovered that his idol has feet of clay.

A whole week passed before Patrick finally decided to tell Annabel what he had found out. He did so uneasily, not sure what her reaction might be. She was an Invertebrate Man herself, and had no particular fear of spiders, but she still turned white at the thought of what was lurking beneath her floorboards.

'You have to tell Nijssen,' she said.

Patrick shook his head. 'They'd sack him. Can you imagine what this might do to the company's image?'

'The hell with the company's image,' she replied. 'And to hell with McBride, too. Those things have to be destroyed.'

Patrick gritted his teeth, and said: 'Why?'

'Because they're an obscenity, and because they'd set the genetic engineering business back twenty years if anyone found out.'

'An obscenity?' Patrick queried. 'Do you know what they're doing out on Cape Clear? Research in biological warfare. They're making bacteria, microsporidia, HIVs and other assorted viruses, and nerve gases. Everything John does at the warehouses is for the betterment of the human condition. He may have a lot to say about the benefits of human extinction, but those boys at the Cape are actually trying to do it. Are you telling me that a few big spiders are obscene, and that McBride ought to be ruined?'

'Damn right,' she said.

After a pause, Patrick said: 'It's good work, Annie. Pure genius.'

'So is the work they do on the cape, no doubt,' she observed, drily. 'Christ, Pat, these things are in our house. Do you seriously want to live with them? If you don't want to stop McBride, then you have to make him destroy them himself.'

'He'd never do it. Never in a million years.'

'Then someone else has to. You must see that.' She paused, and studied him through slightly narrowed eyes. 'You do see that, don't you?' she went on. 'You just aren't prepared to do the dirty work yourself. Do you want me to tell Nijssen?'

Patrick squirmed in discomfort. 'I don't know what to do,' he complained. 'He's not just my friend; he's the best Invertebrate Man in the world. Okay, so the Flynns and the Flanagans of the world see him as a mad scientist – but they see us the same way. We're supposed to understand. We're all Invertebrate Men together. He only told me because he thought I'd understand.'

Annabel stared at him, still with a hint of contempt in her gaze: 'But you don't understand,'

161

she said, pointedly. 'Do you?' It was a challenge as much as a question.

'Maybe I do,' he said. 'It's like the way I used to keep spiders when I was young. A kind of bravado. I didn't keep them in spite of the fact that they were horrid, but because of it. The more horrid, the better. He's just taking that to its logical extreme, that's all. And in its way . . . it's pure genius, Annie, pure genius.'

'Is this some kind of test?' she asked him, in a softer voice. 'Are you trying me out, to see if I'll recoil in disgust? Or are you testing yourself, to see whether an impartial observer thinks that you're as crazy as he is?'

'I don't know,' said Patrick, unhappily. 'I don't know what to do.'

'Well I do,' said Annabel. 'You tell that bastard that if those things aren't gone by the end of the week, you'll call in the vermin exterminator. And if you won't, I will.'

Patrick looked her mournfully in the eye, and said: 'I don't know if I can do that to him.'

'Well,' she replied, cuttingly. 'I guess it's okay for an Invertebrate Man to be short of backbone – but we Mollusc Girls have hard shells. You have five days, Dr Frankenstein.'

These words were deliberately calculated to wound, but only at a superficial level. Annabel was, after all, in love with Patrick O'Connell. She had no idea what the reference to a lack of backbone meant to him, and would never have said it had she known how deeply it would cut him. But instead of urging him to action, as she had intended, her remarks threw him into a pit of gloom. For the next three days he avoided her completely.

Whether he would have let the five days elapse, and left her to do her worst without so much as a word, it is impossible to say. Matters came to a head before that, and though what transpired was a disaster for John McBride and the corporate image of IBEX, it probably saved Patrick and Annabel's love-affair from ruination.

On the fateful day, Patrick stayed late to work in the laboratory – more because he was reluctant to go home than because there was urgent work to be done. Because there was no one to give him a lift he had to walk home. The sun had set, it was already beginning to get dark, and it looked like rain, but in his masochistic mood he was quite content to get soaked.

He was unaware of any trouble until the police car roared up to him, siren blazing. For a few dreadful moments, as he was hurried unceremoniously into the back seat, he thought that he was under arrest. The Garda were more intent on getting him to the house than they were on explaining, but when he saw the smoke and the fire engine skewed across the lawn, he realised that the trouble was far worse than that.

Annabel was in front of the house, with a milling throng of Flynns and Flanagans, many of whom were shouting and caterwauling extravagantly. They didn't seem pleased to see Patrick – even Annabel, as she grabbed the door of the police car, was more angry than grateful.

As he stepped out on to the gravel driveway, looking round at the uniformed firemen, Patrick felt like a specimen in a cage. Every eye was upon him, aggressively expectant.

'What happened?' he asked, his anxious eyes looking at the oily smoke oozing from the cracked windows of the ground floor apartments.

'The Flanagan kids,' Annabel said. 'The boys broke into the basement. What they found there scared them so much they panicked – tripped over the cables, pulled oxygen leads loose. Electrical fire started – burned like crazy with all that oxygen. Pressured cylinders started exploding.

'The boys got out; there was smoke everywhere. I started to get the people out – there was panic enough with just the fire. Then the wolf spiders started coming out, and all hell broke loose.

'Mrs Flynn had hysterics . . . so did the girls. McBride went down into the bloody basement – bloody stupid! He didn't come out.

'The Flynn baby's still on the top floor. The fire didn't spread far; the brigade filled the cellars full of foam. When they went in, they found one of McBride's solifugid specials straddling the staircase. I don't know whether that thing's deadly, but I do know there's not a man here is going to go past it. God only knows how many of the things there are upstairs, but *somebody* has to fetch that baby.'

Patrick looked round at the firemen and the Garda. They didn't seem apologetic. They were just resentful.

'You know about those things,' said one of the firemen. 'Don't you?'

That just about said it all. They weren't necessarily saying that it was his fault; they were just saying that it was his job. He was the Invertebrate Man. He knew all about giant spiders.

Curiously, Patrick didn't feel scared – not yet. He looked at Mrs Flynn's tear-stained face, and at one of her daughters, sitting on the grass with her arms about her knees, sobbing wildly. In the distance, he could hear another siren; it was probably an ambulance.

'I'll need a mask,' he said to the fireman who

had spoken. 'And a flashlight. Have you got a small fire-extinguisher, light enough to carry in one hand?'

The mask was handed to him, and a fireman moved round behind him to strap on the bladder-pack which contained the oxygen/helium mixture.

'The fire's out,' said one of the policemen, nodding toward the building.

'Just give me the extinguisher,' said Patrick.

Another fireman brought him a metal cylinder, not much bigger than an aerosol can, with a thumb-operated trigger. 'That'll give you three or four squirts of foam,' he said. 'Make sure you get the bugger between the eyes.' Patrick took the extinguisher in his right hand, and the flashlight in his left.

As he went through the doorway, it began to rain. *At least*, he thought, *I'll not get wet*. But his unnatural calmness didn't last. There was no light at all inside the house, and the beam of the flashlight seemed fearfully weak as he moved it back and forth, searching for the spiders.

How dangerous they would be he could not guess. McBride had assured him that they couldn't breathe normal air for long, and the atmosphere here was still thick with nasty smoke. But they'd been strong enough and quick enough to get out of the cellar when the shards of exploding gas cylinders smashed their tanks. That couldn't have been easy, with the fire running wild. The wolf spiders and the solifugids weren't poisonous species in their normal forms, but a bite from their overgrown fangs might inject enough venom to kill. And there were the two black widows, which hadn't been mentioned.

As he moved toward the staircase the flashlight picked out the solifugid straddling it, two legs on the banister rail, two on the wall and four on the stair-carpet.

In the bright light of the cellar, when first he'd seen such a creature, the imitation of a severed head had seemed poor and impressionistic, but in this light it was a fragment of nightmare. He could hardly blame the firemen, unwarned and unprepared, for not wanting to take it on. His heart was pounding now, and his body was beginning to shiver, though the night was not particularly cold. He sucked in the oxygen/helium mixture through the mouthpiece, and paused, fighting for self-control. Then he walked towards the unmoving solifugid, pointed the fire extinguisher at it, and pressed the trigger.

The jet of foam struck the body, and to Patrick's great relief there was no purposive response. The great spider convulsed, pulling in its legs the way a spider does when wet, and tumbled from its perch. Patrick kicked it out of the way, though the feel of it on his shoe made him shiver. He went slowly up the stairs, scanning with the flashlight, searching the walls and the ceiling as well as the floor.

There was a wolf spider on the first floor landing. It didn't move, but he squirted it anyhow, then crushed it under his heel. He went through the open door of the Flynns' apartment. He could hear the baby inside, not yelling but whimpering, as though too tired to cry at full strength. It was in a back room, whose door was also open.

As he came to the doorway and shone the light through it, he saw two more wolf spiders. They had fled as far as possible from the smoke, which was quite thin here – only a grey foggy haze in the beam of the torch. One was crouched under the legs of a chair. The other was between the wheels of the pram, which was rocking very gently as Baby Flynn moved inside.

Patrick wasn't sure that he could get two more squirts out of the miniature extinguisher.

He aimed first at the one beneath the pram, and saw it draw its legs in as the foam hit it. It continued to thrash about, desperately, and Patrick felt a wave of sympathy for it. He moved to the side of the pram, and aimed at the spider beneath the chair. It moved, making him freeze in horror, but it could only move slowly. There was something infinitely pathetic about the drunken way it walked toward him.

He pressed the trigger of the fire extinguisher. A little foam flew out, like a blob of spittle, but then there was a moist wheeze. The blob missed the approaching spider by a foot.

Patrick leapt forward, and brought his heel down hard on the wolf spider's black body. It crunched beneath his weight, dry and brittle, and red ichor flooded out over his shoe. He felt suddenly sick, but quickly got a grip on himself. He threw the extinguisher away, picked up the baby, and walked steadily back the way he had come.

The baby squirmed in his arms, still wailing feebly, and he could not help the thought coming into his head that it was like a great helpless spider.

Outside, he passed the baby to Mrs Flynn, feeling heartily glad to be rid of it. He looked around at the ring of faces, weirdly lit by the stroboscopic blue lights of the various vehicles. There were fewer now – some of the Flynns and the Flanagans had been loaded into the ambulance. He was astonished by the change in their expressions. They were no longer hostile, angry or resentful. Instead, they were positively flooded with relief and admiration.

Patrick realised, to his surprise, that he was a hero.

He looked for the fireman who had found him the extinguisher, and took the breathing apparatus from his mouth in order to speak.

'Got another?' he asked.

The fireman shook his head. Patrick turned back to the door, and was surprised when Annabel darted forward to take his arm.

'McBride's still in there,' he reminded her.

'He can't be alive,' she said. 'You don't have to go.'

Patrick shrugged off her restraining hand, as gently as he could.

'Yes I do,' he said. 'And without a backward glance, he went back into the house, heading for the basement door.

The smoke was thick about the cellar steps, and the flashlight was almost useless. The mouthpiece of the mask was tight against his skin, and he could taste nothing but the leaden dryness of the oxygen/helium mixture. He picked his way very carefully down the stairs.

He had no idea whether McBride might be alive. No one could have breathed the smoke-laden air for long, but there were several rooms, and the fire must have affected some worse than others. He knew that there were enough oxygen cylinders to allow McBride to rig up his own supply, if only he had had the time – and provided that the spiders had let him. There had to be half a dozen solifugids down there, and there was no way of guessing how many had died in their tanks. There were also the two black widows, though he was praying that their vivaria had not been smashed in the multiple explosion.

The room where the solifugids had been was in a dreadful state. The fire had started here, amid the greatest quantity of equipment. The room had frosted-glass windows set high in the wall; there was a pit outside which let light reach them even though they were below ground level. It was through these windows – smashed now – that the firemen had directed their hoses.

He shone the flashlight beam around. One vivarium, miraculously, was still intact. The creature inside was unmoving, apparently dead. Three other spiders were dead inside their smashed tanks. One dangled grotesquely from the seared ceiling, and though it was clearly no threat it looked horrible, like a human head hanging from a meat-hook, swaying slightly in the smoky air-currents stirred by the heat from the charred electrical cables on the floor.

There was no sign of McBride.

Patrick kept well clear of the dangling horror, and made his way with the utmost care through the room where the wolf spiders had been lodged. The fire had barely spread into this room before being choked by the foam. Four of the vivaria had been broken. He had already killed three wolf spiders, and he had no difficulty picking out the dead body of the fourth – a victim of the fire.

McBride's body was not here. He had to be in the furthest room, with the black widows. Patrick began to pick his way over the littered floor, but he was less careful now, because his attention was already fixed on the smoke-stained door ahead, which stood slightly ajar. A length of cable snaked around his ankle, as he moved reflexively to free it his other foot – precariously lodged on a litter of broken glass – turned sideways. He fell forwards, but had sufficient command of his balance to make sure that he only fell on to his knee.

There was an upturned thumbtack on the floor. It was driven into his flesh just beneath his right kneecap.

Shock and pain went through him with such astonishing force that it seemed to Patrick as if he had been hit by lightning. As though released by some secret trigger, tears began to course from his eyes. He was amazed, not so much by the fact that he was crying, but by the sheer volume of his tears and his complete inability to stop the flow.

He did not lose his ability to think clearly. It was as though the tears were a detached phenomenon, no more integral to his state of mind than the raindrops which dripped on to the floor near the frosted windows. Carefully, he pulled out the thumbtack, and got to his feet, wondering whether his legs would still support him.

They would, and they did – but he could only limp towards the door behind which McBride must be.

Supporting himself on the lintel, he pushed the door open, and shone the flashlight inside. There did not seem to be much smoke, but McBride was unconscious on the floor. An oxygen cylinder lay beside him, with a length of plastic pipe attached to the nozzle – clearly the scientist had made some attempt to rig up a breathing apparatus, but had not managed to close the door.

Patrick wanted to go to McBride immediately, but forced himself to pause and shine the beam of the flashlight at the two vivaria. Both seemed intact, though he had to blink furiously to see anything at all, and he could not make out anything inside them.

He staggered to McBride's side, and let himself painfully down on his good knee. He groped for McBride's neck, and tried to feel the pulse; it was there, and not so very faint. McBride responded to his touch, turning slightly away. Patrick grabbed the oxygen cylinder, and turned the release-wheel. Hearing a satisfying hiss, he moved the end of the plastic hose close to McBride's face, playing the jet on to the stricken man's lips.

McBride was still breathing, and the oxygen quickly revived him. Half a minute passed, and then he stirred, coughing desperately as he rolled on to his side.

'Oh Jaysus,' he said, weakly. He looked up at Patrick, taking a moment or two to recognise him. 'What the hell are ye weeping for?' he demanded.

'Shut up!' said Patrick, fiercely – the words muffled and distorted by the breathing apparatus. He moved the mouthpiece, and said: 'Get up, you bastard. Get up, and get out!'

'Well,' said McBride, coughing harshly. 'Ye don't . . .'

At that precise moment a black widow dropped from the ceiling, where she had taken refuge after squeezing out of the hole opened in the side of her tank when the oxygen-lead had been ripped away. She landed on top of Patrick's head, and he felt her unnaturally long legs

174

trying desperately to get a grip on his hairy pate.

Patrick froze. If he could stay absolutely still, he thought, she would not bite him. But the tears were still spilling from his eyes, and he was terrified that at any moment his whole body might be seized by a racking sob.

McBride was frozen too; there was just enough torchlight reflected from the whitewashed walls to show him what had happened.

Very slowly, Patrick passed the flashlight to McBride. The older man took it, and had sufficient presence of mind not to point it directly at the spider.

Patrick could feel a sob welling up inside him, and held his breath with fierce determination. He reached up with both hands, offering a platform to the spider's grappling feet. Had the feet already been entangled in his hair, she would have had difficulty, but as it was she moved gratefully on to the levelled fingers. Carefully, he moved his hands forward, and then down in front of his face. Blinking furiously to rid himself of the stinging tears, he kept his eye on the creature as he lowered her gradually to the floor. She moved off his hands and on to a patch of bare concrete, between Patrick's knees and McBride's recumbent body.

She did not seem so very large, now. She was very much smaller than the wolf spiders, although she was a giant among her own kind.

McBride smashed her dead with one blow of the flashlight. It went out, leaving them in darkness.

For a moment, there was no sound but the drumming of the raindrops. Then McBride said: 'Poor little bugger.'

Patrick found himself feeling sorry for the spider. She had not attempted to bite him, and it seemed to him that she must have recognised in his touch a kind of sympathy. He felt that in delivering the spider so tenderly to destruction he had betrayed her.

'Let's get the hell out of here,' he said to McBride, through his mask. 'Do you think you can walk?'

'I can,' McBride assured him. 'Can you?'

They both could, after a fashion. Patrick was limping, but he managed to support McBride as they made their unsteady way through the pitch-dark rooms to the stairway, then up and out into the rain.

Patrick was still crying, and when they came to the doorway he hung back, ashamed to be seen. He need not have worried. Tears mean nothing in themselves, and he had just brought a man from a cellar filled with acrid smoke. No one thought that his weeping eyes were evidence of anything but courage in awkward circumstances. For the first time in his life, he felt that he had backbone enough, in spite of everything that had gone into the making of him.

As Annabel hurried to his side, and an ambulance-man came to take McBride, Patrick felt suddenly certain that until the day he died he could be proud to be an Invertebrate Man.

And so, as things transpired, he was. Even John McBride, in due coure, was able to work again, extending the horizons of applied science further still. Annabel and Patrick were married, and eventually returned to the happier climes of California to raise their children. The Flynns and the Flanagans continued to send them Christmas cards for many years, although – in their own sweet sardonic fashion – they always addressed them to Dr and Dr Frankenstein.

The Furniture of Life's Ambition

'Jesus, Jude,' complained William Morris to his wife one night, as they lay cuddling in bed. 'I've got to get out. I've just got to.'

Judy Morris strangled the sigh which rose unbidden to her lips, as it did every time William had one of his moods. She loved him dearly, but he could be *very* tiresome. She opened her conflower-blue eyes and passed a tired hand through her silken blonde hair.

'You don't mean that, dear,' she said. 'You've just had a bad day, that's all.'

'Bad day!' said William. '*Bad day!* Jude, we're on the threshold of a whole new scientific revolution here. Our entire technological repertoire stands to be transformed in the space of a single lifetime – *my* lifetime. But all Plasmotech care about is meeting consumer demand! You know what they want me to work on now? Fish, that's what! I've been summoned to see Curtis and

Wilberforce tomorrow, and I know exactly what they're going to say. They're going to talk about cod fillets and caviar, and make stupid jokes about Moby Dick. It'll be kids' stuff, Jude, a five-year-old could do it. It's just one bloody supermarket novelty after another. Is this the future, Jude? I mean, Jude, *Jesus!*'

Judy knew that she must at all costs avoid making jokes about loaves and fishes. William, as his finely-chiselled, delicately pre-Raphaelite features implied, was rather over-sensitive, and was prone to overract to any slight, real or imagined. As a child he had been spoiled dreadfully because of his marvellous intelligence and stunning good looks, and in adult life he remained petulant, horribly jealous and prone to outrageous tantrums. Those who loved him had to learn to handle him very delicately.

Most people were willing to learn. After all, one has to make allowances for genius, and William was certainly a genius – possibly the best geneswitcher in the entire world. His employers at Plasmotech were aware of this, and were careful to pay him a very handsome salary. Judy knew it too, and she adored him as much for his fine and reckless mind as for his remarkably beautiful features and lissom body. William was absolutely certain of it, and saw himself as a combination of Albert Einstein and Thomas Alva Edison, without peer as theoretical scientist or practical man.

Plastmotech dealt in factory-produced food: meat and dairy products manufactured biotechnologically, without the aid of animals. Geneticists of an earlier generation than William's had figured out how the genes in an animal egg-cell provided the blueprint for the structure of a mature animal, and how genes were selectively switched off in different kinds of specialised cells to produce organs and tissues. These discoveries had opened up a scientific Klondyke for the geneswitchers whose business it was to design useful organic structures and then to control the switching of genes in developing embryos so as to produce those structures.

It was no longer necessary, in William's day, to allow a cow's fertilised egg-cell to develop into another cow, which would have to graze for years in open fields in order to produce milk or beef. Technical control of the geneswitching process meant that a cow's egg could be instructed to develop into a gargantuan milk-making organ or a single huge muscle. Such entities could easily be kept alive in nutrient baths, fed on an organic cocktail of carbohydrates, proteins and trace compounds which was manufactured in bulk by genetically-engineered fungi.

The earliest food-producing entities had been limited in size. Tissue-cultures, like organisms, age and die; cells cannot keep dividing for ever, and as they become more specialised they age more rapidly. At one time, therefore, a cow's ovum could only be induced to develop into a lump of solid muscle approximately the same size as an actual cow. William Morris's first breakthrough had been to find a way to overcome this limitation. He had discovered how to 'neotenise' the developing tissue-culture, so that the onset of specialisation could be delayed. The early phase of the development of the quasi-embryo could then be extended to produce a huge spherical 'superblastula' before the switching of genes need actually begin. This allowed the growth of very large tissue-cultures. The meat-producing ones were quickly nicknamed skyscraper steaks, while the ones which produced milk attracted less dignified titles.

William's second discovery had been just as dramatic. Plasmotech had had profitable meat-producers and milk-producers even before William joined the company, but they had failed to develop a really efficient substitute for actual chickens as producers of eggs. Co-ordination of the different kinds of specialised cells involved in egg-making became very problematic if the egg-making apparatus was not situated within a greater organism equipped with built-in control mechanisms: a nervous system and a hormonal system. William, working with general-purpose silicon chips and standard organo-metallic synapses developed for medical purposes, had managed to fit simple multi-tissue entities with appropriately simple inorganic 'brains', adding just sufficient control to allow the entities to function. He was thus enabled to design an egg-producer the size of a family car, fuelled by a mammoth drip-feed, which could spew out 400 standard eggs an hour. William called it his 'Heavyside Layer'.

With achievements like this to his credit many a lesser man would have been contented, but William's imagination was of the kind which loved to reach out into vast vistas of half-glimpsed possibility; he had bold dreams and brave ambitions, and he felt that his job was becoming a kind of straitjacket preventing him from fulfilling his true destiny. He was not a happy man, and Judy had often to listen to the outpourings of his anguish.

'Well, dear,' she said judiciously, in response to William's complaints, 'Plasmotech are a food company. 'It's an important job, discovering new ways to make cheap food. There are still two billion people in the world who don't have enough to eat. You used to find the job exciting.'

William groaned. 'That's because there used to be problems to be solved. Important problems, like superblastularisation and silicon-organic integration. Do you have any idea how useful those techniques might be, once their true range of application is explored? Skyscraper steaks and the Heavyside Layer are just scratching the surface . . . but Curtis can't see any farther than the next bloody delicacy! A thousand other geneswitchers will be picking up the threads of my discoveries and doing really interesting things, while I'm supposed to fart about with fish.

'The stupid thing is that Plasmotech will make billions in spite of their blindness, because they own the goddam patents. My patents, Jude! I won't make as much out of it as Wilberforce and Curtis, and I bet they won't even give me a Nobel Prize, because I'm just a vulgar commercial engineer. Jesus, Jude, I've got to get out. Somehow, I've got to go solo, work for myself. I've got to.'

'Well dear,' said Judy, caressing him soothingly with her gentle hands, in her own peculiarly distinctive fashion, 'I think that's a wonderful idea, but you've said before that it would be very difficult. All that equipment you work with – the

DNA-thingumajigs and the advanced electronic doodahs. It's such a heavy investment just to get started.'

'I know that,' said William, who was beginning to wind down under the palliative pressure of Judy's stroking, and was gradually becoming plaintive instead of angry. 'But I've got a first class record, second to none. God knows, I've done enough to show my worth. If I lived in America, big-dollar men would be queueing up to finance me – I've got American biotech firms headhunting me all the time, though Plasmotech try their level best to keep them away from me. I'd need six or seven million to start up – ten at the most. That's petty cash in the City. *Somebody* should be willing to finance me.'

Judy didn't like the idea of moving to America. She was part of a big, close family, and had an enjoyable job of her own at the BBC. She was also genuinely devoted to England's countryside and the nation's sense of history. Her heart sank at the prospect of giving it all up.

'We did a financial documentary last week,' she said, pensively. 'There was a rather charming man on it – very striking red hair. Name of Marshall. He's part of a firm of investment managers and financial consultants. He talked about multimillion dollar deals as if he fixed them up every morning before breakfast. I've got his card at the office. Shall I bring it home?'

The stroking was by now having such an effect that William was quite relaxed. He seemed ready to forget the whole matter for the time being, in order to turn his attention to a more pleasant occupation.

Judy permitted herself a discreet sigh of relief, and abandoned herself to passion.

She did remember, though, to keep her promise to fetch home the card, thus helping destiny to point William in the direction of his portentous first meeting with Peter Peregrine Marshall of Marshall & Faulkner.

'The trouble is,' said P P Marshall, leaning back in his fancy swivelling chair and flicking cigar ash on to the shag-pile carpet, 'that you haven't really thought this through.'

William was not in the least disturbed by the other man's casual *savoir faire*. He stared into Marshall's brilliant blue eyes, noticing how like his wife's they were. 'Actually,' he said, 'I think I'm the only person in the world – or at least the only person in Britain – who has thought it through. I've just explained to you that these techniques are the basis for a whole new industrial revolution. Do you know how many scientific breakthroughs have been made here, then blocked and mishandled by the obtuseness of the financiers, so that the Americans and Japanese stole all the thunder?'

'That's an old story, Dr Morris,' Marshall replied, 'and you'd be surprised how many people try to tell it to me. Don't mistake my meaning. Marshall & Faulkner do have access to the kind of money you need, and would be happy to put it into the kind of industrial enterprise that you're talking about. When I say that you haven't thought it through, I don't mean that you lack vision – far from it; you can see the far horizons very clearly indeed. What you can't quite see, it seems to me, is the road that will take us there.

'You've said yourself that the difficulty with this kind of research and development is the high cost of the equipment you require. DNA manipulation is so difficult and so delicate that the technology which Plasmotech have laid on for you is phenomenally expensive to purchase and run. You may be able to work miracles, Dr Morris, but you need a very costly magic wand. Plasmotech may seem narrow and unimaginative in the range of applications to which they put your discoveries, but in order to generate the income they need to sustain your research they must have products which they can sell on a very large scale.

'You've talked to me about some amazing possibilities – kinds of organic machines that you might be able to build *one day*. You've talked about new kinds of houses, new methods of mining, new transport systems. I don't doubt that in the fullness of time you might make those dreams come true, but you can't move to those levels of complexity in the short term. In order to keep your project going for 30 or 40 years you have to make it show a return in two or three years, four at the most. I can understand why you want to work for yourself, and why you're contemptuous of the idea of using your talent to make cheaper fish fingers, but you can't really afford that kind of contempt. If you're to start a new company, you need a *product*, and it must be a product which you can start to manufacture quickly and sell to a mass market. That won't be easy, especially as Plasmotech hold the patents on your research work; they won't let you set up in competition to them without a very hard fight, which means that the food market is effectively closed to us.

'So what can you make, Dr Morris . . . not in twenty years' time, but *tomorrow?*'

William smiled. He had not been taken by surprise by the line of argument. He was, after all, a genius, and he understood something of the wicked ways of the capitalist world.

'Furniture,' he sid.

'Furniture?' Marshall echoed.

'Chairs, couches . . . that sort of thing.'

Marshall raised a quizzical copper-coloured eyebrow, assuming an annoyingly contemptuous expression which made William writhe inwardly with resentment.

William did not approve of P P Marshall. He knew that the man was deemed by some to be a genius in his own field – Marshall was known in the City as the 'copper-crowned certainty' – but William could not bring himself to accept that the field of finance was a proper arena for the deployment of true genius. He detested casual smoothness and polish, and he despised people who made fortunes by playing games with other people's money. He knew full well, though, that he *needed* someone of Marshall's kind, and that he could only win his scientific independence by tying himself to such a man.

He knew that he simply had to grit his teeth and get on with what he had come here to do.

'We don't just get beef from cattle,' William explained, patiently. 'I've been looking at the price of leather. The Americans have begun producing it in sheets for the clothing and furnishing industries, the way they produce furs. They've helped

to sustain the fashionability of leather uphol-
stery. But their leather-upholstered furniture is
just ordinary furniture with a biotechnologically-
produced covering. It's not so cheap, despite the
cheapness of the leather, and it's crude. I can
design a superblastula that will mature into a
single armchair or couch, with its own leather
skin. An elementary silicon chip connected to
a primitive nervous and circulatory system –
simpler than the ones in my chicken substitute
– would allow the chair to alter its shape to
accommodate a particular sitter, to recline as
desired, and vary its softness and its tempera-
ture. The ultimate in home comfort: adaptable
furniture with inbuilt central heating.'

William could see that P P Marshall was
impressed. He was pleased with himself for
keeping this trump card up his sleeve, and
felt that he had chosen the right psychological
moment to play it.

'This would use existing technology?' Marshall
queried.

'Elementary,' William assured him. 'But the
application is sufficiently novel for us to be able
to establish a new set of patents. Plasmotech
couldn't touch us. Only I know my methods well
enough to do it. We'd have six or eight years' clear
start on any possible opposition.'

'Those things would need nutrition.'

'Minimal. Once-a-month injection.'

'I don't want to be a wet blanket,' said Marshall, 'but I have to play the part of devil's advocate. Is the world really ready for living furniture? Mightn't it make people uneasy? A whale-sized piece of meat in a factory is one thing – all the consumer sees is the same old package on the supermarket shelf, and she doesn't have to think about superblastulas any more than her mother had to think about abattoirs. But to have something like this in your living-room, to sit on . . . that might be scary.'

'If it's properly marketed,' said William, firmly, 'it won't be. If we have an advertising agency with imagination, we can put it across. My furniture would have a lot of selling points. The ultimate in comfort, utterly safe. Do you know how many people still have furniture stuffed with foam that gives off toxic gases, because they begrudge the expense of replacing it?'

Marshall looked at him ruminatively. 'How expensive would this stuff be?'

William shrugged. 'To develop . . . well, you've already looked closely at the cost of equipment, sites, manufacturing capacity. To produce, once the groundwork is done . . . I can do for the price of chairs what the Heavyside Layer did for the price of eggs.'

The russet eyebrows ascended again toward the remarkable fringe. '*That* cheap?' said P P Marshall. He had the air of one who had scented a proposition as copper-bottomed as he was copper-crowned, and William knew that he was hooked. Marshall fingered the arm-rest of his own high-tech executive chair, speculatively. 'Everyone sits on chairs, don't they?' he mused.

'First the chair,' said William. 'In time, the entire environment. Do I get my 20 million?'

P P Marshall stubbed out the butt of his cigar. 'I think I can arrange that, Dr Morris,' he replied. 'In fact, I'm certain that you and I can do business.' He stood up and offered his hand. William rose, too, and reached out to clasp it.

Thus began one of the most remarkable partnerships ever forged between scientific and financial genius.

Even as the two men looked one another so frankly in the eye, though, it was plain from their manner that the relationship would never develop into a genuine friendship. In some ways, they were too different, and in others, too similar.

William despised the financier for his cupidity, but he could tell that Marshall, in his turn, despised *him* for his unworldliness. This was a presumption which he found deeply offensive. P P Marshall was one of the few men in the world who was almost as handsome as he was, and one of the few who was every bit as competitive and ambitious; these factors served to compound the insult.

On one level, William knew that he would *hate* working with Marshall, but on another level, he was rather looking forward to finding out which of them would come out on top in what was bound to turn into a personal struggle to be top dog.

The firm of Morris, Marshall & Faulkner (Furniture Manufacturers) started small, but soon grew very considerably. P P Marshall's anxiety as to whether the public was ready for superblastular entities in the home proved to be fortunately unfounded. The world, with a little help from an advertising agency with imagination, proved quite willing to welcome the new biotechnology into the inner sanctum of the home.

The new Morris chair passed rapidly through the classic stages of product evolution. At first it was a novelty. Soon it became a status symbol (not of wealth status, because it was so cheap, but of cultural with-it-ness, of biotech chic, of futurist foresight). In remarkably quick time it became a standard fitment. It so caught the popular imagination that it seemed to be a perfect embodiment of the spirit of the age.

With the arrival of the Morris chair, biotechnology crossed the threshold of social intimacy. The move from factory to salon was one small step for a chair, one giant leap for superblastulakind.

William Morris became his own boss, the steersman of his own researches. He revelled in his self-appointed status as an unfettered pioneer. His name became a household word. The public delighted in the fortuitous combination of circumstances which allowed him to echo, on so dramatically amplified a scale, the achievement of that earlier William Morris, who had also lent his name to an adaptable chair. That earlier Morris, it was recalled, had been a Utopian, who had brought *News from Nowhere* of a finer and happier world to come. The new William Morris, it was widely said, was a Utopian in a more impressive sense, who was actually bringing a finer and happier world into being.

William became rich. Then he became very rich. It was rumoured that it could only be a matter of time before he received his knighthood. His phenomenally handsome face grew even more finely-chiselled with age, and was – in spite of his love of privacy – to be found on magazine covers everywhere. The snatched snapshots of the *paparazzi* showed him often in the company of his equally handsome wife, who was perenially pestered for the 'secrets' of her milky complexion and silky, honey-blonde hair.

Despite the closeness of their financial relationship, though, William was very rarely seen in the company of Peter Peregrine Marshall, the flame-haired golden boy of the City.

Marshall was just as famous as William; he was fêted as the entrepreneur extraordinary, and was universally regarded as England's most eligible bachelor, not even excluding the princes of the realm. But William always considered Marshall's fame to be undeserved, because it was essentially parasitic upon his own. He was resentful (though never in public) of the fact that Marshall often gathered applause which ought to have been his, simply because he had perforce to spend so much time in his beloved laboratory, while Marshall was always abroad in the world.

Although William would not play to the crowd, he still loved being a celebrity, after his own fashion. So did Judy.

William did not allow his celebrity to distract him from his work. Indeed, he threw himself into his researches with ever-greater zeal. He wanted to be the Isaac Newton of genetic science —

the man whose efforts paved the way for the building of a new world. He was fearful that his intellectual prime would not last for ever, and was determined to exploit it to the full before the inevitable decline set in.

While the Morris chair went through the phases of its success, therefore, William worked longer and longer hours on more advanced techniques of genetic manipulation. Morris, Marshall & Faulkner hired dozens of brilliant young men to work out commercial applications for the basic techniques derived from his patents, while he did his best to operate on an entirely different level, paying as little heed as circumstances would allow to issues of immediate applicability. William was committed boldly to do what no man had done before in the usurpation of godlike power.

'A century ago,' William told a reporter, in one of his rare interviews, 'men looked at the wonders of nature, and were awed by the power of the hypothetical being who might have wrought such marvels. Now, the intelligent man can only wonder at the poverty and narrowness of that Creation, and must reserve his awe for contemplation of the things that men will make, given their mastery of DNA.' William never actually claimed, when he indulged in such reveries, that

DNA had no other master as virtuous, as adept or as ingenious as himself, but no one who heard him speak doubted that it was true.

And yet, in spite of everything, William was not altogether happy. Resentment and dissatisfaction had not yet been banished from his everyday existence.

'Jesus, Jude,' complained William one night, as they lay side by side in bed, 'I've got to get out. I've got to.'

'You don't mean that, dear,' said Judy, stifling that same old sigh. 'You've just had a bad day.'

'Bad day!' William retorted. 'I'll say I've had a *bad day*! You wouldn't believe the way they keep trying to drown me in paperwork. They want me in on *everything*: planning committees, product development, public relations, foreign buyers, franchises. I mean, for Christ's sake, what does a man have to do to get rid of that kind of crap? What's the point of being the boss if the pressure from underneath is even greater than the pressure from on top used to be? I'm trying to run a bloody scientific revolution here, and I keep getting tangled in red tape. It's all around me, tying my hands and strangling me. I lock the door . . . I don't even have a phone in the inner sanctum . . . but they lie in wait for me outside the door like a flock of vultures. I mean, Jude, *Jesus!*'

Judy knew that she had to refrain from making jokes about disciples and the hazards of being worshipped, and must at all costs refrain from colourful word-play featuring crucifixion or other styles of martyrdom. William was as sensitive as ever, and reacted badly if he suspected that she was not taking his anguish sufficiently seriously. If anything, success had made him even more of a prima donna. He had recently taken to making camera-smashing assaults upon the *paparazzi* — a well-known badge of unstable temperament.

'Well, dear,' she said, 'it is your company, and everyone in it does rely to such an extent on your methods and your ideas. They depend on you, and you can't blame them for wanting to consult you when you get so angry if they do anything wrong, or anything you don't like. You do have a responsibility to them, you know.'

'Responsibility!' groaned William. 'If Prometheus had had as much to cope with as I have, the fire of the gods would still be in Heaven. Marshall, who ought to protect me from the flak, is the biggest battery firing at me. I've made that red-haired bastard a multi-millionaire, but he thinks he has a mortgage on my bloody brain, and he always takes first place in the pestering line. Jesus,

Jude, sometimes I think I ought to get out of Morris, Marshall & Faulkner and set up a nice little research establishment in the middle of the Arizona desert. I've got the money, you know. I could do it.'

This was an idea of which Judy disapproved very strongly. She would still quote all the old reasons for wanting to stay in England — family ties, her work in broadcasting, her sense of belonging — but nowadays there was even more to it than that. She had done everything possible to conceal it from William, whom she still loved very dearly, but she had come to treasure exactly what he had come to loathe: the attentions of Peter Peregrine Marshall. Marshall and Judy had been enjoying a passionate love affair for some years, aided and abetted by the nobility of commitment which kept William out of the way in his laboratory for such long hours.

In consequence of the strain which keeping this secret placed on Judy, her patience was not quite as endless as it once had been. Her sex-life with William had lost much of its old magic, especially when it was compared with her more romantically energetic encounters with her other. Nevertheless, whenever she began to stroke him in her own distinctive fashion with her uniquely gentle hands. William's anxieties still ebbed gradually away.

She stroked him now, to soothe away his pain. There was something a bit mechanical about the way her hands moved but she was certain that William was too wrapped up in himself to notice. The tokens of her love for him had, inevitably, become matters of routine, which no longer engaged her full consciousness, and no longer carried the meaning they once had had — but he would surely never know the difference, even if he *was* a genius.

'You mustn't worry so much, dear,' she told him. 'I'll speak to Peter for you, if you like. I'll explain to him how desperately important it is that you shouldn't be bothered while you're working. But you mustn't fret, because that's hurting you just as much as all the pressures on your time.'

'The trouble is,' said Marshall, leaning back against a work-bench in William's laboratory suite, 'that you haven't really thought this through.'

William stared into those frank blue eyes, reflecting on the incompetence of nature, which allowed such an innocent expression to mask chicanery and double-dealing. Here, he thought, was a man who could betray his best friend without a flicker of conscience. (His private detective had handed in a very full report, and William had read every word of it several times over.)

'Actually, Peter,' he said, 'I've thought it through very carefully. I want to retire from this kind of life, so that I can concentrate entirely on pure research. No more chairs, no more waste-disposal units, no more living light systems, no more biotech batteries. In fact, no more *products* at all. No more rat race. I shall continue to work for the scientific revolution in my laboratories, but I shall no longer man the barricades.'

Marshall spread his hands wide, as if he were about to embrace his colleague in a spirit of pure camaraderie, and favoured him with the kind of look that had melted many a heart.

'Billy,' he said, 'I understand how you feel. Believe me, I do. I know that your eyes have always fixed on those far horizons. I know how the everyday business of Morris, Marshall & Faulkner gets you down, how sordid it all seems to you. I do my best to protect you – far more than you can possibly realise. I've kept a lot of weight off your back, shielded you from so much hassle, stood in for you in every way that I could, though I don't really understand the nuts and bolts of biotech at all.

'I know you're a genius, Billy, and I also know

that because you're not like ordinary men you don't really know what's good for you, what you really need. Judy knows, Billy, and we've talked about it. Trust her, Billy. Trust me. We can take care of things for you, and together we can bring about this fabulous revolution of yours. Side by side, each with our part to play. Together we can do it, but apart . . . each of us amounts to less than we'd like to think. We're not as young as we once were, you know – we're both past our best. All the City whizzkids I started out with have burned out, and all the geneswitching geniuses of your day are on the downhill side now. We still have a great thing going here, Billy, if we can just keep it on the rails, but it needs work. Trust me.'

'Well,' said William, carefully, 'I've trusted you for a long time, Peter. I know how much I owe you; I really do. And to show you how much I appreciate all we've meant to one another, I've got something I'd like you to look at, which will demonstrate to you exactly where I'm up to right now . . . to make it clearer what I've been working on, and what the fruit of my labours has been. It's in my inner sanctum.'

William's inner sanctum was the very heart of his private empire, inviolate even to his most intimate co-workers. Marshall had never been inside, and William knew how much it would surprise him to be invited now. Surely, he thought, even P P Marshall would deign to feel a little bit proud as he stepped across this strange threshold.

Marshall went through, and William followed him.

The inner sanctum was quite cramped, because of the vast quantity of equipment which had been crammed into it over the years. William knew that to Marshall, as to Judy, it was simply an array of 'DNA-thingumajigs' and 'electronic doodahs'.

In the middle of the room was a Morris chair.

'Sit down, Peter,' said William, amiably.

Marshall sat, relaxing into the chair. It was warm and (of course) supremely comfortable. William watched while Marshall's fingers ran appreciatively over the armrests. The chair accommodated itself to its occupant's shape, moulding itself snugly to his contours.

'Nice texture,' Marshall commented. 'New, isn't it?' He continued to stroke it with his fingertips, testing its quality. 'It's got a really nice feel to it – it should do well as next year's model. How long have you been hoarding it away in here?'

'Oh, it's new all right,' William told him blandly. 'I only made it this week. Entirely new design – tricky, in its way, though I'd practised the basic techniques a lot. Programming the chip wasn't too difficult, but any manufacturing process is delicate when you use new raw material for the first time.'

'New material?' queried Marshall, interestedly. 'It's not grown from a cowball, then?'

William had never liked the way that Marshall referred to superblastulas as cowballs. 'I didn't grow it at all,' he said. 'You see, I've progressed quite a bit in the matter of making superblastulas. I've found a method of producing them, as it were, the other way round. I can now switch on the genes of specialised cells, neotenising a mature tissue by reducing its cells to the undifferentiated embryonic stage. A superblastula made from a mature organism doesn't have quite the same capacity to grow, of course, but it can be redifferentiated into an entirely different structure.'

'My God!' said Marshall. 'You mean that you made this thing from a mature cow? You reduced an actual carcase to protoplasm and then reshaped it?'

'Oh no!' said William, permitting himself a tiny smile. 'I didn't use a cow.'

'Good,' said Marshall, shifting his position slightly. 'That would have been rather too macabre. Another chair, then?'

'It wasn't a chair,' William told him, calmly. 'It was Judy.'

There was a moment's deadly silence.

William watched those familiar ruddy eyebrows lift, as the alarmed realisation dawned on Peter Peregrine Marshall that this might not be a joke.

Marshall tried to stand up, but found that the chair, which had so conveniently modified itself to accommodate him, was actually folded about him rather tightly. He began to struggle, but the more he struggled the tighter the grip of the chair became. His arms gripped the rests more tightly, and William watched his face change as he realised that the chair's colour was the delicate hue of Judy's wonderful complexion, and that the tiny silken hairs with which it was covered were honey-blonde in colour.

William waited calmly for P P Marshall to stop writhing, and to start remembering Judy's embraces, and the special texture of her flesh.

Eventually, Marshall was forced to accept that he was not to be allowed to rise to his feet, and he looked up at William, with horrific questions trembling on his tongue.

William smiled, angelically.

'This is a very advanced Morris chair,' he said, quietly. 'If you pay careful attention, you might be able to discern a slight pulse. This is a chair with a *heart*. It has a more complex nervous system than the standard model, better circulation, and – as you've probably realised – much better musculature. But the chip – oh, my dear Peter, you can't imagine the cleverness of that tiny, tiny brain!'

William took a small gadget from a nearby drawer. It looked rather like the kind of remote-control device issued with TV sets and other automata. William began pressing the buttons, and the chair began to grow hands. One pair grew by Marshall's wrists, and promptly gripped them; two pairs grew on either side of his torso and began to run their fingers lightly over his ribs and belly; a further pair grasped his calves and more fingers began groping about in his crotch. William could see, though his prisoner could not, that more hands were emerging beside Marshall's head.

P P Marshall, golden boy of the City, wet his pants.

'Don't worry about that, Peter,' said William, lightly. 'The chair can take care of it.'

The hands set about undressing Marshall, and being many, made light work of it. He was soon stark naked.

'I understand that you have frequently benefited

from my wife's caresses,' remarked William, in a strangely abstracted tone of voice. 'I have always felt that her touch has its own quite distinctive quality. No doubt you agree. I have treasured that talent of hers, and I assume that you do too. We two are the only connoisseurs, I think – the only people in the world who would appreciate this particular Morris chair. What wonderful opportunities this new Judy presents, don't you think? I've tried her out, and found her really quite exquisite. An experience to be savoured. I think you're going to find this a real privilege, don't you?'

Marshall made no reply to this. In fact, if appearances could be trusted, he was feeling rather sick when the chair began its foreplay, making love to him with all the mechanical tenderness of which it was capable.

P P Marshall, flame-haired darling of the media, began to scream.

Nobody could hear him. William's inner sanctum was soundproof. After a minute or so, though, the screams began to distress William, so he directed one of the hands to clamp itself tightly over Marshall's mouth. Marshall resisted this stifling clutch fiercely, biting at the hand and making it bleed terribly. But the chair had no mouth or throat, and could not cry out in pain; it could only quiver. It continued, though, with its insistent caresses and its lascivious appreciation of the naked body which it held captive.

William watched the orgy for some time, with mixed feelings. He was glad that his victim didn't seem to be enjoying himself much – though Marshall did manage eventually to demonstrate that he was the last man in the world who needed to worry about the humiliations of impotence.

'Can you see the product potential, Peter?' asked William, earnestly. 'Can you see the kind of market that this opens up? We have the seed of a sexual revolution here, you know.'

P P Marshall was unfortunately past the stage where he could give this line of thought his full attention. He was sobbing desperately. William could only presume that he was suffering from a rather extreme case of post-coital *triste*.

William's delicate fingers brushed the buttons of his remote-control device once again, and the hands relaxed their grip on Marshall. The one that had clamped over his mouth withdrew, throwing off blood and saliva with a contemptuous flick of its fingers.

'Damn you, Morris,' grated the copper-crowned certainty, retreating into cliché as though he were an actor in some tired old sci-fi movie. 'You'll never get away with this!'

*   *   *

Marshall was right, of course, as he usually was. William didn't get away with it.

People of the social standing of Peter Peregrine Marshal and Judy Morris cannot simply disappear without questions being asked. When it came to the consideration of motive and opportunity, it did not require a Sherlock Holmes to figure out who was responsible. Eventually, the police obtained a search warrant and invaded William's inner sanctum, where they found sufficient evidence to prosecute.

The Crown versus William Morris became one of the longest and most confused criminal trials on record, bogged down by unprecedented problems of definition as the jury struggled to decide whether his victims were legally dead.

In the end, William was found guilty, but only of Grievous Bodily Harm – a verdict which many observers thought eccentric. Cynics concluded that the jury (which included eight women) had been swayed by the defendant's amazing good looks, and had sympathised with his jealousy. Optimists pointed out that the light sentence he received would allow him to resume in a matter of months the researches which might easily lead to future benefits for all mankind.

When it was all over, though, those conscientious officials who sheltered beneath the grand title of 'The Crown' found themselves faced with an altogether unprecedented problem: what on earth were they to do with Exhibit A?

Exhibit A was an entirely new design of Morris chair, resembling two armchairs facing in different directions but intimately fused together: a 'love-seat'. Half of the love-seat was decorated most gloriously with silken blonde hair; the other half was upholstered in a remarkable shade of coppery red.

And somewhere deep inside it were two hearts, beating as one.

The Fury That Hell Withheld

'Heaven has no rage like love to hatred turned,' Congreve assures us, 'Nor hell a fury, like a woman scorned.'

Congreve was a man much preoccupied with the romantic passions, and we discover this observation in a poem called 'The Mourning Bride'. In the Classical World things were seen differently, and it was held that ties of blood were more vital than those of amatory attachment. The Furies of Classical mythology were not unleashed to punish faithless lovers, but to persecute undutiful children. In that tarnished Golden Age the fiercest hatreds and most awful jealousies were stored up in the bonds of maternal and filial affection. The most celebrated victim of the Furies of old was the mother-murdering Orestes.

It is a matter for argument whether our own era has more in common with the age of Congreve or the era of gods and heroes to which Classical mythology makes its reference. In purely historical terms, Congreve is closer to us, but our nascent Golden Age, when men are beginning to acquire godlike power over the organic and inorganic alike, is in its fashion a Promethean Era. The old order is not merely in decay but liable to be turned upside-down. The tales we must tell of the time that is soon to be may echo in many ways the tales the Greeks and Romans told of the time behind them, and it is a question again to be asked what kind of Furies Hell has saved for the special damnation of the men of the future.

The names of the heroes of the biotechnological revolution have already become legend, and prominent among them is the name of Adam Emden, who was a doctor of medicine in the early years of the New Millennium. He was one of the first men to involve himself with the applications of techniques of genetic engineering in the treatment of physical injury; he was primarily interested in mobilising and augmenting the body's own powers of self-repair, by accelerating the healing processes which mend wounds, and by persuading the body to regenerate lost limbs or damaged organs.

Natural selection never provided the human

body with abilities of this kind because nature unaided could not contrive to keep the whole human entity alive while drastic reconstructions of particular parts occur. Modern technology, however, can sustain the blood supply to a human brain even in the absence of a heart, thus buying the time for drastic repairs to be carried out, if only the genes in the tissue-cells can be persuaded to co-operate. Adam Emden became their most cunning persuader; he was a sculptor of human clay, forcing the cells of human tissues to revert to an undifferentiated state of blastular innocence and then causing them to multiply and re-specialise themselves into the desired structures.

In this way, Adam Emden helped deformed children to acquire physical perfection; he saved the victims of many spinal injuries from paralysis; he gave new eyes to the blind; and to those who needed them he gave new hearts, new kidneys and new livers, skilfully drawing these gifts from the hapless flesh of the victims themselves.

Had there been no more to say than that he did these things, Adam Emden would have been hero enough. But there was more. His fellow men were by no means united in helping to ease his path to these triumphs. Many of the processes of gene manipulation that he put to these uses were first developed by companies involved in food technology or drug manufacture, and the directors of these companies fought long and hard to protect their discoveries with patents. Thus, having first learned the arts of genetic reconstruction, Adam Emden had then to go into battle in the courtrooms of the world in order to establish his right to use them.

The so-called Patent Wars, which were fought to determine what rights could and should exist in this new area of technological development, extended over ten long years. Throughout those years Adam Emden was one of the most prominent warriors in the field, driven by a powerful determination to secure what he considered justice for all the people who needed his help. He came to be seen by the public at large as a tireless crusader: a champion of the weak against the strong, a man who cared for the rights of all instead of the wealth of the few.

In the eyes of the world, Adam Emden's opponents were fighting for greed and the power of exploitation, while he was a speaker for the helpless. His case was that the lame should not need to pay for legs; that the blind should not have to pay for eyes; common humanity, in his view, demanded that all people must have the opportunity of equality which cruel fate had hitherto denied to so many.

When he began his long campaign, Adam Emden was neither a lawyer nor a politician. While the Patent Wars ran their course, he was forced to become both. He tried as hard as he could to keep up his 'real work' – by which he meant his list of pseudosurgical operations – but he was manoeuvred by circumstance into a situation where he had to follow two other professions as well, spending as much time in court as in the operating theatre, and as much time again in campaigning and propagandising.

The effect of all this on his private life was devastating. A hero of the New Millennium has little life that is private in any case; television has all but obliterated the very idea of privacy thanks to its self-appointed licence to intrude and the remorseless intimacy with which its cameras zero in on the personality of its celebrities.

Adam Emden was a family man before the Patent Wars began; he had a wife named Clementina, two daughters named Phoebe and Alexia, and a son named Aristide. When fame first closed in on their father, the three children were beyond infancy but still far from maturity, and all three had to grow up in the full glare of public interest.

The three children of Adam Emden suffered mixed fortunes as a result of this pressure. Had they been shadowed from the light of popular attention they might have found their own interests and projects, but as things were they could not help but be involved in their father's crusades.

Alexia, the youngest child, became more tightly enwrapped by it all than the others. It was she who became her father's constant companion and helper, his emanuensis and his shield against the bombardment of enquiry to which he was constantly subject. In this role she quickly displaced her mother Clementina, who tried for a while to cope with such duties but had neither the skill nor the commitment necessary to carry them off successfully.

Aristide, in his turn, tried hard to model himself upon his marvellous parent, whom he idolised. He studied medicine and the techniques of bio-engineering, with a special kind of fervour, setting himself standards to achieve that were almost too high to permit success. It may be that no one has ever desired more ardently to be a genius than Aristide Emden, and it is certainly remarkable that he did not come apart under the pressure to which he subjected himself. Whether or not he achieved genius must remain a matter of opinion, but he certainly became brilliant, and those in a position to judge considered him even more adept in the operating theatre than his father. As a researcher he interested himself particularly in the treatment of cancers, and tried hard to bring nearer the day when his father's techniques would be adequate to the task of making the body repair itself after a cancerous attack – one of the most intractable of the medical problems of his day.

The elder sister, Phoebe, was not so successful; or perhaps she was simply not so fortunate. Her character was already well on the way to formation when the Patent Wars began, and she had not the same opportunity as her siblings to adapt to the peculiar circumstances of Adam Emden's celebrity. Her attempts to find a role which she could adequately play within the circus of her father's destiny came to nothing, and she suffered from a terrible sense of failure which led her to such reckless self-disregard as to fall victim to a black market psychotropic drug of particularly vicious character. Once she became physically dependent the path of degeneracy leading to death led steeply downhill.

When Phoebe was terminally ill, her father tried to operate on her, desperately using techniques which he was virtually inventing as he proceeded, trying to regenerate the tissues of her brain. But there was nothing he could do to save her; her self-inflicted injuries were far beyond the scope of his art.

The tragedy of Phoebe Emden's death was a brief *cause célèbre*, and the publicity which it generated had at least as much effect on those to whom she had been near and dear as the death itself.

Adam Emden was not permitted to indulge himself much with grief; he had more important things to do, a heroic status to live up to, and it was therefore necessary for him to put the incident behind him as quickly and as totally as possible. Aristide and Alexia, by the same token, had not time or energy to spare in exhausting themselves with sorrow. Clementina, by contrast, found a strange kind of opportunity in grief. She found it all too easy to identify with her firstborn daughter's predicament.

Like Phoebe, Clementina had made a life of her own, and acquired an identity of her own, long before the Emden Patent War bandwagon began to roll. Indeed, she had sufficient identity and purpose of her own to carry on even though she could not ride the bandwagon – but this did not prevent her nursing a strong sense of failure and resentment when she was left to one side while her younger daughter took the chief supportive role. Circumstance had led Phoebe to despise, and abuse herself; following her death it began to lead Clementina to feel justified in despising and abusing Adam Emden. She began – perhaps subconsciously – to blame Adam for Phoebe's death, and to blame him too for her own feelings of wretchedness, which were monstrously fed and inflamed by her grief.

Clementina never did set that grief aside, and felt herself wounded by the fact that all the other members of the family did so with such efficient alacrity.

It is not surprising, given these circumstances, that Clementina Emden took a lover, nor that this lover should also be a man who had cause to hate her husband. Joseph Hess was undoubtedly an attractive man in his own right, and Clementina had conserved her own beauty into late middle age, but what drew the two together was not so much spontaneous passion as the awareness that knowledge of their association would hurt the feelings of Adam Emden.

Hess was not directly involved in the Patent Wars – not, at any rate, as a courtroom combatant. He was, however, a bioengineer working for one of the multinational corporations who were Adam

Emden's adversaries. He had been intimately involved in the work which had generated some of the key patents relating to the blastularisation and respecialisation of tissue cells, and had conducted some spectacular experiments with animal subjects. Some of these experiments, indeed, had gained him a notoriety which few scientists would have envied.

In a time when most experimenters were conscientiously wary of the Ethics Committees which watched over all adventures in vivisection, Hess sneered at them for alleged moral cowardice. His publicity-conscious employers would normally have tried to restrain an employee from expressing such opinions, but Hess was unrestrainable, and his work yielded such rewards that they elected instead to defend him from his critics and from the assaults of the law.

Hess's most famous series of experiments involved the decomposition and re-differentiation of brain tissue in living animals which had been taught various skills and responses; by this means he sought to discover the extent to which behaviours were hardwired into the brain, and in what ways learned behaviours were stored. He was never allowed to work with a human subject, but he said in public on more than one occasion that if anyone in the world could have helped Phoebe Emden in the last stages of her addiction, then it was he and not Adam Emden. Adam, who already despised him, found this statement uniquely objectionable – Clementina, on the other hand, believed it.

The affair between Joseph Hess and Clementina Emden quickly became the subject of comment in the yellow press. They did not strive very hard to be discreet. Adam at first simply disregarded the reports, though he probably believed them. When the speculations became too open to ignore, he still refused to be moved by them. He did not sue for divorce, nor did he discuss the possibility of divorce with his wife. He moved out of what had been the family home – though in truth he had spent little enough time there during the past two or three years – and left Clementina to enjoy or modify her solitude as she pleased.

This indifference annoyed Clementina more than any action would have. She felt herself scorned, and that stirred a kind of fury within her – but hers was not a hot temper and her anger simmered rather than burned. It was a sullen nursling that never left her, but seemed rather to drain her vitality, becoming gradually murderous.

Alone, Clementina would never have formed a serious resolution to murder Adam Emden, though she certainly would have brooded on the possibility and fantasised about the action, but she was not alone. Such murderous feelings as she had achieved a curious coition with the feelings of Joseph Hess.

Hess's hatred of Adam Emden was by no means strong enough in itself to prompt him to consider murder, but hatred had never figured large in his motivation. What moved Hess to think in terms of assassination was more a kind of pride, not in his work *per se* but in his capability as an exercise of power. Such pride might easily be compared to the Classical sin of *hubris*, for what Hess loved was an imagined godlike quality in his experimentation. His contempt for the Ethics Committees and other organisations which tried to interrupt him was allied with a covert delight in the blasphemous aspects of his research; that it caused outrage in others was one of the things he most loved in it.

What attracted Joseph Hess to the possibility of murdering Adam Emden was not that it would appease some wrathful lust within him, but firstly that it would be an act of unholy bravado to bring down the nearest thing to a saint that the modern world contained, and secondly that he was convinced that he could get away with it. Hess believed, in fact, that despite the obviousness of his and Clementina's motive, the two of them could – given the aid of his technical skills – avoid all suspicion. He believed that he could commit not merely a murder, but a perfect murder, and the aesthetic attraction of that possibility was something which moved him very powerfully indeed.

This combination of motives proved irresistible. Each alone might have proved impotent, but their connection was synergistic. Within days of first mentioning the desire to destroy her husband, Clementina Emden was caught up in a plot to achieve that end. She knew her husband's ways intimately enough to decoy him into returning to the family home, arranging the circumstances and the timing so that even Alexia did not know that he had gone.

There, in a tiled bathroom which was very easy to clean, she and Joseph Hess stabbed him to death.

Afterwards, Hess removed the body to his laboratory, and set about repairing the damage. A body does not die all at once, and he did not need any complicated machines to maintain it; his aim was not to revive it, but simply to make it whole again, removing every sign of violence.

When this was done, there was no trace on Adam Emden's corpse to betray what had been done to him. He was, however, a corpse; though Hess made the unclotted blood course through his brain again, the blood could not restore that brain to function. The mind of Adam Emden – the soul of the saint – was gone, and the body in this vegetable condition could be sustained for only a few hours before it simply stopped again.

Clementina Emden and Joseph Hess put Adam Emden's body in a place where it might plausibly be found, but which had no connection with them. Then they sat back to wait for the public distress which would follow the discovery of the body. They knew that no doctor in the world, however puzzled, could possibly come to any conclusion but that Adam Emden's heart had simply failed.

In this assumption, of course, Joseph Hess and Clementina Emden were right. An inquest recorded a verdict of accidental death, and left only two people in all the world suspicious and dissatisfied. Those two people were Aristide and Alexia Emden – but they remained mute at the inquest because they had not a shred of real evidence to justify their suspicions.

At first, even Aristide and Alexia suspected themselves of being unreasonable in not being entirely satisfied with the official version of their father's death. Aristide was, after all, a scientist, and a scientist who set himself very high standards. He was not a man who could easily cherish and lend credence to vague feelings unsupported by proof. Alexia wondered whether her own unease might be a mere side-effect of her terrible feeling of loss; after all, with her father's death her entire *raison d'être* had been suddenly withdrawn. But the public and private ceremonies which followed the death brought them both into frequent contact with their mother, and in her behaviour they gradually became convinced that they could read signs of guilt.

They could not have specified precisely what it was that they saw, and it is perhaps surprising that they saw anything at all. Clementina was a strong woman, by no means the kind to be overcome by the enormity of what she had done. Whatever remorse she felt in respect of her crime was well-controlled. She made no very strenuous effort to feign grief, but in the circumstances that could hardly be required of her. When it transpired that Adam had not bothered to change his will in order to accommodate the change in their circumstances, so that Clementina inherited the bulk of the estate, she received the news with a reasonable degree of indifference, and made no extravagant plans for herself.

One consequence of what had happened, though, was that Clementina conceived a strong dislike for Joseph Hess. The two had been bound together more by their mutual opposition to Adam than by honest affection, and though their motives for murder had cross-fertilised one another they remained different and distinct. Clementina did not much like Hess's overweening pride in his accomplishments, and he thought her hatred a rather pitiful thing. They ceased to see one another, and began to react to the thought and mention of one another with reflexive distaste.

It might have been this which provided Aristide and Alexia with subliminal clues. In any case, something did, and once they confided in one another, their suspicions fed one another in much the same way as the murderers' motives had.

Once an awareness of possibility was planted in his brain, Aristide was quick to realise that skills such as his own might have repaired a damaged body to present the appearance of a natural death. Once such an idea was born in his mind, he quickly began to consider whether he might find evidence which the coroner had overlooked. The scientific rigour ingrained in his thought, which had earlier forbidden him seriously to entertain a hypothesis without evidence, not required him to put the hypothesis to the proof, so that it might be properly falsified.

Aristide applied to the court to have Adam Emden's body exhumed from its honoured grave, inventing as a pretext certain anonymous letters, sent both to the family and the press, claiming that the body in the grave was that of another man. To the court and the interested world at large he expressed the opinion that there was not a shred of truth in these letters, but that it must be his distasteful duty to prove the fact. That he volunteered to carry out what would undoubtedly be an unpleasant second autopsy himself was considered by many to be an act of heroism such as could be expected in the worthy son of a great man.

Clementina Emden and Joseph Hess were not unworried by this turn of events, and Clementina publicly opposed her son's capitulation to the innuendo of the crank letters – an opposition which seemed reasonable enough even to the anxious children. Clementina was not so foolish, though, as to get in touch with Hess over the matter.

Hess, meanwhile, suppressed his own anxiety ruthlessly, his pride asserting itself privately as powerfully as it so often did in public. Hess was not afraid of Aristide; he had full confidence in the perfection of his achievement. This confidence seemed to have been borne out when Aristide, having carefully examined his father's body, announced to the press that — as he had always believed — the wicked allegations of the anonymous letters were completely unfounded, and that everything was at it should be.

Hess's confidence was, however, misplaced. Aristide was lying. He had not found that everything was as it should have been.

It was not that Hess had made some dreadful mistake, or even that he had overlooked something trivial but vital. Ironically, he had done his job too well.

Hess had restored Adam Emden's body to perfection, but Adam Emden's body had not been perfect before the knife-wounds were inflicted by his murderers; like every other mature body it had accumulated a small burden of scars and benign skin cancers — moles and other such growths. Pretty women, and some vain men, had such blemishes repaired by cosmetic pseudosurgery of exactly the kind which Adam Emden practised, but he had always disdained such wasteful use of resources. There was nothing so large or obtrusive that it might have qualified as a distinguishing mark in a police file, but Alexia had lived so closely with her father that she knew his appearance very well – better, in fact, than her mother, who had shared his bed but had never paid the slightest attention to such trivial matters. She was able to tell Aristide exactly what to look for, and when he failed to find it they both knew that the body had been tampered with, and that it had been reconstructed by someone almost as expert as himself.

Aristide and Alexia never gave serious consideration to the possibility of going to the police. Though they knew that their evidence was conclusive, they suspected that it was not sufficiently powerful to convince a jury to find the two murderers guilty. In any case, they had their own ideas about justice.

From Alexia's and Aristide's point of view, what Hess and Clementina had done was not mere murder but a more heinous crime. Just as Clementina had not forgiven her husband for Phoebe's death, so Alexia and Aristide had not forgiven their mother her lack of forgiveness.

Alexia had been happy enough to sacrifice herself to the service of her father's ambitions, but in doing so she had always been conscious that she was doing a duty that should have been Clementina's. She had always felt that she was, in her father's eyes, a substitute for Clementina — a substitute who could never really be adequate, because even though she did everything she could to the best of her ability, there was one aspect of her mother's role she never could take. She could not be a sexual substitute. She had always believed, probably correctly, that Adam Emden nursed a secret bitterness about his sexual estrangement from Clementina, and felt deeply that he could never love *her* as much as he had once loved her mother. This belief had fed Alexia's resentment of her mother: a resentment which she justified as a resentment of Clementina's failure to do her duty, betraying not merely Adam Emden himself, but the ideals which he stood for as well.

Aristide had not the same idolatrous attitude toward the person of his father, but he did have a worshipful regard for the work and the mission which he had shared with him. In his eyes, the guiltier of the two killers was Hess, who had spoiled and corrupted the art and science which, in Adam Emden's hands, had always been used for the good. In Aristide's view, what Hess had committed was not simply homicide but a Satanic desecration of all that a man such as he should have held dear.

When Aristide and Alexia began to plan revenge,

therefore, they were not simply seeking reparation for a common crime. Each was possessed by a more ambitious fury, and because the two furies were different their mingling was as synergistic as the mingling of murderous motives which had propelled their intended victims.

'We must,' said Aristide, 'serve them as they have served our father. We should turn their own evil upon them. I must use the art that Hess used to conceal his actions to conceal my own. Instead of exposing their crime we must make certain that it remains hidden, and we must hide its reparation too. That way, the memory of our father will remain untainted, and this will be the end of the matter. Only I could have detected Hess's crime; when he is dead there will be none who can detect mine. I can, if necessary, restore his body as he restored our father's, and no matter what agonies and mutilations we inflict upon it, no trace will be left. All may be cleansed, washed away by the baptism of my art.'

'Amen to that,' replied Alexia, and they began to plan exactly what they might do.

'This must be our father's vengeance,' Aristide insisted, 'and we are but its instruments. If the murderers are to be rent as they rent him, then it should be his hand which wields the knife, whether it be a literal or a metaphorical knife.'

'On the matter of principle,' said Alexia, 'I agree, but I do not see any possibility.'

'I saw such a possibility as soon as I knew what Hess had done,' her brother told her. 'He took advantage of the fact that the body does not die all at once; when the personality is obliterated there remains enough life in the cells of the body's tissues to regenerate them. He brought our father back to life, hours after his death, though it was a mindless life that could not endure.

'By the time the body came into my hands, weeks had passed, but still the cells were not entirely beyond recall. Perhaps one in a hundred still retained the capability of biochemical functioning. I knew what had happened as soon as I had examined the surface of the body, but I still proceeded with a thorough autopsy. I recovered tissues of every different kind, and immediately placed them in culture-solutions in order to revive and reblastularise them. The cells which were able to come back to life cannibalised their dead neighbours.'

'Do you mean that you can grow an entire new body?'

Aristide shook his head. 'Alas, no. Cells have a limited power of self-reproduction because errors accumulate in their nucleic acids and their structural proteins. Reblastularisation cannot repair the DNA itself – merely the switches which operate the genes within different kinds of cell. The cells which I have taken have some capacity to grow, but even when I combine them all they will not be able to produce a body any bigger than an apple – nor will that body be able to differentiate itself into any kind of manikin or homunculus, much as I would like to model it into that appearance. I think it possible that I could make a pair of hands, but nothing larger.'

For a moment, the macabre image of a disembodied but living pair of hands eclipsed Alexia's desire to find some extraordinary means of destroying the murderers. 'My God!' she said.

'The problem,' Aristide continued, patiently, 'is to give to a pair of disembodied hands any semblance of function. The idea is old, in the context of supernatural fiction, but without magic to aid me I cannot make the sinews pull and the muscles grip. Death by strangulation, I regret to say, is out of the question. And there is no way in the world that a disembodied hand can wield a knife. I believe that I could make each hand capable of one convulsive clutch, but that would be all. There is no real leverage, you see.'

By this time, Alexia was beginning to understand. Though it was difficult for her to assume the same attitude of clinical detachment which came easily to her brother she was by no means immune to the fascination of the subject.

'If a disembodied hand cannot wield a dagger,' she said, eventually, 'then we must look beyond the imagery of old-fashioned horror stories. Your art must surely permit possibilities of which the Gothic imagination never dreamed.'

'Indeed it must,' Aristide agreed, readily. 'And I hope that you will feel, as I do, that the poetry of the justice in what I am about to suggest transcends any trivial issue of tit for tat. I cannot make a homunculus, or even a fragment of a whole body, to do our bidding; but it would be silly to require that the instrument of our dispensation would be that kind of crude image of the murdered victim. We are scientific sophisticates, you and I, and we know that the identity of a man is contained in his genes, not in the appearance of his face, or in his fingertips. The cells themselves, suitably engineered, can be our agents. We need not assemble them into any kind of crude pastiche of the individual to whom they once belonged.

'Of course, the murderers will not then be able to see with their immediate sensory apparatus what it is that is being done to them, but we should remember that they are as sophisticated as we are. If we can explain to them what we

233

have done, when it is too late for them to do anything about it, then that knowledge will have as profound an effect upon them as the sight of any avenging face or disembodied hand ever had upon the villain of an ancient horror story. They will see all the more clearly with the mind's eye – do you not agree?'

Alexia did agree, and Aristide then told her what it was in his mind to do.

It was no more difficult for Aristide and Alexia to plot their execution than it had been for the two murderers to plot their crime. Aristide had simply to tell his mother that he wished to bring about a reconciliation of the family in the wake of the tragedy which it had suffered. He begged her to give him the opportunity to heal old wounds, to repair the body of the family much as Adam Emden himself had repaired the damaged bodies of individuals. He could be persuasive when he wanted to, and his mother was willing enough to be persuaded. She felt herself very much alone, now, and hoped that much might be gained from an orgy of mutual forgiveness. So Aristide invited his mother and his sister, with much ceremony, to a symbolic feast at his own home.

Without telling Clementina, he also issued an invitation to Joseph Hess.

This required greater diplomatic skill, but the story which Aristide told Hess was in essence the same one: he said that he wanted all to be forgiven and forgotten. Aristide claimed that he had been disappointed by the fact that his father's death had apparently interrupted a relationship which had given his mother much solace, that he understood now how much strain the love affair had placed on everyone, and that he thought that the time had come for an all-round reconciliation.

Hess was tempted by the invitation, not so much because he wanted to restore loving contact with Clementina, but because the whole idea amused his colossal pride. He easily allowed himself to fall into the error of believing that Aristide was too naïve to understand the hatred that had existed between Adam Emden and himself. He could not help but be attracted by an invitation to be wholesomely reconciled with the unsuspecting family of a man he had been pleased to kill. And so he delivered himself up into the jaws of the trap that had been laid for him.

When the time came Clementina was, of course, surprised to see her ex-lover, but she too accepted the reasons which Aristide was quick to offer her, and the four of them sat down to dine together.

Afterwards, when Aristide stood up to make

the speech which Clementina and Hess expected to be sentimental and pleading, Clementina was genuinely touched and Hess thoroughly pleased with himself. Their contentment was short-lived.

'There is in Classical mythology,' Aristide told them, 'a tale of a man who was summoned by another, who was secretly his enemy, to a great feast. There, unknown to himself, he was served the flesh of his own children.

'If my memory serves me correctly, it was Atreus who served up the flesh of the children of his brother Thyestes, who had deceived him with his wife; the blood-feud thus originated extended over several generations – Aegisthus, the son of Thyestes, later murdered Agamemnon, the son of Atreus, after seducing *his* wife Clytemnestra, after which Aegisthus and Clytemnestra were killed by Agamemnon's son Orestes. But the details are unimportant, save to dramatise the chains of consequence that an evil act may have.

'The vengeance of Atreus had been the basis of several famous horror stories and tempted even Shakespeare to its use, but we live in a more sophisticated world now, where such crudities have no place. Nevertheless, I have to tell you that there was in what you have just eaten something which you could not know about, and I think I can say with confidence that you might rather have dined on the flesh of your children.

'I hope that you will by now have guessed that I myself sent the anonymous letters that gave cause for the exhumation of my father's body, and that they were a mere pretext, enabling me to satisfy myself that he really had been murdered. The crime could have been committed and concealed only by two particular individuals working in association, and those two individuals were also the only persons who had a sufficiently strong motive for the crime. I am sure that you will forgive me for not boring you with formal accusations and careful arguments in proof, because you are doubtless hungry for information as to what distressful thing it is that you have just consumed.

'It was, of course, the flesh of my father, which I removed from his body when I conducted my autopsy and revived using much the same methods – more cleverly – that you, Dr Hess, used to repair his body when you removed the signs of whatever injuries you inflicted upon him. You were too polite, I noticed, to comment that the courses were a little too cool; they had to be, in order not to injure the living cells that were hidden within them.

'The knowledge that you have committed the

sin of cannibalism probably does not worry you overmuch – you have, after all, already killed my father, and are bound to be less distraught at the thought of eating him than Thyestes was at the thought of feasting on his murdered children. But those cells which you have consumed were no mere meat. Each one carried into the depths of your own bodies a massive supplement of nucleic acids; new genes and active chromosomal fragments of the kind we usually call viruses.

'These living cells are cancerous, and will take tumorous root wherever in your gut they may come to rest. They are armed, moreover, with powerful biochemical defences which will keep them safe from marauding phagocytes and the instruments of your immune systems. All my life I have tried to serve the ideals of my father, learning to protect the body against such enemies as cancer; but everything that I have learned is easy enough to turn on its head, so as to equip cancer cells with powerful protection against their enemy, the body.

'Nor will your troubles end with the tumours themselves, for as they grow they will spew out more genetic material into your bloodsteams, which will infect your own cells and make them cancerous too. This added dimension of the problems which now face you is, I believe, an important one. It is unnecessary from the point of view of ensuring your death, but it confers a certain propriety on your fate. At the cellular level, you see, the cancers that will spring from your own flesh will be the daughters of your own cells. Tonight, although you have not devoured your children, you have innocently set in train a chain of causation which will result in your being devoured, at least in sophisticated metaphor, by your children. I hope that the logic of this parallel is not too convulted for you.

'You may leave here now, if you wish. You, Dr Hess, are perfectly welcome to unleash all your knowledge and skill upon the task of trying to undo what has been done to you, and, if generosity moves you, you might even try to cure my mother. I am confident that you will not succeed; this is, after all, my field and I am sure that I could not save you myself. If you can heal yourself, then I will be pleased to acknowledge you a better physician than I.

'I think, on balance, I might prefer it if you did try to save yourself. I trust that you will not take the easier way out — to kill yourself, as an act of tormented euthanasia, might endorse the ancient opinion that whom the gods destroy, they first make mad, but I think we live in more civilised times nowadays, and you are a man of science, are you not? I will have slightly more respect for you if you try to secure your salvation, even though we both know that the task is hopeless.'

There is perhaps no better testament to the fact that our new Golden Age of biotechnology is infinitely to be preferred to the mythical Golden Age of heroes and blood feuds than the fact that Joseph Hess and Clementina Emden did go to their homes, without trying to do violence to their killers.

Joseph Hess did try everything he could to save Clementina and himself, but it was all to no avail. They did not make public what had been done to them; shame prevented them from attempting even that meagre vengeance. And so the matter ended with their deaths, which were relatively painless, by virtue of modern analgesics. No blood feud extended itself into future generations.

Aristide Emden became in the fullness of time a great man, regarded by all as a kind of saint. He followed up the victories won by his father in the Patent Wars, saved many a life, and made many others more worth the living. His sister Alexia became his constant companion and helper, performing for him the same role that she had performed for her father. Neither ever married, though there was nothing literally incestuous about their relationship.

No Erinyes ever appeared to harry Aristide and Alexia, despite the fact that they had murdered their mother. If, in some secret recess of their minds, they were troubled by guilt, they gave no outward sign of it. Hell, it seems, is nowadays constrained to withhold its Furies, at least until death delivers us to the court of divine justice; and given that we live in such civilised times, how can we possibly believe that it does?

The Engineer and the Executioner

'It's my life,' said the engineer. 'Mine. Can you understand that?'

'I understand,' replied the executioner calmly.

'I created it,' said the little man with the spectacles and the unsteady eyes, persistently. 'I made it, with my own hands. It wasn't entirely the creation of my own imagination; other men can take credit for the actual plan, and the theory which allowed them to make the plan. But I made it. I put the genes together, sculptured the chromosomes, put the initial cells together. I provided the time, the concentration, the determination. The others played with ideas, but I actually built their life-system. I made a dream come true. But you can't possibly understand how I feel about it.'

'I understand,' repeated the robot. Its red eyes shone unblinking from its angular head.

The engineer's name was Gabriel Samarra. The

executioner, because it was only a machine, had no name at all.

'Look at it,' said Samarra, waving an arm toward the great concave window that was one wall of the room. 'Look at it and tell me it's not worth anything. It's mine, remember. It all grew from what I built. It all evolved from the cells I created. It's going its own way now. It has been for years. But I put it on that road.'

The man and the robot stared through the glass. Beyond the window was the hollow interior of Asteroid Lamarck.

From space, Lamarck looked like any other asteroid, with crater-scars and jagged crags and waveless lakes of dust, but it was hollow, and inside it was a tightly-sealed, carefully con-trolled, Earth-simulation environment. It had air and water, and illumination produced by cells which trapped solar energy on the outside of the planetoid and released it again on the inside. The light was pale and pearly. It waxed and waned as the asteroid turned on its axis. At this particular moment it shone bright and clear – it was the middle of inner-Lamarck's day.

The light shone upon the edge of a great forest of silver, made up of shimmering elements like great wisps of cobweb. The elements were so slight and filmy that it seemed as though one ought to be able to see a long way through them, but in fact visibility dwindled away within a dozen metres of the observation window.

Half-hidden by the silvery web-work were other growths of many different colours and forms. There were red ones like sea anemones, which moved their tentacles in a slow, rhythmic dance, as though fishing for prey too tiny to be seen by human eyes. There were pale spheres of lemon yellow, mottled with darker colours, suspended within the framework of the silver filaments. There were tall, ramrod-straight spikes of blue and gold which grew in geometrically regular clumps at random intervals.

There were things which moved, too – airborne puffballs and tiny beings like tropical fish floating in a gigantic bowl. There seemed to be no crawling life; nor anything that walked. Everything mobile flew or floated. There was no gravity in the vast chamber. There was no up and down; there was only surface and lumen. It was different in the living-quarters, where a local 'gravity-field' was induced by mysterious engines – mysterious, at least, to Gabriel Samarra, who was a genetic engineer, and knew little of any other kind of machinery.

'The life-system is somewhere between community, organism and cell,' said the engineer.

'It possesses certain characteristics of each. The method of reproduction employed by the life system is unique. Light is the only thing which comes in from outside, to provide the energy which keeps the system in operation. Water, air and minerals are all recycled. There is no more organic matter there than there has ever been. Everything is used and re-used as the life-system evolves and improves. As it grows, it changes, and day by day it evolves. It was designed to evolve, to mutate and adapt at a terrific pace. The cycle of its elements is a spiral rather than a circle. Nothing ever returns to a former state. Every generation is a new species, nothing ever replicates itself. What I have instituted here is ultra-evolution — evolution which is not generated by natural selection. My life-system displays an alternative kind of evolution, not covered by Darwin's theory.'

He paused, casting an expectant glance at the robot. The machine did not react.

'It's the most wonderful thing that men have ever made,' continued the little man dreamily. 'It is the greatest of our achievements. And I built it. It's mine.'

'I know,' said the executioner, irrelevantly.

'You don't know,' said the little man. 'What can you know? You're metal. Hard, cold metal. You don't reproduce. Your kind has no evolution.

245

What do you know about life-systems? You can't know what it's like to live and change, to dream and build. How can you claim to know what I mean?'

'I try to understand.'

'You came to destroy it all! You came to send Lamarck toppling into the sun, to burn my world and my life into cinders. You were sent to commit murder. How can a murderer claim to understand life? Life is sacred.'

'I am not a murderer,' said the robot calmly. 'My instructions are to remain here while you take my place in the capsule which brought me here. It is programmed to rendezvous with station K6 in one month's time. You must take your place in the capsule very soon, and activate the machinery which will place you in artificial hibernation. You will come to no harm. No one is to die.'

'I'm not talking about the murder of a man,' said the bespectacled man, in a low, petulant voice. 'I'm talking about the murder of an entire life-system. They *can't* deflect it into the sun. It's worse than mere murder. It's worse than genocide – it's the destruction of an entire Creation.'

'It is considered too dangerous to permit Asteroid Lamarck to exist,' quoted the robot. 'It has been decided that the dangerous experiment begun here should be obliterated with all possible speed, and that no possibility of contamination should be tolerated.'

'Why was it decided?' complained Samarra.

'It was agreed that Asteroid Lamarck harbours a danger which threatens life on Earth,' explained the machine. 'It is believed that the life-system might one day produce spores capable of crossing space after leaking from within the planetoid. It was pointed out that if such an eventuality were to come about, there would be no way of preventing the Lamarck life-system from destroying all life on Earth. The life-system, according to your own reports, is a genetic predator which could consume all organic matter with which it comes into contact.'

The little man wasn't really listening. He had heard it before. He was staring hard through the window, at the silver forest. Little teardrops were leaking into the corners of his eyes. He was not crying for himself, but for the life he had created in Lamarck.

'What are they really afraid of?' he asked, of himself rather than the robot. 'Are they afraid that my life might evolve intelligence? That it might become cleverer, better in every way than a man? Are they afraid of being superseded?'

'I know nothing about fear,' said the robot. 'I know what I have been told. There is a danger

of infection from Asteroid Lamarck. The consequences of such an event are so terrible that no
such danger can be allowed to exist for a moment
longer than is inevitable.'

'My life could never reach Earth.'

It is felt that there is a danger of the evolution
of Arrhenius spores.'

'Arrhenius spores,' sneered the little man.
'What could Arrhenius know?' He died hundreds
of years ago. His speculations are nonsense. His
supposition that interstellar spores might be
responsible for seeding new planets with life
was naïve and ridiculous. There is no evidence
that such spores could ever exist. If the men who
sent you used Arrhenius spores as an excuse, then
they are fools and liars.'

'Your life-system, if it ever got to Earth, could
destroy the planet,' said the robot, patiently. 'Every
organism here is unique, and each carries two sets
of chromosomes. Each set of chromosomes carries
a complete genome. One set determines the present
form of the organism, the others are attached to
gene-sequences which can act as viruses. When
an organism reaches senility, the virus-augmented
chromosomes pre-empt control of protein synthe-
sis from the organism-chromosomes. Billions and
billions of virus particles are produced and the
organism dies of its inbuilt diseases. The virus

particles are released and are universally infective. Any protein-synthesising system is open to their attack.

'On infection, the viral chromosomes fuse with the chromosomes of the host. The fused chromosomes induce metamorphic changes in the host body, which mutates serially through a chain of forms, each one of which lives only for a matter of hours or days. Forms which are registered as viable are "recorded" in different chromosomesets, most of which become dormant, each attached to viral gene-sequences. When the process ceases and an "adult" form of the organism is stabilised, the cycle is completed.

'The key property of the life-system is the means by which the virus may infect absolutely any living creature, irrespective of whether or not it is already a part of the life-system. There is no possible immunisation.'

The little man nodded. 'So you know it all,' he conceded. 'You know what it is and how it works – parrot-fashion, at any rate. Your masters have accused me of the Frankensteinian sin of creating a monster which is just waiting to destroy me and conquer Earth. Can't you see how childish and ludicrous it all is?'

'There exists a danger,' said the robot obstinately.

'Utter nonsense! My life-system is absolutely bound to the inside of Asteroid Lamarck. There is no possibility of its ever reaching the exterior. If it did, it could not live. Even a system as versatile as mine could not live out there, without air or water. Only robots can do that. There is no escape from Lamarck, as far as the system is concerned.'

'If, as you have claimed in your reports, the evolution of the Lamarck life-system is directive and improving, then it would be a mistake to limit the presumed capabilities of the system. There is a finite probability that the system will gain access to outer Lamarck, and will evolve a mechanism of interplanetary dispersal.'

'Arrhenius spores!' spat the little man. 'How?' Just tell me, how? How can a closed system, inside an asteroid, get spores to Earth, *against* the pressure of the solar wind? Surely, even the idiots who sent you must realise that Arrhenius spores must drift outwards, *away* from Earth.'

'It is impossible to make predictions about the pattern of drift within the solar system,' stated the robot implacably. 'I must warn you, Professor Samarra, that time is limited. I have followed my instructions carefully, and have already set the gravity-field device which will reduce the momentum of the asteroid. When the timer is activated Lamarck will begin its slow spiral into the sun. It is necessary that the capsule detaches before the field is activated, and I am instructed to make certain that you are aboard.'

'I won't go.'

'You must go. Asteroid Lamarck is to be tipped into the sun. There is no appeal against the decision. You cannot remain here.'

'No appeal,' sneered the genetic engineer. 'There is no appeal because they did not dare allow me a voice. There is no justice in this decision. There is only fear – the fear of some monstrous ghost. That's all it is – a crazy, stupid, pathological fear of something they can't begin to understand or appreciate. Fear that can be made to breed fear, to infect others with fear. Fear that can be used as a lever to make death sentences. They say that some infection might reach Earth – it is there already. Fear infects everything, and its second generation is murder.'

'Fear is a natural defence-mechanism,' said the executioner.

'They have passed a death sentence upon you too,' said the genetic engineer.

'I accept the necessity.'

'Is that supposed to make me accept it too? You're a robot. You don't put the same value on life that I do. You're programmed to die. You're only a machine.'

'Yes,' said the robot demurely. 'I am a machine.'

The little man stared through the glass wall, forcing back the nausea, the frustration – and the fear.

'I won't go,' he repeated. 'It's *my life*. It's everything I've done, everything I believe in. I don't want to die, but I don't want all this to die either. It's important to me. I made it. You can't possibly understand.'

'If you say so,' conceded the executioner. 'But you must leave now. I have been instructed to ensure that you are placed in the capsule. I have permission to employ discreet force in placing you in a state of artificial hibernation. You cannot refuse.'

The little man turned away from the glass wall, towards the door.

'There is nothing you can do,' said the robot. 'It is futile to attempt resistance.'

Samarra stopped and turned his head.

'There are some things I must fetch,' he said. 'I will do what you wish, but you must wait a few moments.'

'As you wish,' said the executioner. 'You must do whatever you need to do. But I must ask you to hurry. There is little time left.'

The little man left the room, and the robot

turned its red eyes to the glass wall. It stood in silent contemplation, watching the silken forest. Beyond and within the silver threadwork – which was all one creature – were other organisms. Some moved; most remained still. All seemed very peaceful. The robot watched without curiosity; it was not interested.

The little man returned, having been gone less than three minutes. He held a revolver, so heavy that it required both hands. He had small, delicate hands and thin arms.

'What are you going to do?' asked the robot, quietly.

The little man peered through his thin-rimmed spectacles, sighting along the barrel of the gun. It was obviously an unfamiliar experience.

'It won't help you to shoot me,' said the robot.

'What do you care whether I shoot you or not?' demanded Samarra. His voice was sharp and emotional. 'You're metal. You don't understand life. You kill, but you don't know what you're really doing.'

'I know what it is to exist,' said the robot.

'You *exist*,' sneered the engineer. 'You don't know what life means. You don't know what *that* means,' he said, pointing at the great window, 'to me, to science. You only want to kill. To kill life, to kill knowledge, to kill science. For fear.'

'Put the gun down, Professor Samarra. There is no way to save the asteroid. If you destroy me, you will only succeed in placing your own life in danger. It would be a futile gesture.' The machine's gentleness was infuriating.

'Everything's futile. I'm a condemned man. Whatever I do, it's a waste of time. I'm a dead man. You're a dead robot. But you don't care.'

The executioner remained silent.

The little man raised the gun, and pointed it at one of the robot's red eyes. For a few moments, man and machine stared at one another. The robot watched impassively as a thin, unsteady finger pressed the trigger of the gun.

The hands that held the weapon jerked as the recoil jolted the genetic engineer. There was a loud bang. The bullet clanged off the metal ceiling and ricocheted into the window. The glass did not break.

'It's pointless,' said the robot softly. Somehow, after the sharp report of the gun, its calmness seemed plaintive.

The little man fired again, squeezing the muscles round his eyes and mouth as he struggled to keep his hands still. The bullet splashed the robot's electronic eye into tiny red fragments. The metal man moaned, and went over backwards. There was a moment when the balance adjustment in its double-jointed knees compensated for the impact, and held the robot in a backward kneeling position. Then the moaning ended in a sharp gasp, and the engineer winced as the robot fell full length on to the floor.

The fallen robot uttered what sounded very like a laugh, which rattled harshly out of the uncoordinated vocal apparatus. The engineer stared at the crumpled heap of metal. It was no longer a parody of a human form. It was just metal. It was dead.

The little man walked slowly over to the large window. He fired from the waist, gunfighter style. The bullet rebounded from the glass and grazed his thigh. His face went pale, and he winced, but he did not fall. He fired three more times, at the same spot. At the third attempt the glass cracked, but there was still no breach in the wall.

The engineer felt tears easing from the corners of his eyes, and a trickle of blood on his leg. He smashed the butt of the gun into the glass again and again. The cracks spread. Finally, the window gave up the fight and shattered.

Once the gap was there, it was not very difficult to enlarge it. The little man allowed the artificial gravity of the laboratory to pull him to the floor, resting his injured leg while he chipped away at the lower edge of the hole until he had made a doorway in the wall.

He crawled into the world of his life-system. Once there, beyond the scope of the gravity-field, his leg stopped hurting him, and his body was filled with an exhilarating buoyancy.

He breathed the air, and imagined that he found it cleaner and fresher than the cold, sterile air of his own quarters. He felt nothing, but he knew that in the air he breathed, and through the wound in his leg, virus-particles were invading his body.

He pushed himself away from the window, to get away from the murdered robot, and found that he could move with amazing rapidity and with little expenditure of effort.

The geneticist wanted to leave the window far behind, because it was a window into a world that had sent an executioner to take away his Creation. He grabbed at spongy alien flesh, and used the leverage to pull himself further and further into the body of the silver forest, and on, and on.

He found another forest – another single being with many individual aspects. This was a con-glomeration of tree-forms which consisted of twisted, many-branched stalks, each of which seemed to have arisen by a process of bifurcation and spiralling away of elements from a single point of origin. Each of the branches terminated

in a small, eye-like spheroid. The branches were
of equal thickness, and of a glass-like smoothness
and hardness. At first sight, the entire forest
seemed petrified, but there was life here in abundance, and growth. Nothing ever petrified in the
Lamarck life-system. Nothing ever really died.

Within the globes at the ends of the branches,
the engineer could perceive movement, and when
he stopped to look more closely, he saw a shifting
and pouring like swirling smoke, which could
only be cytoplasmic streaming. He perceived
darker regions that were nuclei and organelles.
He concluded that the spheroids were the living
elements of a colonial being or hive, and that
they constructed the stalks which bore them from
purely inorganic matter.

Then he pulled himself on, half-flying through
the small forest, and into another kind of forest,
and another. He had lost sight of the smashed window, and he could not see any of the batteries of
solar cells which were the only other evidence of
human interference with the Lamarck life-system.
He was alone, a stranger in the world which he
had made. He floated to a stop, and sank slowly
to the carpet of tiny unique organisms. He lay,
exhausted, listening to the beating of his heart
and admiring the wonders which his genetic
engineering skill had produced.

There was a strange lurching sensation, and his head reeled with sudden dizziness. The gravitational wrench was gone within a few seconds, and then his weightlessness was restored, but he knew that the device which the robot had brought to tip Lamarck into the sun had been activated. There had been no way to prevent its activation. It was all over now; he and his life-system were doomed to die together. He was overwhelmed by a sense of tragedy, and he mourned. He was beginning to feel sick and feverish. His body was trying, hopelessly, to mobilise its defences against multitudinous infections.

He saw a giant plant, not far off, which must have covered a much larger area of ground than any of the so-called forests. It was of such complexity that it was built in tiers in the air. The lowest layer consisted of a dense tangle of light-coloured tendrils of an even continuity, not unlike the filaments of the silken forest. The slender threads were woven into cushions of varying density. Above this region was a looser serial carpet of thicker elements, which were darker in colour but of a similar even texture. The threads stirred gently, and appeared to be very flexible. From this stratum there extended towers of small spherical elements, held vertical by the pressure of inner turgor. These spherical cells were being continually produced by budding from the filaments. The topmost spheres continually lost the adhesion which bound them to the mass, and drifted away, very slowly, dipping and soaring on gentle air currents. Eventually, each one exploded into a cloud of invisibly small particles.

In the opposite direction, the engineer could see another vast growth, which had the appearance of a tree bearing fruits like precious stones. The growth arose from a deep bed of slime – a great morass which would have seemed hostile to life had it not been part of the Lamarck life-system. When he squinted, the little man could perceive thousands of rod-like bodies moving randomly within the slime body. The tree itself was slender and extremely beautiful in the manner of its curving and branching. The branches were translucent, but not wholly clear, for at certain points they contained encapsulated rod bodies, entombed like flies in amber. The engineer imagined that the tree was formed of crystalline slime. At the tip of each branch was a large spherical or elliptical jewel, each enclosed by a thin membrane. There was movement within each gem, and they looked like the many faceted eyes of some strange beast.

The engineer looked, and marvelled, and loved.

Later, the engineer slept, and while he slept he died.

The viruses worked within him. They invaded his cells, penetrating the nuclei. They fused with his chromosomes, and pre-empted protein production within the corpse – for the cells did not die all at the same time, and there were processes of life which continued even though the man was dead. The viruses had killed, but even while they were killing, they began rebuilding and regenerating. The passenger chromosomes carried by the viruses began an elaborate mating dance with the forty-six human chromosomes. The DNA within them began to undergo chemical metamorphosis as bases shifted and genes were remodelled. As new genotypes are created, they mutated and replicated.

The generation of the new entity which was being born, phoenix-like, from the carcase of Gabriel Samarra was an unsteady process. There was much in the engineer's genes which was entirely new to the Lamarck life-system, and though there was nothing in that system capable of 'knowing' or 'thinking', there was at the biochemical level a process of discovery unfolding. As Lamarck's ecosphere absorbed the hopeful monster which had somehow erupted into it from another world, it obtained the potential for an evolutionary leap of marvellous scope.

Had Gabriel Samarra been able to guess that this would happen, he would have been rapt with joy. In godlike fashion, he had made the ultimate gift to his Creation – he had donated his substance, his power, his inner fire. He was his own Prometheus, his own Christ.

In conjunction with chemical metamorphosis came physical change. The body of the genetic engineer began to flow and dissolve. A new being was forming inside the old, and was growing within it, feeding on its latency as well as its flesh. The process which was going on inside the corpse of the little man was more complex than the elementary mode of genetic exchange which the engineer had initially incorporated into the life-system at the time of its creation. The rapidity of the life-system's evolution had increased the speed, the smoothness, and the efficiency of its metamorphoses considerably.

The new being absorbed the engineer, and came slowly to the first of its many maturities.

The body of the little man had lost its substance. His face widened into a skull-grin, and his ridiculous spectacles lay lop-sided across the gleaming white bridge of the crumbling nose. His brain was completely gone from the skull, and the whole of his lower abdomen gradually disappeared. His legs decayed into thin ropes of wiry muscle. His ribs were reduced to tiny studs attached to what had once been the spine. Only organic dust remained where the heart and lungs had once been.

From the corpse there emerged a winged thing, which took off and hovered in hummingbird-like fashion, testing its strength. It was small-bodied but large-skulled. It had a tiny wizened face, without eyes, but which nevertheless retained some faint echo of human expression. The face moved continuously as though experiencing unknown emotions, and the creature made a small, thin sound like a rattling laugh.

The creature soon flew away from the remains of its 'father', zooming through the weird forests of inner Lamarck in great circles. Finally, it found the silver forest, and settled on a branch very near to the smashed glass wall. It lay still. It had never eaten. It was not even equipped to eat. It was already changing again into something new, and it had many changes yet to undergo, and many cousins yet to meet.

In time, the plants of inner Lamarck passed through the doorway which the engineer had made for them. They 'explored' his laboratories, his library, his bedroom, his office. They slipped under doors and through keyholes. Things grew upon the inert mass of the robot, consuming the plastics and synthetic proteins in his body. In due course, they consumed the metal, too. There was only one place that the organisms could not easily reach, and that was the world of outer Lamarck, beyond the great iron airlock that had neither crack nor key.

Organisms 'died', and were 'reborn'. They were changing, ever changing. New types of creature formed around and on the iron door – entities which built their cell walls out of pure iron. With vegetable efficiency, they began to dissolve the airlock.

All kinds of new winged creatures evolved within the gravity field of Samarra's living quarters. Crawling creatures made their first appearance in inner Lamarck. They experimented with endothermy and exothermy, with chitin and with bone, with blood of many colours. They lived and passed on in legions, forever sprinkling tiny offspring from strange organs. Sphincters pulsed and pulsed, and every pulse-beat was a measure of the inventiveness of Samarra's Creation.

Millions of tiny organic motes floated in the air, far too light for the weak gravity to pull them to the ground. The air within the lumen of the asteroid also became filled with them, and their effect upon the silvery forests was remarkable. The entire ecosphere became unquiet with constant mutation. Everywhere there was movement, catalysis, metastasis. Having absorbed the corpus of its creator, the life-system of inner Lamarck had become fervent with ambition, biochemically inspired by that unprecedented martyrdom.

In the months that followed, Asteroid Lamarck spiralled slowly inwards towards the sun. It crossed the orbit of Mars, the orbit of the Earth, and the orbit of Venus, but it was still tens of millions of miles away from the sun when pinpricks first began to appear in the outer airlock door. The inner door was by that time completely gone.

Air began to seep away, slowly at first, but with increasing rapidity as the holes were enlarged. Like all the other creatures of the Lamarck life-system, the iron-eaters were fast and efficient. The seepage ultimately became a rush. As it erupted into the void, the air took tiny particles produced in thousands of millions by all manner of exotic organisms.

Lamarck was far too small to hold the atmosphere which flooded out into the desolation of its outer surface. The air was lost and the particles with it. While Lamarck plunged on towards the sun, in its ever-decreasing spiral, it left behind a long, long trail of grey dust.

Of every million micro-organisms, only a bare handful could function as Arrhenius spores, but there were very many millions.

Those few cells which were viable even in these extreme conditions began to drift lazily on the solar wind, carrying their infinitely precious cargo of gluttonous chromosomes – the gift of a new Creation – slowly outwards . . . towards the orbital path of the Earth.

The Growth of the House of Usher

It was a dull and soundless day on which I approached by motor-boat the house which my friend Rowland Usher had built in the loneliest spot he could find, in the southern region of the Orinoco delta. There are plenty of lonely spots to be found there nowadays, after a century and a half of changing sea levels due to the greenhouse effect.

The edifice which Rowland was raising from the silt of that great stagnant swamp was like nothing I had ever seen before, and I am morally certain that it was the strangest dwelling ever envisaged by the imagination of man.

It loomed out of the swamp like a black mountain, without an angle anywhere, and without a single window – though that, of course, is the modern fashion. Near its crown there were soft crenellations, mere suggestions of battlements, and a number of projections that might have been balconies, but the whole seemed languidly shapeless. To what precise extent Rowland had been inspired by the coincidence of nomenclature that linked him with the famous story by Edgar Allan Poe I do not know, but there is surely some sense in which one of the true architects of that remarkable tower was a long-dead 19th century fantasist, even though the other was a 22nd century civil engineer.

Rowland had always wanted to erect a House of Usher that could not and would not fall into ruin.

I could not help but wonder whether the letter which had summoned me – which gave every evidence of nervous agitation and spoke of 'mental disorder' – might also be construed as a kind of satire on Poe. I had never thought of Rowland as a joker, but I could not quite believe that his protestations were entirely serious. I obeyed his summons, of course, but I was uncertain what to expect.

I had first met Rowland Usher at college, where we studied civil engineering together. We had been partners in practical classes, where we both became adept in the deployment of the Gantz bacteria which are used in modern cementation processes. These engineered bacteria, which can be adapted to almost any kind of raw materials, had already wrought their first revolution, and were helping to transform whole vast areas of land where it had been impossible to build in the past: deserts, steppes and bare mountains alike. While the ecological engineers were transforming the world's environments, Gantz-inspired structural engineers were building entire new cities for people whose ancestors had never known adequate shelter; thanks to Leon Gantz, there need be no more mud huts – great palaces could be raised from any kind of matrix, whether it be mud or dust or sand or shale.

Rowland and I had been fired with a similar sense of mission, determined to use the tools which our education provided to their very best purpose, to play our part in a Utopian remaking of the world, which would save it from its multiple crisis. We shared a sense of vision and an ambition which many of our fellows lacked, and this brought us closer together. We both became increasingly interested in the techniques of genetic engineering involved in the manufacture of Gantz bacteria, and we dreamed of imparting further powers to these living instruments, which would equip them to perform more astounding miracles.

Pioneers in our field were even then experimenting with living systems integrated into the walls of Gantzed structures, so that houses could put down tap roots into the ground on which they stood, securing their own water supplies. Living systems for the disposal of human wastes had been in use for some time, and ingenious engineers were trying to adapt these systems to the production of useful materials. These were the kinds of projects which had seized our imaginations, and we often collaborated on the design of imaginary living dwellings which would serve every human purpose.

As I approached the remarkable house which Rowland had built for himself, I could not help but recall these flights of fancy, and I wondered how much progress his genius had made. The castles in the air which I had built in our discussions had been without exception edifices of considerable beauty and profound charm, but no one could say that about the thing which Rowland had elevated from the silt of this great swamp. It retained the blackness of that silt and possessed an outward form which reminded me of the great termite mounds I had seen in southern Africa, where I had been working in recent years. When I came closer I saw that the walls seemed slightly less than solid, as though capable of a certain sluggish protoplasmic flow, and this appearance gave me an uneasy feeling as I neared the threshold, recalling to my mind the story of Jonah who was swallowed by a whale.

Rowland met me at the open door and greeted me with enthusiasm. He conducted me through black, smooth-walled corridors which curved eccentrically into the bowels of the house, to a study where he obviously spent much of his time; it boasted three telescreens, a well-stocked disc library of miscellaneous publications, an integrated sound system and two well-worn sofas. The chamber was lighted by artificial bioluminescence, which was oddly ruddy and subdued.

A pot of China tea was waiting for me, timed to perfection, and we sat together drinking from small cups, exchanging platitudes. I had not seen Rowland for more than seven years, thanks to the reclusive habits which kept him apart from human society. I had expected to find him changed, but in spite of his letter I was surprised by the difference in him. He was very thin and pale, and his hair was quite white. His voice was uncertain, sometimes stumbling over simple sentences, and he gave the impression of slight intoxication, though there was no wine to be seen in the room.

I asked him if he was ill. He confirmed that he was, and incurably. Even the most modern diagnostic computers had failed to determine the biochemistry of his malaise, despite the most comprehensive sampling and analysis of his bodily fluids. He was continually in touch, electronically, with the medical research foundation at Harvard, but there was little the doctors could do for him.

'You need have no fear for yourself,' he assured me. 'This is no virus, or other infectious agent; the fault is integral. This is the same malady which destroyed my father before me, and my beloved sister Magdalen; somehow, it is written in our genes. It seems strange that in an age when we have won such powers of command over the formative powers of DNA the cunning double helix should still harbour mysteries, but it does. We have not entirely conquered those inner blights and pestilences which rot the very core of our being.'

I inferred from this rather florid speech that Rowland was suffering from some exotic form of cancer, associated with a heritable chromosomal abnormality.

'Your sister died of this same illness?' I remarked.

He favoured me, as he answered, with a peculiar smile. 'Oh yes,' he said. 'Many years ago, before I knew you at college. She was 17 years old – she was born a year before me. The disease afflicts females more severely than males; my father lived to be forty, and I am now 47. My grandfather's sister, the last female sufferer I have been able to identify, died at 19. You will readily understand why the disease is inherited through the male line. It is an Usher complaint, like the one which afflicted my famous namesake. Did I not know he were a fiction, I would suspect a line of actual descent.'

I think I might have been alarmed if Rowland had told me that his sister were still alive, and had I seen her flitting ethereally through the apartment just then. This would have been one Poesque parallel too many for my tired mind to bear.

'With Harvard on your side,' I said, earnestly, 'there must still be hope for you.'

'No,' he replied. 'It is too late now to hope for a cure. Modern medicine has helped me to ameliorate the symptoms of my condition, but it has failed to identify its biochemical nature, and there is no hope of permanent remission. The point of origin of my symptoms is the brain, which is that least understood of all the organs, perhaps the last great mystery of human nature which remains to be revealed by our new Age of Englightenment. You will have noticed that my speech is affected, and my sight too, which is why, I fear, the lighting here will seem a little eerie to your eyes. The mental disorder of which I spoke in my letter is increasingly perceptible, and I know that my working days are almost over. That is why I asked you to come to me – I want to explain to you what it is that I have been doing all these years, in my solitude, while you have been helping the poor in Africa.

'I want you to get to know my house, to understand what I have achieved here. I want you, in brief, to be the executor of my will. My personal possessions are worthless, but my additions to the sum of human knowledge and creativity are not. I leave everything to mankind in general, for the joy and benefit of all future generations – and you, my old friend, must convey my legacy to those heirs.

'There are full records of my data here, of course, but you know as well as I that the world is laden down beyond endurance with stored data, and that knowledge needs human champions if it is to be properly disseminated and developed.'

I told him that I understood, though in truth I was not entirely sure that I did, and gave him my most earnest promise that I would try to do as he wished. He was delighted by this response, but his enthusiasm seemed suddenly to weaken him, and when we dined he ate almost nothing. Soon afterwards he begged leave to desert me, and after showing me to my bedroom he left me alone, begging me to make full use of the facilities of the house and apologising profusely for not being able to give me a more thorough introduction to them.

Because the room had no window I could not ascertain whether the threatened storm had begun, but when I lay silently in my bed I thought that I could perceive a vibration in the dull, warm walls which might have been an echo of lashing rain and howling wind – or which might, instead, have been some mysterious internal process at work within the living fabric of the fabulous structure.

After a time, I came to find it strangely comforting, as if it were a subliminal lullaby, and I allowed myself to be carried off by it into peaceful sleep.

When I awoke the next day Rowland seemed better, and we breakfasted together. He told me, though, that he did not feel well enough to guide me about the house. He promised that he would show me its wonders at a later date, and offered instead to tell me something of the researches which had led to its construction, and which formed the substance of his intellectual legacy.

'You may recall from discussions we had nearly

a quarter of a century ago,' he said, 'that I was always impatient with the traditional Gantz techniques which were in common use in our youth, and which we were expected to learn in a more-or-less slavish fashion in the course of our education in civil engineering.

'One of my chief interests, which we shared, I think, was the possibility of integrating better artificial living systems into the structure of buildings. It will not be long now, I am sure, before biotechnologists develop methods of artificial photosynthesis, and truly sophisticated living dwellings will then come into being. Houses will one day be living machines harvesting the energy of the sun as plants do.

'My own house simulates, by necessity, a more primitive kind of organism: a lowly scavenger which draws its energy from the organic detritus of the silt out of which it is constructed. It is no more sophisticated than many sedentary creatures which live in shallow seas, filtering food from the murky waters which overflow them. Its closest analogues, if you wish to think in such terms, are coral polyps, barnacles, and tubeworms. Nevertheless, however primitive it is, it lives and grows. The Orinoco feeds it with all manner of decayed vegetable matter *via* the network of filters which extend from the foundations.

'You will probably remember another of my fascinations, which is similarly embodied in this house. Ordinary Gantz processes involve the use of inert moulds – the cementing organisms simply bind the material brought to them, and the architect controls the shape of what they produce by crude mechanical means. I was always impressed, though, by the way that certain living organisms are themselves genetically equipped to construct complicated edifices: the nests of wasps and termites, of bower-birds and ovenbirds; the supporting structures of corals; the astonishing forms of flowering plants and trees. I designed this house, therefore, by programming into the genes of its micro-organic creators the kind of structure it should be.

'Its main structure is, of course, built primarily from non-living tissue, like the xylem of a tree or the shell of a mollusc; but that structure retains its connections with living cells, and is formed more-or-less precisely by the pattern of their activity.'

'Your house, then, is really a gargantuan living organism?' I observed, rhetorically.

'Strictly speaking, no,' he corrected me. 'It's builders are micro-organisms, which associate and collaborate like the members of a beehive or the individual cells in a slime-mould. If it is to be seen as a single entity, then it is a *colony* – a colony which consists of trillions of quasi-bacterial cells. In adapting it for habitation, though, I do have cause to use other engineered organisms, which might be regarded as symbiotes of the elementary cells. The structure is naturally honeycombed by tunnels and chambers, but the precise design of the corridors and the rooms, not to mention the various connecting conduits which carry water, electricity and optical fibres, requires supplementary work.'

Such work in ordinary Gantzed structures is usually carried out by de-cementing bacteria whose work is precisely the opposite of the cementers, but from Rowland's reference to 'other engineered organisms' I inferred that he was using 'worms' more akin to the artificial organisms used to pulverise rocks like granite and basalt. Most such organisms are, though vermiform, not really worms at all – the vast majority are the larvae of insects, akin to 'woodworm' and 'wireworms', which are frequently equipped with jaws and rasps powerful enough to cope with stone and metal.

'I have always been interested in insect larvae,' he explained, when I asked him to elaborate. 'They have in them so much latent potential –

the phenomenon of metamorphosis has always fascinated me.'

This was an interesting sideline to the discussion, and I pursued it. 'None of the larvae which are conventionally used to tunnel through rock are capable of metamorphosis,' I said. 'They are of such a size that the insects which would emerge from their pupae would be inviable giants, incapable of breathing or of locomotion.'

'That is because Gantzian engineers have not been interested in those genes which the larvae would only switch on during and after metamorphosis,' Rowland told me. 'They have made only feeble efforts to modify such genes, and the giant insects which they have managed to produce are mere grotesques. No one has tried to explore fully the real metamorphic potential of these larvae. Crudely utilitarian research into rock-breaking organisms can do no more than scratch the surface.'

'But you have gone further?'

'I have . . . taken an interest. The humble servants which help to hollow out my rooms have been my only companions for many years, and I have used them in certain unorthodox experiments quite unconnected with their more obvious purpose.'

I could see that this was a point upon which

Rowland was, as yet, unwilling to elaborate. He seemed very tired and strained.

'Would it not be a good idea,' I asked, 'if we were to return together, however briefly, to the United States? I know you are in touch with medical researchers there, and can transmit information gleaned from analysis of your blood and other fluids, but if you are suffering from a tumour in the brain, you surely need a sophisticated scan, which must be beyond the capacity of your own facilities.'

'Although my illness has its origins in the brain,' he told me, 'it is not a localised tumour. It is some kind of genetic defect which is capable of affecting all the neurones, and will eventually affect enough of them to kill me, as it killed my sister. The researchers at Harvard have quite enough samples of my cells – and, for that matter, my sister's cells – in their freezers to allow them to continue examining the chromosomes for many years. Eventually, I feel sure, they will map and identify the anomaly, though by then the knowledge may be redundant as the last known sufferer will be dead. I shall leave no children of my own.

'I hope that the work done on my cells after I am dead will serve to pave the way for their successful treatment and cure. I have been doing my own research, too, using the apparatus that permits me to engineer my bacteria and my worms to do what I can to study my own chromosomes. I have my own cryonic chambers, and my own tissue-cultures – my father made the first contribution to my stocks before he died.'

'I wonder that you have not devoted your life to that research,' I said, 'instead of spending so much time on your other project.'

'Ah!' he said. 'My other project will assure me something worth far more than an extended lifespan – it will provide a kind of immortality. Even had I succeeded in curing myself I would have died after seventy or eighty years, but this house will live for centuries, perhaps for millennia.

'The Usher family will die out with me, but this House of Usher will continue to grow for many generations, and will be one of the wonders of this world when your descendants have discovered and colonised new worlds which orbit distant stars. You see, my friend, that I have lost none of that Romantic imagination which drew you to me all those years ago!'

Indeed he had not, and as we talked further he waxed rhapsodic on the subject of the futures that were already nascent in the genetic technologies of the present day, his inventiveness vaulting across the centuries with talk of the miracles that godlike genetic engineers of the far future would work.

'It is not given to us to see such things,' he told me, after some while, 'but your grandchildren will come into a world whose science will offer them immortality, and they will see the world transformed in ways we can hardly imagine. I will have my monument then, as Khufu has his; it will be one of the last and greatest achievements of mortal mankind. We are members of one of the last generations to need tombs, my friend, and I intend that my sister and I shall have one of the very finest!'

His speech was becoming slurred and his tone was feverishly excited. I knew that his illness was taking hold of him, and I made every effort to calm him. In the afternoon, though, he had to leave me again, and I dined alone that evening.

The hours before I retired to my bed I spent in reading, but I was not tempted to begin the work of making my way through the discs which contained the long record of Rowland Usher's experiments. Instead, I sought solace in more familiar works, in the poetry of Blake and Byron, and (how could I avoid it?) Edgar Allan Poe. I say solace, but I really mean distraction, because the more time I spent in my tiny apartment deep in the heart of that utterly strange house, the more uneasy I began to feel about my virtual captivity.

I did not like to be so cut off from the world outside, and the sound of the everpresent murmur in the smooth, warm walls which surrounded me no longer seemed quite as comforting as it once had. When I finally went to my bed I had a turbulent night, full of vague nightmares in which the imagery of Poe's poems mingled with the dreams and achievements of Rowland Usher. Conqueror Worms continually triumphed in an uncertain tragedy, from whose toils I could not escape until I woke in a cold sweat, many hours before morning.

My nightmare had had such a profound effect on me that I did not like to close my eyes again for fear of its return. I reached out to activate the bioluminescent strips that would light my room, threw back the quilt and rose unsteadily to my feet. I went to the sink on the far side of the chamber, and filled a cup with water.

No sooner had I taken a sip than my attention was caught by a sound in the corridor outside. Though there was nothing sinister in the sound itself I had not yet escaped the effects of my evil dream, and it drew from me a gasp of pure terror.

I knew, at the level of reason, that I ought not to be afraid, so I forced myself to go to the door and open it. Such was my state of mind, though, that it was only by the merest crack that I pulled it ajar, and as I peeped out into the corridor my heart was pounding in my breast.

The corridor was not quite dark, though its bioluminescence was considerably toned down, so that what remained was a faint bluish radiance. Because the corridor curved I could see only a few metres in either direction, and could see only one other door, that of Rowland Usher's bedroom.

That door too seemed to be ajar, but there was darkness within. Moving away from the door, though, just disappearing from sight around the gentle angle of the tunnel, was a human figure. I caught no more than the merest glimpse of it, but I had the distinct impression that it was a young female, perhaps fourteen or fifteen years of age. She was quite naked.

The idea that this must be Rowland's sister Magdalen, somehow risen from the dead, sprang into my mind, provoked by my dream even though I knew full well that it could not be. The power of the thought, even as I fought to dispel it, was sufficient to make me close my door again, and I found to my disgust that I was actually trembling. I, a scientist of the

22nd century, was infected by the morbidity of the Gothic Imagination! I cursed Rowland Usher and his absurd termitary of a house, and resolved to demand an explanation in the morning.

When morning came, though, the matter seemed far less urgent to me. I had slept again, more restfully, and when I awoke at the proper time my experience in the corridor seemed rather to belong to the realm of my nightmare than to the realm of reality. I honestly could not tell whether or not it had been part of my dream, and even though the cup from which I drank was still on the side of the sink, I could not take seriously what I thought I had seen. Perhaps I simply did not want to.

In any case, I asked no questions of Rowland over breakfast regarding the possibility of his being haunted by the ghost of his sister.

That day, Rowland felt well enough to conduct me on a tour of his abode, and so we set forth into its amazing winding corridors. He showed me several other guest-rooms, none of which showed the slightest sign of ever having been inhabited, and several storerooms, some of them crammed with collections of objects which he had obviously inherited from past generations, as well as hoards of his own.

There were many antique books, some with

acid-rotten pages that should have decayed a century ago, some even dating back to the 19th century. There was a collection of minerals, one of medical specimens, one of ancient navigational instruments, and a particularly quaint assembly of display screens and keyboards from the early days of information technology. I asked if these devices were in working order, but Rowland simply shrugged his shoulders; he did not know.

When we descended into the lower strata of the house I found things much more coherently organised, and there were clearly many rooms in active use. First he showed me the laboratories and his transformations of Gantzing bacteria. His equipment was reasonably modern, though no private individual, however rich, can possibly keep up with the larger research institutions.

His fermenters, where his bacterial cultures grew, were built into the fabric of the house, and it was not until he told me their total cubic capacity that I realised how much of the house was hidden, circled by the spiralling corridors. Clearly, that space was not wasted.

I marvelled that any one man could possibly make use of the extensive laboratory facilities, but he assured me that the high level of automation made it reasonably easy. He kept relatively few household robots, regarding the motile varieties as inherently unreliable examples of the mechanician's art, but some routine domestic tasks were contracted out to service personnel who operated their machines by remote control.

At a lower level still he showed me other holding tanks, where he kept his many varieties of burrowing worms. Most of the species needed special containers of some substance which they could not break up or digest. There were observation-windows which let us look in upon the creatures, though sometimes we could see little enough within because of the difficulties of providing lighting systems immune from their ravages.

Rowland allowed a few species of these worms to live freely in the structure of the house as benign parasites, because they could not damage its structure and they performed useful waste-disposal functions as they foraged for food. At first it was disconcerting to come across these creatures at irregular intevals, but I soon got used to it.

'How do you direct the burrowing of the more voracious species?' I asked him. 'Surely, any kind of escape would be desperately dangerous – the worms could devour the entire fabric of the house.'

'Elementary cyborgisation,' he told me. 'These

creatures have little or no brain, and are guided through life by simple behavioural drives. It is a relatively easy matter to fit them with electronic devices which deliver the appropriate commands by electrical or biochemical stimulation. I handle them with great care. They cannot live, of course, on the materials they are designed to tunnel through, and their diets are deliberately exotic. I feed them what they need in order to execute a particular task, and no more. They cannot escape, and could not live wild if they did.'

Watching these curious creatures, whether roaming loose or confined in their tanks, made me slightly nauseous, though I had often seen their like before. Most were like blowfly maggots – big and soft and white, their body walls so transparent that one could see the organs inside them. Rowland's were the biggest I had ever encountered, a metre and a half in length and at least 80 centimetres in girth. Their internal organs were not themselves coloured, but were enwrapped in a webwork of blue and pink. I asked Rowland to explain this, and he told me that he had equipped their circulatory systems with haemoglobin in order to serve the oxygen needs of their organs; like us these creatures had deoxygenated blue blood in their veins and oxygenated red blood in their arteries.

Some others looked more like elongated centipedes than maggots, being bright yellow in colour and equipped with hundreds of pairs of limbs along the length of their plated bodies. These too were the largest of their kind I had ever encountered, being at least four metres long, though they were only as thick as a man's wrist. On the other hand, a few of Rowland's living machines were surprisingly small: there were black, hard-skinned creatures that were only a few centimetres from head to tail, though they had vast heads that were almost all jaw. Rowland informed me that these were very difficult to rear because of the enormous amounts of food they had to consume in order to work those massive jaws. In their womb-like holding tanks they were virtually submerged in high-protein fluid.

These marvels impressed me tremendously, and we spent many hours in these lower regions. He showed me something of the 'roots' which the house extended into the substrata of the swamp, and the apparatus for gathering in organic materials from the silt. He also showed me the biological batteries which produced the house's electricity, which had a potential output, Rowland boasted, equivalent to 30 billion electric eels. Most of this, however, remained inevitably hidden; what could be seen of the house's systems was far less, in metaphorical terms, than the tip of an iceberg.

Rowland assured me that there was much more to be seen than could be taken in during a single day. He reeled off statistics in an impressively casual manner, telling me that the biomass of the house was greater than ten thousand elephants, and that if it *had* been a single organism then it would have been the vastest that had ever existed on Earth.

In the afternoon it became clear that Rowland was tiring, and becoming light-headed. His graphic descriptions began again to diversify into flights of fantasy, in which houses such as this one would gradually replace the plants and animals making up the world's ecoystems, so that in a thousand years the entire ecosphere might consist of nothing but organic artifacts, not merely houses but entire cities, all locked into a careful symbiotic relationship controlled by men.

In such a world, he hypothesised, sexual reproduction would be the sole prerogative of mankind, everything elese in the organic realm being capable only of vegetative growth or of being cloned and transformed by human genetic engineers.

I confess that I did not find this a wholly attractive prophecy (or speculation, for Rowland was talking of opportunity rather than destiny), but there was something very attractive in the sheer grandiosity of Rowland's ecstatic voyages of the imagination, and the magic of his ideas took a firm grip on me, encouraging my own mind to the contemplation of vistas of future history extending toward infinite horizons.

I joined in, for a while, with his game, and I became so carried away that I did not notice that Rowland's condition was becoming desperate until he was on the brink of losing his power of motor co-ordination. He demanded that he should be allowed to show me the upper parts of the house, above our apartments, and uttered dark hints about there being more in the basements than I was yet prepared to imagine, but I had to forbid any further wandering. I was forced to support him while we made our way back up to the dining room.

For once, dinner seemed to revive Rowland's spirits, and he ate a good deal. After he had rested for a while he was restored sufficiently to conduct a longer conversation than had been possible on the evenings of my first two days as his guest.

He set out to tell me more about the history of his researches, but soon progressed to more personal matters, including secrets which he had hesitated to share with me when we were intimates in our younger days. In particular, he spoke of Magdalen, and I listened in fascination as he gradually peeled away the layers of inhibition which had hitherto concealed the inner mainsprings of his motivation. He granted me then such an insight into his character as he would surely never have conceded if he had not been certain that he was very close to death.

Alas, he was closer than he knew!

'Magdalen lived always under the shadowy threat of death,' said Rowland, his voice weakening almost to a whisper as the process of recall carried him into a trance-like reverie. 'My parents treated her with extraordinary indulgence; she was never sent to school because there seemed little point in trying to secure the kind of education that would be useful only as preparation for a later life which would not be her privilege. Instead, my father educated her himself, after his own theory, trying to equip her to obtain the greatest enjoyment from the years she actually would have. She was a beautiful child, who won the admiration of everyone, and of my father's eccentric tutelage I can say only that it seemed to work magnificently, for she was the happiest being I have ever met.

'Although I was allowed a more conventional schooling, I was also much involved in her life.

My father sought to provide her with what he considered to be an ideal companionship; I too was a part of his scheme, though at first I did not know it. As he sought to mould her, so he sought to mould me, to build between the two of us such a bond of affection and community as to make us the lights of one another's lives. Such a uniquely close companionship he considered to be the greatest treasure which any human life is capable of discovering. I have not had cause to disagree with him in the decades through which I have lived since I lost that perfect relationship.

'I am a little sceptical now of my father's motivations. I wonder why, knowing that he was the victim of a heritable disease, he chose to have children at all. At the time, I thought the way he took such careful and absolute control over our nurture was a measure of his heroic desperation in trying to save us from a misfortune of fate. Now I suspect that he had children precisely in order to carry out this remarkable experiment, and that we were his guinea-pigs. Nevertheless, I do know that he loved us very dearly indeed, and that the grief which he felt when Magdalen died robbed his life, as it robbed mine, of almost all meaning.

'You see around you the extraordinary lengths to which I have been driven in my attempts to find a meaningful project in which to absorb myself. He never did find another; he lived and died a sad man, save for those years when Magdalen gave him a reason to exercise his unusual powers for creativity. You and I work with the elements of physical heredity, and cannot fully understand the difficulties which attended his work of manipulating the psyche and the environment, but I think you can appreciate what a triumph was his when I say that I whole-heartedly believe that Magdalen's was the most joyful, the most compassionate, the most *complete* life that I think a human being might live, in spite of, or perhaps because of, its brevity.

'He taught her only those things that might stimulate her sense of beauty and her sense of wonder, to give her the fullest measure of delight in the world where her mayfly existence was to be lived. He controlled all that she saw, and heard, and felt. When I became old enough to understand what was happening, he made me his collaborator instead of his instrument, and towards the end I conspired with him in planning her last few months.

'We were determined that there should be no joyful aspect of human experience denied to her and we discussed carefully the question of whether it should be he or I that would introduce her to sexual love. Despite the value of his experience in such matters, the responsibility was given to me – old taboos against father/daughter incest still have some power, while brother/sister intercourse is widely accepted, and we were scrupulously respectful of prevailing social attitudes even though we had established for Magdalen a private society in which the world at large could not interfere

'There is a sense, I think, in which the climax of my life had already passed when you first met me. You found in me a man who felt he had already finished one life, attempting the impossible in trying to make another. All I can say is that I have done my best, and that I am proud of what I have achieved. I do not regret having become a recluse, separating myself as far as it has been practicable from the society of other men. My memories of Magdalen are far more precious to me than any other relationship with a woman or a man could ever have been.

'I realise that you are bound to think this unusual, but if you are to be the interpreter of my achievement, who must explain to the world the measure of my genius and its productions, then you must try to understand it all.'

Indeed, I did try to understand. He was correct in saying that in our enlightened times we are no longer so fearful of the taboos which preyed upon the consciences of our ancestors. We are no longer horrified by the idea of incest, so I was not particularly shocked to find out that Rowland had been his sister's lover. Nevertheless, the tale he told was so singular that I did have to struggle imaginatively to accommodate it.

How odd and uparalleled, I thought, *the life of Magdalen Usher must have been!*

Quite frankly, I doubted Rowland's assurances about the perfection of his sister's existence. I could not believe that this experiment in eupsychian engineering could possibly have been as successful as he claimed. No human being can be kept so utterly insulated from the darker side of life – from the ominous aspects of our own inner nature – as to be held inviolate from all dread, all sorrow, all splenetic impulse. Nevertheless, I did not doubt that he believed it, and that in his mind his sister's image must have a significance of purity great than that of any saint or other idol.

I remembered then the apparition of the previous night, of which I still feared to speak. I could not help but touch upon the subject, but felt compelled to do so elliptically, without directly saying what I had seen.

'She must be very much in your thoughts now,' I said. 'You must feel her nearness very acutely.'

'I do,' he said, dreamily. He seemed now to

have been overcome by a tremendous tiredness, which carried him off into a kind of euphoric altered consciousness. Despite the fact that he had resolved to tell me his secrets, I do not believe that he would have told me any more at that time had he been in full possession of his faculties. He had surely planned a more gradual process of revelation. He was in the grip of his disease, though, and in a state of mind that few humans can ever have attained.

'At first,' he said, 'I dreamed of re-creating her. So many of her cells, including oöcytes from her womb, were taken from her even before death, to make the tissue-cultures that would be used for the study of our freakish disease. I wanted to clone her, to bring her back from the dead, to make her anew. I soon realised, though, that it would be a dreadful thing to do. All the best efforts of my father and myself had gone into giving her a perfect existence within its prescribed limits. To create another of her would be to spoil our design, as if we were to take a great painting and daub over it an inferior copy. She could never be re-created, and to make another individual out of her genes would be an appalling subversion of all that my father and I had done.

'When I went to college, therefore, I deliberately elected to stay away from medicine, from human engineering. I went into the kind of work that would help me to transform the human environment rather than the human body. I wanted to build houses, not people – places for people to live, where they could live well, in privacy. I soon realised that it would not be enough to build the kind of houses that are now being built; I wanted to create something much more ambitious. But I could not entirely forget Magdalen, and there remained a sense in which my own house, my private world, must in some way contain her.

'That was when I first conceived the notion of working with the larvae.

'These days, we are so proud of our own bio-technic miracles that we tend to forget nature's. We forget what a colossal bounty was made available to our early genetic engineers, in terms of the raw materials with which they began to work. I have always been fascinated by metamorphosis: by the fact that a maggot or a caterpillar can carry within it genes which code for an entirely different creature, so that when the time comes it builds itself a temporary tomb from which it will one day emerge anew.

'It struck me as a terrible waste that structural engineers should breed hundreds or thousands of new kinds of larvae to work for us, without sparing a thought for the fact that their eventual pupation would now be the end of their story. No one cared, it seemed, about the fact that these modified larvae could no longer advance to a final stage in their development, because the imagos programmed into their altered genes were hopelessly inviable.

'Thus, when I began engineering larvae for work within my house, I also began engineering them so that they would be able to pupate and metamorphose successfully. I knew that they could not produce giant insects, with wings and exoskeletons, so I set about reprogramming them to produce creatures which would be viable at that size.

'The creatures resembling blowfly maggots which I showed you today have approximately the same biomass as a human being. They lose much of that in pupation, but can still produce something the size of a young adolescent: mindless creatures, of course — but very beautiful, in their way. They do not live long, at present, but I have laid the foundations for work which has limitless scope. In time, the engineers of the future might produce another human race.

'I have tried hard to gain sufficiently refined control over the features of these individuals, and I regret to say that I have not succeeded in producing one which bears more than a passing wrapped the body in preparation for interment. By this time I had located Rowland's actual last will and testament, and I set in motion the legal machinery needed to put it through probate. The will provided for burial of the body beneath the house, and I knew that this was a task which I would have to carry out myself, but it was one that could safely be left for another day.

It was late when I finally dimmed the lights and returned to my own room. Midnight had long gone, but because I was insulated from any awareness of the setting and rising of the sun my sense of time was confused, and I did not feel tired until I actually took the decision to stop and rest. Then, fatigue suddenly swept over me like a wave.

With darkness and fatigue, though, came an inevitable relaxation of reason, and when I slept, my self-control, so carefully maintained by the iron grip of consciousness, was banished. I dreamt more nightmarishly than I had done the previous night, and my dreams were pure Poe.

I dreamt that I buried Rowland not in his own house but in that other — that haunted purgatory of fantasy. Our journey to the grave took us through rotting passages weeping with cold slime, lit only by smoky torches whose flames were angry red. I dragged the coffin behind me, supporting only one end, and I think that Rowland somehow spoke to me from dead lips as we went, mocking my slowness.

This was bad enough, but after I had immured him in a vault behind a great metal door I remained anchored to the spot, listening for an eternity, waiting for the sound that I knew would come – the sound of the body risen from its rest, its fingers tapping and scratching at the door.

Inevitably – there was probably no real lapse of time, but simply an aching false consciousness of time passed – the sound began, and taunted my soul with echoes of dread and anguish which reverberated in my being until I felt myself literally driven insane, and howled at myself in the fury of my hallucination: *'Madman! Madman! Madman!'*

Then I woke in a cold sweat, thirsting.

And I heard, outside the door of my chamber, a faint tapping and scratching.

For a moment, I convinced myself that I was still asleep, and struggled manfully to wake. Then I could deny my senses no longer, and knew that the sound was real.

I dragged myself from my bed. I felt very heavy, as though my body required an agony of effort to move at all. I stumbled to the door, and opened it, at first by the merest crack wrapped the body in preparation for interment. By this time I had located Rowland's actual last will and testament, and I set in motion the legal machinery needed to put it through probate. The will provided for burial of the body beneath the house, and I knew that this was a task which I would have to carry out myself, but it was one that could safely be left for another day.

It was late when I finally dimmed the lights and returned to my own room. Midnight had long gone, but because I was insulated from any awareness of the setting and rising of the sun my sense of time was confused, and I did not feel tired until I actually took the decision to stop and rest. Then, fatigue suddenly swept over me like a wave.

With darkness and fatigue, though, came an inevitable relaxation of reason, and when I slept, my self-control, so carefully maintained by the iron grip of consciousness, was banished. I dreamt more nightmarishly than I had done the previous night, and my dreams were pure Poe.

I dreamt that I buried Rowland not in his own house but in that other — that haunted purgatory of fantasy. Our journey to the grave took us through rotting passages weeping with cold slime, lit only by smoky torches whose flames were angry red. I dragged the coffin behind me, supporting only one end, and I think that Rowland somehow spoke to me from dead lips as we went, mocking my slowness.

This was bad enough, but after I had immured him in a vault behind a great metal door I remained anchored to the spot, listening for an eternity, waiting for the sound that I knew would come – the sound of the body risen from its rest, its fingers tapping and scratching at the door.

Inevitably – there was probably no real lapse of time, but simply an aching false consciousness of time passed – the sound began, and taunted my soul with echoes of dread and anguish which reverberated in my being until I felt myself literally driven insane, and howled at myself in the fury of my hallucination: '*Madman! Madman! Madman!*'

Then I woke in a cold sweat, thirsting.

And I heard, outside the door of my chamber, a faint tapping and scratching.

For a moment, I convinced myself that I was still asleep, and struggled manfully to wake. Then I could deny my senses no longer, and knew that the sound was real.

I dragged myself from my bed. I felt very heavy, as though my body required an agony of effort to move at all. I stumbled to the door, and opened it, at first by the merest crack and then, in consequence of what I saw, much wider.

There in the faintly-lit corridor, prostrate at my feet, one hand still groping for the door, was what seemed to be a teenage girl.

I knew, of course, that it was not. How many human genes were in it – Magdalen Usher's genes – I could not guess, but I knew that it was only a sham and a phantasm. It was no more human than the maggots which would soon consume Rowland Usher's body – and one day, no doubt, my own. But still, it was a pitiful creature, and in such a form it could not help but attract my sympathies. I remembered what Rowland had said about their not living long.

Some insect 'adults' are born without digestive systems, unable to feed; they exist only to exchange genes in the physiological ritual of sexual intercourse. These creatures of Rowland's had not even reproductive organs inside them. They existed neither to eat nor to breed, having been equipped with the very minimum of a behavioural repertoire in order to serve their maker's purpose.

They existed to cling and caress, to soothe and be soothed, and that was the entirety of their purpose. Like mayflies they were born and they died, innocent and ignorant of time, space and the world at large. Their universe was the House of Usher, and one can only hope that they passed their brief existence in a kind of bliss.

I was awake again now, and though startled and a little appalled, I found no alternative but to pick up the poor creature and carry her to my bed, where I stroked her gently and calmed her. I say 'her' because I could no longer think in terms of 'it' once I had touched her.

She died before morning.

Later, I visited the caverns deep underground – but still within the living walls of the growing manse – where the free-living maggots pupated. There I saw rank upon rank of grey pupae, shaped like the sarcophagi in which the Egyptians entombed their mummified dead. It was a truly awesome spectacle.

For a while, I took care to watch the hatching of the humanoid ephemerae, and studied them as they went through their brief life-cycle, which occupied a mere handful of days. They did not, if left to themselves, find their way into the upper parts of the house, though when I led one of them, as Rowland Usher often must have done, to my own bedroom, she knew both the way back to the deepest cellars and the way to return to the room, unescorted.

They did not really need me, I found, for it was rare that they hatched out alone. Usually, there were half a dozen alive at any one time, and they could obey their inner drives in fondling one another, achieving their fulfilment easily, comfortably, and, by their own standards, naturally.

When the time eventually came for me to leave Rowland's house to convey his legacy to the greater world so that his methods and techniques might be employed for the betterment of mankind, I was sorry to leave these ephemerae. I had grown quite fond of them, in my fashion.

It was in their chamber that I buried Rowland Usher, for it was there that I found the grave of his beloved Magdalen, and I knew that brother and sister would have wished to rest side by side. I left him lightly confined, as I knew that he would have left her, so that in time his decaying flesh might be absorbed, with hers, by the scavenging cells of the house, to become a part of its extending body, dissipated within it, united in substance if not in spirit.

When I finally did come out of the house again, and found myself in the full glare of the tropic sun, I had to wrinkle my nose against the stench of the swamp, for I had become used to breathing clean and sterile air. The sky seemed very blue, its light wild and abandoned, and my eyes ached for the gentle roseate light of the house's artificial bioluminescence.

As the motor-boat sped away toward the main stream of the Orinoco I looked back at the astonishing edifice, and saw that in this light its ebon walls gleamed and sparkled like jet, and that its softened shape resembled a Daliesque hand reaching up as though to touch the sun with molten fingers.

I saw that it was not ugly after all, but perfectly lovely.

The first House of Usher – that shameful allegory of the disturbed psyche – was burst asunder and swallowed by dark waters. In stark contrast, Rowland's house still stands, soaring proudly above the tattered canopy of the twisted trees. It is still growing, and though it stands today in a noisome swamp there will come a time, I know, when it has purified the lakes and the islands, absorbing their stagnancy into its own vitality.

I was afraid, for a time, that the mysterious canker which was implicit in Rowland Usher's being might in some curious fashion be replicated in his house, perhaps by infection as the house absorbed his mortal remains. I am glad to say, though, that in the ten years since I quit that house it has shown no outward sign of any malady, and

I become more confident with every year that passes that it will truly stand the test of time.

In one of the notes which he appended to his data discs Rowland contrasted his own house with Poe's imaginary one, damning the fictitious original as a typical product of the 19th century imgination and its myriad demonic afflictions. His own house, he claimed, belongs not merely to the 22nd century but to the third millennium, and he was bold enough to hazard the speculation that its life might not even be confined by a thousand years, but might go on for ever, into that far-off Golden Age when the entire ecosphere of his planet – and who knows how many more? – will be subject to the dominion of the mind of man.

We can only hope that his faith will be justified.

And He Not Busy Being Born

It was in September 1973, shortly after returning from his honeymoon, that Adam Zimmerman began to read *Sein und Zeit* by Martin Heidegger. Although he was a native New Yorker, he read German fluently; he was the grandson of Austrian Jews who had fled Vienna with his father (then an infant) in 1933, and a perverse estrangement from his parents had made him more enthusiastic to retain his national roots than his religious ones. For this reason he had always remained aloof from *schmaltz* while being self-indulgent in the matter of *angst* and he was ready-made for that sanctification of self-pity which is the existentialist's red badge of courage.

While he read Heidegger, a couple of chapters at a time, on those nights when he elected not to claim his conjugal rights, Adam felt that he was not so much being instructed as helped to bring to consciousness knowledge which had always lain within him, covert and unapprehended. He hardly needed to be told that *angst* is the basic mood of existence, because it had always nested in his soul. When Heidegger explained how our awareness of possible death, though unfathomably awful, is carefully repressed to a subliminal level, so that the threat of nothingness can be held at bay, Adam felt a surge of tremendous relief. It was as if a truth which had been captive in his mind was suddenly set free.

When he finally laid the book down on his bedside table for the last time, the silken caress of his expensive sheets seemed infused with a new meaning. For 25 years he had been a stranger to himself, but now he had been properly introduced.

He woke Sylvia, his bride of eight weeks, and said: 'We're going to die.'

Although distressed at being hauled back from gentle sleep in this rude manner, Sylvia naturally adopted a tone of loving sympathy. 'No we're not, Adam,' she said. 'We're in perfect health.'

'The one constant of our existence, Syl,' Adam told her, calmly, 'is the awareness which haunts us that we may at any moment be snuffed out of existence, forsaking being. It is the fundamental insecurity which weakens the foundations of the psyche.

'We try in our myriad ways to suppress it and defeat it: we invent myths of the immorality of the soul; we try to hide in the routines of the everyday; we try to dissolve our terror in the acid-baths of love and adoration. None of it works, Syl. At the end of the day, it can't work. Heidegger thinks we can break through, liberate ourselves from our servitude to the ordinary and achieve authentic existence, but even that won't work. It's nothing but another cheap trick to try to dodge the issue. The *angst* will always win. What can we *do*, Syl?'

In a year of courtship and eight weeks of marriage Sylvia had already had abundant opportunity to study her loved one's penchant for being abominably pompous, but she still thought that he was wonderful, and didn't mind it too much.

'Go to sleep,' she advised.

Adam loved Sylvia too well to react to this shallow riposte with the contempt it clearly deserved. Instead, he let her follow her own advice, while he continued to brood. The sheer enormity of his realisation denied him escape into the arms of Morpheus. He turned out the bedside lamp and sat in the dark, appalled by the vision of nothingness that was conjured up before him, languishing in the awful sensation of having no hope.

It is useless to speculate as to whether sleep might have saved him; if he could have slept in such circumstances, he would not have needed saving. As it was, Adam Zimmerman became in the course of that insomniac night a man obsessed. Those few rough-hewn sentences which had poured out of him as he tried to explain himself to the sleepy Sylvia became the axioms of his philosophy of life.

Heidegger's analysis of the human predicament – that life is underlaid, limited, subverted and devalued by its own precariousness in the face of possible death – Adam accepted in full; but he denied what seemed to him feeble attempts by the philosopher to find a cure in some shifty sleight of mind.

He went on to read the work of other existentialist writers, and became especially fond of Sartre after reading *Nausea* made him throw up, but try as he might he could attain no age of reason, obtain no reprieve and discover no iron in the soul.

Adam was tempted for a while to abandon his job as a high-powered company accountant, on the grounds that there was something absurdly meaningless about the ceaseless juggling of figures. It seemed to exemplify that desperate absorption in the trivial which was one of the hollowest of false solutions to the problem of being. Because he played the guitar well – it was his one mode of relaxation – he contemplated beginning a new career as a spaced-out folk singer, growing his hair and beard and changing his name to Adam X, to symbolise the falseness of the family as a conduit of intergenerational continuity. He decided against it, in the end, because hippiedom was already *passé,* and because he had thought of a better plan.

Sylvia applauded this decision heartily, but was later to divorce him anyhow, on the grounds that he was too gloomy and could not provide her with essential emotional support.

'The trouble with you,' she said when she left him, 'is that you're deadly dull, over-devoted to stupid speech-making and incapable of enjoying yourself.' *Angst,* as far as Sylvia was concerned, was a marital misdemeanour.

(As things turned out, Sylvia lived comfortably on the alimony which he paid her for the remainder of her days, but failed to escape the ravages of her own *angst* and eventually died an alcohol-sodden wreck in 1999.)

Adam's own plan for escape from the human predicament was a daring one, but it was devastating in its simplicity. If the quality of life, he reasoned, is permanently and fatally impaired by the momentary possibility and ultimate inevitability of death, then the only real solution is to become immortal.

When, before their divorce, he put this proposition to Sylvia, she laughed contemptuously, having long left behind the days when love forbade such indelicacies. This reflected the fact that she really and truly did not understand him. For all his faults, Adam was not given to idle flights of fantasy; when he said he thought that was an answer, he meant it. Nor was he talking in terms of any metaphorical or metaphysical immortality; he did not believe that satisfaction could be found in the thought of 'living on' in the pages of a few books or a few children, and the prospect of being a born-again optimist did not tempt him even when the Fundamentalist revival was at its height in the 1980s. Adam needed something more solid than Christ to put his faith in, so he invested it instead in ice.

By the time Adam became interested in cryonics the Cryonics Society of California and half a dozen similar outfits had already tried freezing newly-dead bodies. Their efforts had come to naught and they had gone ignominiously out of business. Adam was not disheartened by these failures. He could not convince himself, in any case, that future medical science would stretch to actual resurrection, and he knew that contemporary techniques in freezing were inadequate to guard against tissue-damage. He believed, though, that given time and money, cryogenic scientists would soon devise methods which would allow living human beings to be placed in suspended animation more-or-less indefinitely.

There was, of course, a problem of timing to be worked out. Adam wanted to wait until the most sophisticated techniques could be put at his service, but on the other hand he wanted to be hale and hearty at the time. He knew, too, that he was going to need considerable wealth if he were to get the best of care during several centuries of inactivity.

It was not easy to weigh all these things in the balance, but years of devotion to the juggling of figures had given him an unparalleled skill in calculation. He eventually decided that the best option was to be frozen down in the year 2001, when he would be 53 years old. For safety's sake, it would be advisable to have at least a billion dollars at his disposal at the time.

This decision was taken in 1986, two years after his divorce, and he decided that provided he did not marry again, the billion dollars was achievable. He contemplated remaining celibate, but, having studied Bertillon's data regarding sexual activity and death-risk, decided that keeping a string of mistresses was a justifiable expenditure.

There were several ways in which an aspiring company accountant could plan, in 1986, to make a billion dollars by the turn of the century. They all involved helping oneself to other people's money on a grand scale, but at that time the body and spirit of American Capitalism were relatively unfettered by legalistic inconveniences, and it was not necessary to take undue risks. Adam did not, of course, steal from the corporations which employed him, but plundered on their behalf, taking an entirely reasonable commission on every deal.

Adam was fortunate in his dealings, during the 1990s, which many people called the Golden Age of Capitalism. Those were the days of the multinational frontiersmen, the buccaneers of international finance and the software stormtroopers, when hardly a month went by without a whole nation going bankrupt. Adam helped himself to a lion's share during the heady years of the asset-stripping of the Third World, and was one of the quiet men who masterminded the great Tokyo Crash of 1996, which smashed the brittle commercial hegemony of the New Samurai and brought the entire world electronics industry into a corner whose anchorage was in the belly of the corporation which numbered Adam among its brain-cells.

Although his part in these transactions made him one of the wealthiest men in the world, Adam remained modest and unassuming in his dress and his manner. His legion of aides and assistants thought him shy and kind, though he did have an annoying habit of giving them pompous little lectures on the power of positive thinking, the virtues of thrift and the dangers of hedonism.

One of his favourite topics, oddly enough, was fame. 'Fame,' he would tell them, sternly, 'is essentially a matter of attracting attention, and attention is always fatal to men who make their living by dipping into other people's pockets. One should avoid at all costs being *interesting*; it not only renders one vulnerable to the iniquities of inquisitiveness, but makes one susceptible to flattery. Flattery is a powerful force, and its seductions can be difficult to resist.

'One must constantly remind oneself that fame is one of the most awful reminders of one's own mortality. The masses are always hungry for misfortune and disaster, and they love to revel in the tragedy and grief which attend the sufferings of their idols. The public invents celebrities mainly in order to revel in their decay and extinction, and fame always breeds sickness and self-abuse.'

Such speeches as this were taken by his associates as evidence of cynicism, and it was widely assumed that Adam Zimmerman was an unhappy man. The story got round among those who knew him that his life had been blighted when his one great love, Sylvia, had deserted and divorced him. It was sometimes said that his relentless money-making was a pathetic compensation for his failure in the one aspect of his existence which really meant something to him. Even his mistresses believed this, and perhaps with better cause, because sometimes, in the grip of post-coital *triste*, he would weep a few tears of conscience for all the people in the world who were wretched and starving because he and others like him were appropriating the wealth which, in a saner world, might have made them comfortable. In such moods as this, he would make statements of a different kind.

'The thing we have to remember,' he would say, earnestly 'is that we are all dying, with every moment that passes. We begin to die even before we are born; the moment an ovum is fertilised it begins to age. The embryo is aging even while it grows and the period when the forces of growth can successfully outweigh the forces of decay is brief indeed.

'We think that we are still possessed of the bloom of youth when we are in our twenties, but this is a cruel illusion. Death begins to win the battle against life when we are barely nine years old. After that, though we continue to increase the size and number of our cells, the rot of mortality has set in. The moment of equilibrium has passed, and the new cells we produce already show the signs of senescence in the copying errors that have accumulated in the nucleic acids, and in the cross-linkages which disable our functional proteins.

'What we call maturation is the seal set upon us by the Grim Reaper, and until science finds a way to reverse these processes, correcting the nucleic acid errors and obliterating the cross-linkages, there is no hope for any of us, whether we sleep in silken sheets or starve in arid wastelands. We are all equal before the horror of it, whether we have the best of care or none at all. In such circumstances, there can be no honour in conscience, nor any shame in selfishness. In an evil world, we are free to be evil.'

His mistresses usually understood these arguments, because he always picked intelligent companions, but they rarely found it possible to agree with him. Without exception they concluded that he was lonely, bitter and neurotic, and they pitied him as much as they adored him. He had the knack of finding women who loved him passionately for himself, caring little about his money, and he broke their hearts with careless regularity.

Adam never used any of his own funds to support the intensive research in cryogenics which were carried out by the Ahasuerus Foundation of Cincinnati during the 1990s, but he did prompt the various senators and congressmen who were in the pocket of his corporations to divert massive government funding in that direction.

He always considered this to be the humanitarian side of his activity, allowing the people of the whole world – who were, in the final analysis the source of the wealth paid as taxes by the great corporations – to become shareholders in the greatest of all human endeavours: the war against death. Many of them, indeed, were privileged by virtue of his interventions to become casualties in that war.

Adam Zimmerman was very proud, therefore, to become in April 2001 one of the first few volunteers to be frozen down while still in the full bloom of health, using the most sophisticated of new techniques. He left his vast fortune in trust, to pay rent for his body, if necessary for thousands of years, while he waited for the war against death to be won and for immortality to become the common heritage of all mankind.

By virtue of its links with the corporations for which Adam had worked, aided by the trustees of his fortune, the Ahasuerus Foundation rode out the Great Depression of the 2020s, the resource crisis of the 2040s and the plague wars of the 2060s. It remained rich and strong through the Greenhouse Crisis of the 22nd and 23rd centuries, surviving the sporadic hostility of individual saboteurs and Luddite governments. It survived the predations of a new breed of tax gatherers, which was spawned by the strengthened United Nations once it came to dominate the old nation states and vie for power with the cosmicorporations which controlled the world's wealth.

The Foundation was relatively untroubled by the Little Ice Age of the 26th and 27th centuries, though it moved most of its holdings – including its richest corpiscles – along with the rest of the world's elite to one of the fabulous macroarcologies which sprang up on the moon after the elaborate technologies of artificial photosynthesis made it fertile.

Adam Zimmerman's body was moved from the moon to an orbital habitat in 2724, and then back to earth again in 2887 when the UN's ecological engineers finally brought eternal summer to what had, in pre-glacial days, been the temperate zones of the northern hemisphere.

By 3015 Adam, still serenely at rest in his personal freezer, was back where he had started, in the new supercity which had been recently erected on the site of Old Cincinnati.

The trustees of Adam Zimmerman's estate grew very rich, and as generation followed generation they loyally fought off a series of attempts to have him revived.

The first technology of longevity, developed in the 24th century, involved drastic tissue-renewal surgery. It extended the human lifespan to 150 years, but this was far from being the immortality which Adam coveted. The technology which replaced it was based on the genetic engineering of human ova, and was not the slightest use to anyone but the unborn, so that by the year 3000 research into the technology of longevity was entirely concentrated in the area of embryonic engineering. This also was of no use to Adam.

By 3250 the Ahasuerus Foundation had diversified its interests to the point where almost none of its effort was devoted to research which Adam

Zimmerman would have considered relevant to his ambition. Cynical observers suggested that Adam's trustees were showing a marked lack of enthusiasm for the attempt to create the circumstances in which they would have to hand their fortune back to its real owner. The trustees replied by stating, correctly, that under the terms of their trust they could not bring Adam back into a world such as theirs without betraying his dearest wish, and must be prepared to be patient.

When the UN finally broke the economic back of the cosmicorporations in the 34th century, Adam's situation changed. Instead of growing richer and richer, his trust began to grow poorer. In 3453 – by which time none of the old corporations existed as separate entities or reservoirs of power – the Ahasuerus Foundation was absorbed into a minor UN department. The job of deciding what was to be done with its legion of corpsicles became a matter of petty bureaucratic decision. Many of them were restored to the land of the living, but Adam's case was a very difficult one, and it was in the nature of bureaucracy even in this era that decisions were easier to postpone than to make. The tempo of life had slowed dramatically with the extension of the human lifespan, and these postponements stretched over centuries.

Eventually, Adam suffered the ultimate fate of all matters of bureaucratic record: he was forgotten by every living person, his very existence being 'known' only by the uncaring intelligence of computer files. Along with eleven other corpiscles he was consigned to an informational limbo, there to await rediscovery for as long as it might take.

By 3770 all the other people frozen down in the second and third millennia had been revived, and cryonic preservation was no longer employed for any purpose at all, but Adam and his companions, exempted by some whim of chance, slumbered on, the electricity supplies to their cryonic chambers carefully maintained by conscientious automata. The world continued to change around them – rather slowly – but they remained quite unaffected.

It was, in the event, not until the 47th century that the technology of longevity used by mankind reached its ultimate stage, granting its users what they believed to be a limitless lifespan if they remained untouched by violent accident. It was not until the 52nd century, though, that the rebuilding and renovation of Cincinnati IV brought back to the surface of the earth the secret chamber where Adam's body had been concealed for more than a thousand years.

The rediscovery of the twelve corpiscles was a momentous event in a world where hardly anything new ever happened, and it stirred the imagination of the people of the new Golden Age of youth and tranquillity. In this marvellous Utopian era the only need which was conspicuously unfulfilled was the need for surprise, and no greater joy was possible than that occasioned by the uncovering of something wonderfully ancient.

Unfortunately, the cryonic technology of the year 2001, despite all the effort poured into it by the lavishly-funded Ahasuerus Foundation, proved to have been far from perfect. Of the twelve corpiscles stored in the vault, eleven had succumbed to the ravages of putrefaction in spite of everything. Only one could be revived, and the singularity of this seemed a virtual miracle.

There was undoubtedly a certain justice in the fact that the sole survivor was Adam Zimmerman, because he had done far more than the other eleven to make sure that the possibility of their survival was kept open.

When Adam awoke from his long and dreamless sleep he found himself in a comfortable bed, with sheets which felt like the softest and most delicate silk. Beside his bed sat a charming blonde girl, who seemed to be about nine years old. He favoured her with a bright smile, and asked: 'What year is it?'

'By your calender,' she told him, pronouncing the words tentatively and a little clumsily, 'it would be 5186.'

Adam smiled again, but dared not yet rejoice in the feeling of security which he had promised himself when this moment came.

'Are you immortal, little girl?' he asked.

'One cannot be sure of that,' she said, 'but I am three hundred and seventeen years old, and I know no reason why I should not live for ever.'

Adam could not help but laugh at the delightful contradiction involved in a person of three hundred years plus looking as if she were only nine: a blonde-haired, snub-nosed poppet with eyes that radiated innocence! Of course, he believed what she said.

'And I am to be immortal too,' he said, not even phrasing it as a question.

It says a great deal for Adam Zimmerman's strength of character and essential resilience that he did not break into tears when she told him, as diplomatically as she could manage in a language which was for her utterly archaic, that he was not.

The enormity of it all did not become clear

immediately. He learned only by degrees what sort of a world it was to which he had come. His task was made more difficult by confusion, and dogged by a deep depression which was alleviated only by infrequent intervals in which he was simply too overwhelmed by the wonders of the new era to be despairing.

The facts of the matter were straightforward. He had arrived in a world where no one died unless he or she chose to do so. Disease and aging were completely conquered, and the probability of fatal accidents had been reduced by technological ingenuity to zero. Minor wounds could be healed by tissue-regeneration, even to the replacement of lost limbs or smashed organs. Violence and aggression no longer figured in the repertoire of human behaviour. The world was at peace, and it was paradise.

No one was born into the world any longer, although the technology existed to clone individuals from single cells, developing the embryos in artificial wombs. All those who were alive in this world had been shaped to an ideal of physical perfection by genetic engineers. The development of their bodies had been arrested at that point when the forces of growth held the forces of decay exactly in check, and everyone in the world appeared to Adam's eyes to be nine years old. The world was without puberty and without sexual intercourse. Such pleasures of bodily contact as there were required neither arousal nor orgasm.

All that was known in this era about the technology of longevity concerned methods of engineering human egg-cells and early embryos. Immortality had been programmed into human nature. Even the primitive methods of tissue-renewal, which had first given longevity to men of the third millennium, had not been practised for thousands of years, and to attempt them would be a hazardous business. Despite the awesome sophistication of the science these people had at their disposal, there was little they could think of doing to help preserve Adam's life beyond its own programmed span. They could protect him from disease, and from cancer, and they could help to regenerate his tissues as they wore out, but about the copying-errors that accumulated in his DNA and the cross-linkages that were disabling his proteins they could do nothing. He might live to be a hundred, perhaps a hundred and twenty, but then he would die.

Adam realised, slowly, that he was the only person in the world doomed to senescence and death. He was the sole heir of Heidegger's *angst*. He was also the only person in the world possessed of sexual desire, and though the people of the new era were perfectly willing to help him serve these urges if he wished, he was not psychologically equipped for life in a paedophile's Utopia; his sensibility revolted at the thought of intercourse with persons who appeared to be nine years old, whatever their real age might be.

The fact that he was still completely cut off from his heart's desire – though everyone else in the world possessed it – was only one of the ironies in Adam's new situation. He awoke to find himself famous.

By virtue of his nature he was the object of a fascination greater and more widespread than had been attained by any other man in history. There was not a man or woman in the world who did not know about Adam Zimmerman, who did not want to see and touch Adam Zimmerman, who did not want to be kept informed of every detail of his progress through life. The world was hungry for his thoughts, besotted with his actions.

He saw very clearly that what he had cynically said about fame in the distant past was all too obviously true in this startling present. The basis of his celebrity was his mortality; what fascinated these people above all else was his awful misfortune in being a man who one day must die.

They tried, of course, to be scrupulously polite.

They readily acknowledged his right to privacy, and tried not to invade it. They did nothing that involved him without seeking his informed consent. They apologised for every intrusion, and begged his leave for every question they asked. If he asked to be let alone, they left him, but hovered always near to be responsive to his every whim. When he chose not to be alone – and he could hardly bear solitude – there was no way for them to set aside their curiosity, their utter absorption in the mysteries of his fate and fortune.

Adam soon found out that if he were to ask his hosts to have him frozen down again, they would do it. He no longer had a vast fortune to pay for his upkeep and guard his interests, but in this world no currency was needed save need itself. Whatever he asked of these people, they would give him, and though they would be disappointed in the extreme if he chose to leave them, they could not bear to deny him anything.

He realised that he could ask them to dedicate great efforts to the development of the kind of technology of immortality which he – and he alone in all the world! – required. They would be glad to do it. They would work for him while he coldly slept, proudly and gladly, for centuries or millennia, and would delight as much as he in the possibility that he could one day get what he had come so far in search of. Their delight, though, would mask a disappointment, because if he became one of themselves, he would cease to be fascinating.

Adam Zimmerman considered his options, and he hesitated.

For the first time in his life, he had doubts about the prospect of immortality. Was such a reward, after all, a mixed blessing? Could he really bear to have the clock of his being turned back, to revert to being nine years old for ever? Would it really work, as a cure for his existential predicament?

As the days passed, and Adam lived in the supremely comfortable world of the 52nd century, he began to wonder whether *angst* was still the sole and central fact of his existence. Another horror was beginning to compete with his horror of death. It was not the horror of eternal life *per se* – that would have been absurd – but it was the horror of the idea that in winning eternal life the essential Adam Zimmerman would be exterminated just as thoroughly as he would by death.

The people of this new era were healthy, and happy, and wise; theirs was an entirely enviable condition, but it was a condition to which they had been born, and he, if he was ever to inherit it, would have it thrust upon him. It would not be, could not be, the same. He began to see that although the pre-pubescent avatar which would result from such a scientific miracle would be an immortal, it would not be an immortal Adam Zimmerman. The goal he had sought in casting himself adrift on the sea of eternity in the first year of the third millennium – the preservation of *his own being* – was still out of reach.

Adam realised, like so many others before him, that his cure for the human predicament would not work. Like all the old philosophers and lovers, all the artists and hobbyists, all the mystics and martyrs, he found in the end that he couldn't beat the *angst*. He could repress it, ignore it, sublimate it, stare it full in the face or freeze it for thousands of years, but he couldn't get away from it.

Adam did not enjoy this discovery, but he was not utterly defeated by it. Alongside the realisation that he didn't really want the kind of immortality these people might procure for him came the realisation that there was an alternative open to him. Instead of asking to be frozen down again, he could allow himself to fall for the flattery and seduction of his fame. He could give these Golden Age innocents what they longed for: a taste of human dereliction and death. He alone, in all the world, could make them appreciate the privileges which they enjoyed and took for granted, by showing them what it was to be without such privileges.

Adam had spent the greater part of his life trying to find an escape from *angst*; now he allowed himself to be seduced by his fame into a change of direction. He decided to revel in *angst*, in order to show a world that was without *angst* the true meaning of mortal existence: the true significance of his own state of being.

'I am not just a man,' Adam told his greedy audience. 'I am a symbol. You must learn to understand me, for I am not merely famous, I am fame itself.'

They loved it.

They drooled over every second-hand aphorism.

Adam decided to make of the twilight of his life the ultimate dramatic performance. He would show them death with dignity.

He became resolved that he would enable his fascinated hosts to witness both the physical processes of decay which would claim him and the psychological warfare which had been their corollary in the world from which he came. He realised that that which had been trivial and commonplace in his own world, where millions had died because of a few juggled figures on balance sheets, would now be not merely unique, but tremendous.

His death would be the performance to end all performances. It was an opportunity not to be missed.

In the years that followed, Adam's hair turned gradually grey. He let it grow long, and grew his beard as well. He asked his hosts to make him a guitar, and he began to play again, singing songs in German and in English which he remembered from childhood and adolescence, and learning new ones that his faithful admirers found in ancient data-banks. He even composed some songs of his own: sad songs about sex and death, war and poverty, pain and love.

He abandoned privacy, and gave himself entirely to his public. When he was not singing, he talked, frankly and with occasionally painful honesty, allowing all his thoughts to be recorded for infinite posterity as well as being eagerly lapped up by the everpresent listeners. He began to style himself Adam X, to signify the fact that he was the great unknown.

He planned his death meticulously, though the possibility of suicide was ruled out from the beginning. He must die, he decided, of what passed in his own time for natural causes; he must be killed by the cancers which would burst spontaneously within his frail flesh; by the gradual erosion of his tissues; by the failure of the co-ordinating systems that bound his disparate cells into a coherent whole.

He decided that he would use no anaesthetics, suffering the pain which would come with these varied afflictions. This was not a decision which he took out of courage – he had always been something of a physical coward – but out of a sense of responsibility. This was the only chance which the people of the sixth millennium would ever have to understand suffering, and he must not cheat them. His pain, his tears, his shiverings, his sadnesses, his fears – all his precious stigmata – belonged to his audience, because it was these which gave significance to his being.

In planning all this, in carefully preparing for it all and going through it – which was certainly not done without difficulty – Adam X became by degrees a happy and contented man, at peace with himself and his *angst*. He became a prouder man than he had ever been in the days when he took his gluttonous part in the rape of the world. He became a more joyful man than he had ever been, even at the heights of ecstasy which his relationship with Sylvia had allowed him temporarily to reach.

By making death into fulfilment, Adam robbed it of almost all the power it had once exercised over his imagination. He moved his *angst* from the side of moral debit to the side of moral credit in the account-book of his psyche, and with that cunning move – so like in spirit to the legerdemain which had been his forte in days gone by – he turned a potential loss into a handsome profit.

Adam X died on the day which would have been identified in his calendar as 25th July, 5237, at the age of 3289. This was a record, ironically enough, in a world from which death had been banished. He died in a comfortable bed, in sheets which felt to him like the most sensuous silk, and which reminded him pleasantly of riots of sexual excess enjoyed with his most voluptuous mistresses. He had been working on his last words for many years, redrafting and polishing them endlessly, and managed to deliver them all before losing his powers of speech.

'It is my earnest hope,' he told his adoring fans, 'that by the example of my suffering and death I may redeem you all from the innocence which is your fortunate heritage. I have been, during these last 30 years, a stranger and afraid in a world I never made, but I have done my best to remake it, by remaking its understanding of its own origins.

335

The immortality which you enjoy was born out of the efforts of men such as I, made desperate by their own mortality. We could not save ourselves, but we sowed the seeds of salvation for future mankind, paving the road to Heaven with our good intentions.

'I have come out of the mists of time to bear a message, which is that our tragedy and your triumph are indivisibly one, and must be understood as opposite sides of the same coin. I cannot express, in this poor language which every person on earth has learned in order to listen to me, the delight I feel in knowing that mankind has attained an Age of Reason, but I know that you feel it too.

'*Ave atque vale!*'

This speech was to be eternally remembered and treasured by the people of earth, granting Adam Zimmerman the kind of metaphorical immortality that he had once scorned. No one who heard or read it remained unmoved by it; and no one ever thought such an unworthy thing as to deem it pompous.

The innocents of the Golden Age continued to enjoy Adam long after he was dead, granting him the grandest and finest funeral in the history of the human race – whose like, needless to say, was never seen again. They replayed his speeches on TV, again and again and again without end, because those wonderful words remained the only resource mankind had left by which to savour the bittersweet sympathies of tragedy.

Mankind in the Third Millennium

The original version of this essay was a lecture written in response to an invitation from the Japan Science Foundation to address a Symposium for Young Scientists and Engineers, held in Tokyo in May 1986. Its purpose was to introduce a day-long discussion of the evolving relationship between human beings and the products of technology.

By way of introduction to my theme I shall first make some general comments about the nature of man's relationship with technology, and how that relationship has developed in the past. I shall then go on to say something about the problematic aspects of our use of technology in the present, which have generated widespread anxiety about the future and caused some people to become hostile to the prospect of further technological development. Finally, I shall discuss the way in which man's relationship with technology will change in the future, now that we have taken the first steps in a new technological revolution.

The word 'technology' is often used nowadays as though it were synonymous with 'machinery', because machines like aeroplanes, lathes, rockets, computers and combine harvesters are the most impressive products of modern technology. But technology is as much to do with methods as it is with objects; technology consists of all the ways we have of making and doing things. Our machines, the instruments which we use to carry out our plans and projects, are only part of technology; the rest is the knowledge we have which enables us to control and manage our environment.

We have to be careful, therefore, when we talk about man's relationship with technology, not to fall into the trap of thinking that man and his technology are independent and separable. Technology is not merely the means by which men make artifacts, it is the means by which man himself has been made. When we try to say what it is we mean by 'human nature' – when we consider what it is that sets man apart from other living species – we can only do so by talking about the ability to make things. Man is, by nature and by definition, a technologist. The human brain and the human hand were shaped by natural selection to accommodate the activities and possibilities of knowing, of planning and of tool-using.

This is not to say that man's relationship with technology does not change; in the tens of thousands of years through which our species has existed that relationship has changed very dramatically. But we must remember in considering those changes that they have taken place within the context of a basic relationship which is so intimate that the greater part of it is always taken for granted.

The early history of man's relationship with technology is usually described in terms of our gradual mastery of new materials. We divide up the epochs of prehistory according to the materials from which men made their tools: the Stone Age; the Bronze Age; the Iron Age. This is necessary because all that we know, or can know, about prehistoric man has to be inferred from the relics which he left behind, and the most obvious differences between the relics left behind by successive prehistoric cultures are the materials of which they are made. This way of classifying cultures is one of the things which encourages us to think of technology in terms of different kinds of hardware.

There were, however, other kinds of technological development which went on alongside the mastery of new materials, which could not leave such obvious traces. Although they are more difficult for modern archaeologists to track, these other developments were at least as important as aspects of technological progress. The most significant developments of all were the agricultural techniques which permitted and determined the growth and dispersal of human populations throughout the world. These went hand in hand with developments in the domestication and use of animals for food, for transportation, and as beasts of burden. It is very important to remember that technology and human progress have always been concerned with the manipulation and exploitation of living things, not just with the making of inorganic artifacts.

Once the prehistoric development of human cultures gave way to history – thanks to the invention of writing, which was itself one of the most significant of all technological developments – what those cultures passed on to future generations became much more elaborate, and the accumulated wealth of historical records allows modern commentators to take a much broader view of technological progress. Despite its breadth, though, our view of technological development in history is not altogether clear because our historical perspective tends to become preoccupied with the things that the people writing the documents thought important – and they usually paid much more attention to political and religious matters than to their technology. The evolution of technology, which is the principal motor of historical change, tends to be overlaid, and to some extent obscured, by records of empires and dynasties, wars and conquests.

When we extract the submerged story of technological change from the documents of history, we usually pay less attention to mere materials than we do in chronicling the technological development of prehistoric cultures. Instead, we tend to refer first and foremost to sources of energy. Historians of technology describe the supplementation of horsepower by windmills and watermills, and see as a crucial break in history the development of versatile engines which put to many different uses the energy locked up in organic fuels – wood, coal and oil. The first such engines, which were steam engines, brought about such sweeping social changes in Western Europe that we usually refer to their spread as the Industrial Revolution.

The subsequent history of technology becomes much more complicated, mainly because of the rapid development of many new kinds of machines, which became ever more versatile in deploying the energy of fossil fuels: machines using internal combustion engines, and especially machines powered by electricity. In recent times, nuclear power has been added to the list of energy sources, but it is mainly employed as a substitute for coal or oil in the generation of electricity.

The wonderful versatility of electrical energy has allowed the development of a vast range of ingenious machines, whose evolution has inevitably been associated with the production and deployment of many new materials. Just as the evolution of steam engines required the development of new structural materials like steel, so modern electrical machinery has required the proliferation of a multitude of materials which include ceramics and plastics as well as metals.

The evolution of hardware which has taken place since the beginning of the Industrial Revolution, has become so rapid that barely a century of history – about a lifetime and a half in human terms – separates the invention of the electric lightbulb from the development of the desktop computer. This dramatic evolution of technology has allowed machines gradually to take over many tasks which had previously required human hands and human intelligence – a usurpation of human prerogatives which has made many people anxious about the future usefulness of human skills and labour-power.

Because of this astonishing proliferation of new, more powerful and cleverer machines, our attention has been further distracted from technologies which deal with living things. A great many tasks and techniques which once involved living instruments have been taken over by machinery: the horse has been almost entirely displaced from what was once a key role in human affairs; natural fibres like wool, cotton and silk have been supplemented by a wide range of artificial fibres, which have revolutionised the textile industry. New machinery has brought such a revolution to agricultural production in the developed countries that it is common for people to think only of these new practices as 'technological', while the practices of old-fashioned farmers, especially those in so-called underdeveloped countries, are mistakenly excluded from that category.

It is tempting for modern historians of technology, looking back at these vast changes, to see the social and political affairs which provide the surface of documentary history as merely a series of adaptations to new technology. In this view of things societies make progress by making new discoveries, and then adapting their social order to make use of them. Karl Marx, in *The Poverty of Philosophy*, ridiculed starry-eyed reformers who thought that society could be re-designed simply by political planning; he argued that social relationships in the past had been in large measure determined by the means of production which were available in different phases of history. Thus, he argued, the logic of social evolution had required that the handmill produce a feudal society, the steam-mill a capitalist society.

But this too is a drastic over-simplification. It is clear that social forms are not simply the product of different technologies, and that there is not one single path of progress along which all societies must pass. Different kinds of society make different uses of technical knowledge, and societies are obviously different in the extent to which they encourage and foster technical innovation. One must remember that the rapid technological development of the West was greatly facilitated by various technologies imported from the East — gunpowder, paper and printing most conspicuous among them — which had not precipitated similar patterns of change in their native China.

Obviously, then, the relationship between kinds of social organisation and technology is a complicated one, with no simple pattern of cause and effect. That is why it is both sensible and important to hold symposia such as this one for which this lecture was written: the future of our world will not be automatically determined by new technologies which will arise spontaneously within it. It is for us to choose both the shape of societies to come, and the shape of technologies to come, though the intricate interrelationships between the two will inevitably confuse and constrain us.

This brings me to the second part of my argument, which is concerned with those aspects of man's contemporary relationship with technology which have generated anxiety and hostility.

To some extent, it is simply the rapidity of modern technological development which generates this unease. Such has been the pace of this evolution that it has created vast differences both between and within nations, in terms of the access which people have to the rewards of technology. We now live in a world where the real wealth of some nations – the goods they can produce, the value they can add to raw materials in transforming them into products –

vastly outstrips others, and where the wealth of individuals within nations may also differ vastly; one of the by-products of rapid technological progress in the last two centuries has therefore been dramatic inequalities of lifestyle between individuals and groups. At the same time, new technologies of communication have ensured that the poor cannot help but be fully aware of the extent of their disadvantages.

A second consequence of the rapidity of technological development is that every person in the world must now face the probability that the world in which he will spend his latter years will be very different from the world into which he was born.

For the vast majority of people, this adds to the quality of life an intrinsic unease. We cannot help but be anxious about the future when the only thing we can be sure of is that it will not be like the present. The inevitability of change offers us opportunities which our forefathers never had, but it also exposes us to threats which they never had to face. In Britain we have a proverb: Better the devil you know than the devil you don't; and this represents the careful wisdom of common sense. Many people are inclined to think along the lines that although they don't much like the way things are, at least they know that they can get by, because they already do; an uncertain future can offer no such guarantee.

In addition to these general anxieties caused by the pace of change, there are specific anxieties generated by particular technologies.

One set of anxieties arises from the way in which modern technology has transformed the business of war. It is sometimes argued that throughout history the desire to wage war more effectively has been the principal motive force encouraging technological progress, and that the technologies which make modern life more comfortable are largely by-products of discoveries made in the cause of destruction. I do not think that a careful study of history really supports such an extreme case, but there is no denying the fact that the desire to find more efficient means of destruction has been a powerful stimulus to technological research.

Because of this relationship between war and technological development it is easy to be anxious about the fact that the world has now crossed an important threshold. Men now have the resources to wreak such effective destruction that two ideologically-opposed nations each possess enough weapons not merely to obliterate one another, but to wipe out the whole human race. A nuclear war might conceivably set off a chain reaction of destruction which would sterilise the entire biosphere.

Even if we leave aside the awesome might of nuclear weapons, other destructive technologies are abroad in the world which are almost as fearful: wars fought with chemical and biological weapons are no more comforting to contemplate. Wars in today's world are no longer limited to armies of professional combatants – they place entire populations in situations of constant danger of death and mutilation. Given all this, it is not surprising that some people think so fondly of the days when technologies were less powerful that they would bring them back if they could.

There is a further set of anxieties too. War is, at least, a matter of human intention: none need be fought if we can all decide that we will not fight one. Some of the fears which people nowadays have, though, are related to the unintended consequences of technological development – the side-effects and by-products of modern methods of production and manufacture.

Our power stations do not simply generate electricity – the various processes by which they work produce waste-products which are dangerous. If they are atomic power stations they produce radioactive wastes; if they are coal-burning power stations they produce sulphurous fumes which, when discharged into the air, eventually return to earth in acid rain. Nor do our factories simply produce goods; they also generate wastes, which are sometimes released into rivers so that they may be carried away to the sea, but which poison the rivers, and ultimately may poison the sea too.

If what these technologies discharge into the environment is cause for anxiety, so too is what they remove from it. The supplies of fossil fuels – coal and oil – contained in the earth's crust are not inexhaustible, and a technological complex based on their use can only have a limited lifespan. In addition, there is little doubt that we are presently putting too much strain even on potentially renewable resources – on the world's forests, which are being rapidly cut back; and on the world's soils, which may turn to dust and desert if they are used too recklessly in crop-growing.

Human beings are now so numerous, and the technologies they use so powerful, that our endeavours have effects not merely at a social level, or even at a national level, but on a world scale. The biosphere – that thin layer at the earth's surface which sustains all life – is itself a creation of life. The air that we breathe, and the climate which enables us to exist, as well as the food that we eat and the fuels that we burn, are all the products of living organisms past and present. Now that the entire biosphere has become vulnerable to the activities of men – including the unintended and uncontrolled side-effects of those activities – we must be anxious not simply on behalf of individuals and nations, but on behalf of life itself.

Many people feel that the only appropriate response to the anxieties generated by modern technologies is some kind of retreat to a simpler way of life. They call for an abandonment of the technologies of mass destruction, coupled with a scaling down of those technologies which depend on non-renewable fuel-supplies. Such policies would inevitably lead to a slowing down of the rate of change – a restabilisation of the social world.

Others, however, feel that we would be paying a very high price if we were to surrender all the benefits of modern technologies in order to cut these costs. To those who adopt this latter viewpoint, and I am one of them, it seems both unwise and unrealistic to think that the clock can simply be turned back. Hope for the future, in this way of looking at things, must instead be pinned to the possible future development of new technologies which could secure similar benefits at far less cost to the environment.

To those who are fearful of modern technology, the idea that problems caused by past technological developments might be solved by future technological developments seems to be reckless optimism. I want to contend though, that it is not so very reckless, and that there are in fact good grounds for thinking that future technologies might solve at least some of the problems we currently face. They will do this, I believe, because they can be expected to bring about crucial and beneficial changes in man's relationship with technology.

In saying this, I do not mean to imply that we can foresee the future, or that we can accurately predict the future evolution of technology. As Karl Popper has pointed out in *The Poverty of Historicism*, to the extent that the shape of the future depends on future discovery, it is quite unpredictable. We cannot possibly know today what we will discover tomorrow.

We only have to use our imagination to realise how difficult it would have been for men at various stages of social evolution to see how their world might change. The record of human prophecy has been an utterly dismal one, full of failures and miscalculations. No one writing in the past ever issued a vision of his own future which, exposed to the cold light of hindsight, turned out to contain more than a few correct guesses among a multitude of errors.

Despite the past failures of would-be prophets, though, I believe that it is wrong to use Popper's argument too restrictively. If we contrast two elementary examples, we can see that they are not alike. On the one hand, it is true that a man who lived before the invention of the wheel could not possibly speculate about the technological benefits of wheels, because to imagine the wheel would have been to invent it. By contrast, a man contemplating the undomesticated horse might well be able to imagine benefits that would stem from its domestication without having yet achieved it. We must remember, therefore, that the ability to imagine change is actually a necessary stimulus to invention. Without some power of anticipation technological development would be a difficult thing to direct, and yet it is directed after a fashion – it is by no means entirely reliant upon the whims of chance.

In today's world, we cannot know what new possibilities will be opened up by discoveries not yet made. But we do know a great deal more than has ever before been known about how the world actually does work, and we already have abundant examples available to us of the way that theoretical understanding of the way things work in nature may pave the way for technical control of similar processes. We have seen how a theoretical understanding of the physics of radioactive decay paved the way for technologies of controlled nuclear fission. We have seen how a theoretical understanding of the elements of organic chemistry paved the way for the creation and control of a multitude of new organic molecules, for which we have found many and various uses as dyes, fabrics, structural materials and medicines.

In the distant past, technologies tended to be established by trial and error, and theoretical understanding came later, but in recent times that pattern has been inverted. Medical technology provides an excellent example of this, in that we learned by trial and error how to treat many kinds of diseases and injuries even before we knew what caused them – but a more complete understanding of the nature of disease and the biochemistry of the human body paved the way for a vastly more sophisticated and very much more effective battery of remedies and treatments.

What this means is that in recent times we have found a sensible basis for anticipating some future developments in technology. We still cannot predict discoveries, but we can often see where scope for discoveries lies. If we were not able to see this scope, and direct our efforts toward it, then we could not have brought about the rapid technological progress of the last century.

Technology progresses so rapidly nowadays because theoretical discoveries have mapped out areas of profitable research for the practical imagination. In fact, we may be justified in establishing a 'rule of anticipation' which states that as our theoretical understanding of a range of phenomena advances, it becomes more probable that we will be able to find out how to control such phenomena for our own purposes.

This is the kind of thinking that lies behind the future history which David Langford and I constructed for our book *The Third Millennium: A History of the World, A.D. 2000–3000*. Its imaginary history is not a catalogue of predictions, and does not pretend to be. It is a book designed for entertainment, and to that end it has a good deal of humour and whimsy in it. But in our technological anticipations David and I tried hard to be sensible in basing the new technologies we have imagined in theoretical understanding which we already have. We supposed that our understanding in some areas of science – plasma physics and biochemical genetics, for instance – will increase from its presently incomplete state; but we were, by necessity, very conservative in trying to imagine new theoretical developments. What we mostly did was to imagine that phenomena which we already understand fairly well will, in the future, be brought under complete and careful technical control.

The history described in *The Third Millennium* remains only one of an infinite number of possible futures. It contains many matters of concrete detail which are, of course, pure guesswork with no rational grounding at all. But if our work was competently done, the book's anticipation of the nature and scope of future technological change should not be unrealistic.

The idea that a full understanding of natural processes will eventually lead to a technical mastery of such processes encouraged us to be optimistic in thinking that the contemporary problems associated with energy-production might be overcome. Scientists now understand how energy is produced in the sun by nuclear fusion; indeed, people have been trying to build fusion reactors for some time. At present, such reactions can be started, but cannot be sustained and controlled in such a way as to make an energy profit out of them. In our future history David and I do not imagine that these problems will be solved easily or soon, but we do imagine that they will eventually be solved. If and when they *are* solved, that would amount to a significant shift in the relationship between technology and the biosphere, because it would alleviate dependence on non-renewable resources, and would reduce pollution problems.

The kind of changes which might stem from the development of fusion technology are not too difficult to imagine; if we regard that technology mainly as an alternative way of generating electricity, then it takes no great ingenuity to plot out its consequences. The situation is very different, though, with respect to another area of technology which comes in for extended consideration in our speculative history: the biotechnologies which are often discussed under the label 'genetic engineering'.

Scientists now understand fairly well how genes work. We know what they are made of, and we know how they function as blueprints for the proteins which are the principal molecules of life. On the basis of these discoveries, technologists have already learned how to locate and isolate the lengths of DNA which carry blueprints for useful proteins, and how to transplant those lengths of DNA into bacteria, which can then be used as living factories for the production of such molecules as insulin, interferons and growth hormones. We do not yet know how genes carry blueprints for the structure of whole organisms as well as for the materials used in building them, but there is no reason to suppose that we cannot find out. If and when we do, the possibilities of organic technology – technology employing the materials and processes of life – will become very great indeed. Such possibilities *do* require great efforts of the imagination to be appreciated.

David and I tried to be adventurous in making those efforts when we wrote *The Third Millennium*. Since then, I have tried to use short stories to continue to explore the more intimate human consequences of the possible developments there sketched out. The book which you hold in your hands is the result, and I think it would be wrong to close this book without adding a note on the conclusions which (in my view) ought to be drawn from these explorations.

In the early part of this essay I called attention to the way in which our idea of what technology is like tends to concentrate attention on the inorganic technology of steam and steel, coal and electricity. When most people think of 'technology' what springs to mind is machinery of a kind which can easily be differentiated from living creatures in terms of its materials, its energy sources and in terms of one of its most fundamental components: the wheel.

It has become deeply ingrained in our ordinary way of thinking that we can *contrast* the world of machines and the world of living things, so as to speak of technology and nature as if they were things completely apart, and of the mechanical and the organic as though they were mutually exclusive categories. Even where our technology has been invaded by the products of simple organic chemistry, the boundary between the natural and the artificial seems hardly threatened: plastics are not like wood, nylon is not like cotton, even new medicines and food additives are usually considered to be in some way crucially different from 'natural' products and ways of doing things.

This is an error of perspective; the categories are not mutually exclusive and the implied contrast is false. It is an error of perspective, furthermore, which leads to much misguided rhetoric and to conclusions which are, considered dispassionately, not merely stupid but dangerous.

There is a metaphorical sense in which the

biosphere can be said to have its own technological processes of manufacture. Plants manufacture organic molecules by photosynthesis, using the energy of sunlight. Animals harvest and process the organic molecules made by plants in order to sustain themselves. All living creatures reproduce themselves. The most vital component of human technology is that technology which usurps, develops and deploys this 'natural technology' of organic materials and processes.

We employ plants and animals as living instruments, and by selective breeding over thousands of years we have produced very many new varieties of plants and animals which are specifically adapted to our various purposes. In recent years, scientific understanding of elementary genetics has allowed us to be much more thorough and methodical in the business of selective breeding and hybridisation, and the calculated creation of new strains of wheat and rice have helped to bring about a so-called 'Green Revolution' in world food production.

In the past, we have always needed living organisms as middlemen in order to exploit the 'natural technologies' of photosynthesis and protein production. That phase of technological history is now ending, and we are embarking upon a new phase, in which direct manipulation of DNA will allow us to exploit the potential of organic technology much more cleverly. We will, in the early stages of this new phase, be able to recombine genes much more adventurously than selective breeding has allowed us to – we can already transplant genes from mammals into bacteria. This will allow us to create new kinds of living organisms much more quickly and much more adventurously than was possible in the past.

In the fullness of time, we may not need living things to act as middlemen at all – in the later stages of this new technological revolution we may be able to establish artificial processes of photosynthesis and artificial systems of protein manufacture entirely independent of actual organisms.

Scientists have already tried to do something like this, in experiments with tissue-cultures where specialised animal tissues were grown in nutrient baths rather than in the organisms of which they normally formed a part. Those experiments quickly ran into limitations, but it seems probable that if and when we can complete our understanding of the biochemical processes controlling growth, the differentiation of cells into specialised types, and the aging of cell-structures, then it might well be possible to develop an elaborate tissue-culture technology.

At present, we have only a partial understanding of the way in which a seed or an egg-cell contains a blueprint instructing it to grow into a particular kind of body. When our understanding is fuller, the door will be opened to the possibility of instructing seeds or egg-cells to grow into whatever form we would like them to take, whether those forms are organisms capable of independent life, or tissue-structures which can grow and develop only in specially controlled conditions.

The greater part of *The Third Millennium* and the whole of the present book, are taken up by attempts to track the possible consequences of the growth of a sophisticated biotechnology. Such a biotechnology would radically transform food production, the manufacture of materials, and medicine. There are good grounds for thinking it entirely reasonable to speculate about the potential of biological systems of cementation in building, about the possibility of building quasi-living systems into houses in order to take care of water supplies and waste-disposal, about the uses of biological systems in mining essential elements, about biological batteries more powerful than those found in electric eels, about biological illumination more prolific than that produced by fireflies, about biological engines which might allow us to design vehicles combining all the advantages of the motor car and the horse.

None of these things is likely to be seen in our lifetimes, but the true potential of a sophisticated organic technology cannot be expressed other than by the display of such an array of possibilities. How long it will be before these powers are fully available to us we can only guess, but we must talk in terms of hundreds of years rather than thousands.

The medical applications of biotechnology will complete a process of medical sophistication which began with elementary organic chemistry in the 19th century. Scientists have already rendered impotent many of the diseases which used to afflict human populations, and have already made great progress in the repair of damaged bodies. As our understanding of biochemistry continues to increase, we may legitimately hope to defeat many more of the diseases which still threaten us.

If we can understand the process of growth and differentiation in living tissues, then it may prove possible to enhance the body's powers of self-repair, perhaps to the extent that lost limbs and damaged organs might be re-grown. And if we can obtain a thorough understanding of the biochemistry of aging, then there must be a possibility of extending the human lifespan dramatically. Our evolutionary ancestors presumably had much shorter lifespans than we do, comparable to our nearest relatives among the great apes. If natural selection could extend the human lifespan by a factor of three in an interval of time which is short by the usual standards of natural evolution, then sophisticated biotechnology will surely allow us to extend it further, much more quickly.

I am aware, in saying all this, that the contemplation of sophisticated biotechnologies is attended by its own specific anxieties. The idea of genetic engineers tampering with bacteria inevitably raises in the popular imagination the spectre of new plagues. The idea of technological tampering with human genes produces a particularly intimate sense of threat. The recent advancement of such techniques as *in vitro* fertilisation of human ova, and the freezing of human embryos, has already created new moral problems which people have never been forced to face before.

These moral problems do require serious discussion, but we cannot and must not take seriously the kind of blanket opposition to biotechnological experiment which claims to attack all that is 'unnatural'. Everything we now consider to be part of ordinary human life – everything, in fact, that we consider to be part of 'human nature' – is based on some kind of subversion of the order established by natural selection. Agriculture and animal husbandry are usurpations of nature; natural selection does not equip human beings to speak a language, to wear clothes, to build houses. All these things are technologies, which men in the past have invented and which men in the present must learn to use.

Of course there are hazards to be anticipated in the development of new biotechnologies. Even the crude popular nightmares about new plagues might require to be taken seriously. But we must remember that our most powerful armour against the hazards of nature is provided by the biotechnologies which we already have: it is the technologies of agriculture and medicine which secure and preserve human life; indeed, they are what makes *human* life, as we think of it, possible.

It is my contention, therefore, that a more sophisticated biotechnology, based on direct control of biochemical systems of production and reproduction, can and will make it possible for us to live better – more *human* – lives.

In my opinion, we should and must look to

biotechnology to solve and avoid many of the problems which have arisen as consequences of our powerful inorganic technology: problems of industrial pollution, of resource limitation, and of soil exhaustion. It is my hope that such a sophisticated biotechnology would also assist, though it could not of itself ensure, a great equality between the nations and individuals which make up the human race.

The development of fusion power and artificial photosynthesis would help to obliterate many of the economic advantages and disadvantages which nations presently have because of the distribution of natural resources and the way in which they are traded. Such technologies might conceivably produce such an abundance of wealth as to permit the real abolition of poverty.

I contend also that we should and must look to a sophisticated biotechnology to solve the moral problems which arise from our exploitation of other living species. A technology of tissue-culture production, ultimately augmented by a technology of artificial photosynthesis, would allow us to cease entirely our dependence upon and use of other living creatures. We would not only be able to liberate the animals which we use and on which we prey, but the plants too.

It seems to me that these are goals worth

working for – and, indeed, that they are the goals toward which we should all be aiming, as scientists and as human beings.

Only a sophisticated biotechnology can plausibly be expected to solve the problems which we face in today's world. The pattern of progress which I have tried to lay out in my various ventures in speculative future history aims for nothing less than the competent technological control of the entire biosphere. If one can speak of there being an 'end' or 'ultimate goal' of progress, that is what it must be.

In my fiction, at least, that end is not often attained; this is because I take care to emphasise that it is an end which is difficult of attainment. Mankind has no God-given right to win the great game of survival, but if we *are* to win that game, this is what winning must consist of. A fully-elaborated biotechnology will not be the final technology – the expansion of our sciences and our arts is potentially infinite – but it is, in more ways than one, the *vital* technology. It is the one which will determine whether we continue to thrive or become extinct.

There remain aspects of contemporary anxiety which are unanswered even by these ambitious speculations.

The unease generated by the rate of change is probably something which we need to learn to live with, because it is the inevitable corollary of the opportunity which change also offers. The fear that we might destroy ourselves, though, is something which cannot be treated so lightly.

It is not simply the threat of war which needs further consideration here, but also arguments about the impossibility of eliminating human misery first put forward by T R Malthus nearly 200 years ago. Malthus imagined that a world which could produce food in abundance must produce more people in even greater abundance, so that competition for resources could never relax. He proposed that if population growth were not restricted by famine, then it must necessarily be restricted by war or plague. If Malthus had been asked to anticipate a dramatic extension in the human lifespan, then he might well have concluded that it would simply make our problems worse.

In contemplating these matters, I can come up with no other answer than the one which was logically forced upon Malthus, which he incorporated into the second version of his essay on population. According to Malthus's second thoughts, the only alternative to a future of hardship and strife was, in his phrase, 'moral restraint'. That is to say, men must actually take control of their propensity to breed, by collective decision – and, by the same token, must take control of their propensity to make war.

Malthus had not much faith in moral restraint, and he remained pessimistic about the future facing mankind. I am not as pessimistic as Malthus was, and I base my optimism, again, on the development of new technologies. For one thing, we have now technologies for controlling human fertility, and a determination to use them, which Malthus could not have imagined. We may expect in the future that these technologies will improve further, to the point where they will be available for widespread use at the behest of our collective decision-making. In addition to this, we now have technologies of communication far more sophisticated than Malthus could have imagined, and these too may improve to the point where they will bring about a radical restructuring of the human community.

In the distant past, the extent of human community was defined by the family and the village; a community could only consist of people who met regularly on a face-to-face basis. Throughout history, we have seen the gradual extension of communities, by means of technologies like writing and print, aided by ideologies of political and religious solidarity, so that now there is a whole hierarchy of communities, extending from the family to the nation, and from the nation into the world of international relations.

Wherever and whenever men have tried to define a new kind of community they have done so first and foremost by distinguishing that community from others, and then by institutionalising hostility to others, very often in the form of active war. If we are to hope for an end to war – as we must, if we are to hope for the continued existence of the world, then we must hope for the establishment of one great community, which encompasses the whole human race.

I hope that such a community might be established, given appropriate technologies of communication, with the aid of appropriate ideologies of solidarity.

Writers like Marshall McLuhan have already promised us that electronic media of communication like radio and TV would turn the world into a massive Global Village, thus making the whole human race into a single community. Such a development is by no means inevitable, but I believe, sincerely and passionately, that through the future development of communications technology we at least have a chance to create *one community* out of the whole human race – a community whose individuals are *all on the same side*, no matter what racial and cultural differences there might be between groups. In such a world community, I hope, anxiety about the possibility of war might for the first time in history be an adequate guarantee that there would be no wars.

In concluding this polemic, I would like to quote an argument from an impressive essay which was written in 1930 by the British philosopher C E M Joad, entitled 'Is Civilisation Doomed?'

Joad confessed, in introducing his topic, that he had not the least idea whether civilisation was doomed or not, because he had no way to predict the future. However, he went on to say that he felt morally compelled to argue that civilisation *is* doomed, because only by being outrageously alarmist could he hope to make people properly aware of the terrible threats which they faced, and thus rouse them to take action in order to avert those threats.

There are in today's world many people who argue that civilisation is doomed. I agree with Professor Joad that it is entirely proper and necessary for them to do so. It is, in fact, because these others are carrying out the moral duty to alert people to danger that I feel able to carry out what seems to me to be a parallel duty, which is to insist that after all, civilisation might be saved and might be improved, *if we are prepared to work to save and improve it.*

The work which most needs to be done in furthering this cause is work in technological development. It could not be otherwise, because what technology is, according to the best definition we can offer, is the search for human solutions to human problems, and the quest to secure and improve human nature.

We can see, if we have the imagination, what sort of things might be done by future technologists, and there is no more important task that a human being might undertake than trying to discover how to do them.

Acknowledgements

Bedside Conversations first appeared in *Isaac Asimov's Science Fiction Magazine 1990*, Copyright © 1990 Davis Publications Inc.

A Career in Sexual Chemistry first appeared as *Sexual Chemistry* in *Interzone 20*, Copyright © 1987 Interzone.

Cinderella's Sisters first appeared in *The Gate 1*, Copyright © 1989 W Publishing.

The Magic Bullet first appeared in *Interzone 29*, Copyright © 1989 Interzone.

The Invertebrate Man first appeared in *Interzone 39*, Copyright © 1990 Interzone.

The Furniture of Life's Ambition first appeared in *Zenith 2* ed. David S. Garnett, Copyright © 1990 Brian Stableford.

The Fury That Hell Withheld first appeared in *Interzone 35*, Copyright © 1990 Interzone.

An earlier and substantially different version of *The Engineer and the Executioner* appeared in *Amazing Science Fiction* May 1975, Copyright

© 1975 Ultimate Publishing Co., Inc.

The Growth of the House of Usher first appeared in Interzone 24, Copyright © 1988 Interzone.

And He Not Busy Being Born first appeared in Interzone 16, Copyright © 1986 Interzone.

Mankind in the Third Millennium first appeared in Japanese in Japan Research and Technology 249 (1988); it first appeared in English in Social Biology and Human Affairs Vol. 54 no. 1, Copyright © The Biosocial Society.